THE TECHNIQUE OF
THE NOVEL

THE TECHNIQUE OF THE NOVEL

BY

CARL H. GRABO

ASSOCIATE PROFESSOR OF ENGLISH, THE UNIVERSITY OF CHICAGO

NEW YORK

GORDIAN PRESS, INC.

1964

Originally Published 1928
Reprint 1964

Library of Congress Card Catalogue Number 64-8178

Lithographed in U.S.A. by
E D W A R D S   B R O T H E R S ,   I N C .
Ann Arbor, Michigan

PREFACE

In this book on the technique of the novel I have taken the clock apart in the effort to show the functions of the wheels, screws, and levers which compose its mechanism. Or again, to change the figure, I have endeavored to show the manipulation of the strings which guide the puppets in their mimicry of life. To those beyond the footlights witnessing the show, the strings should not be too visible. The spectators lend themselves to the performance, if it is cleverly enacted, and accept it as real. Some even resent the critic's attempt to show how the thing is done. To know how it is done, they contend, lessens their enjoyment. Such is not, however, the attitude of the puppet master.

To dramatist, artist, novelist, the technique of his craft is of never-ending interest. He is not blind to the general effect, the totality of impression, to convey which is the object of his effort. But he is also aware that without the mastery of his medium he will fail of his purpose. In the ensuing pages, the author discusses fictional technique from the view-point of the writer of stories. The reader will remark how often the novels and the critical dicta of Henry James are cited in the illustration of points. James is the most technically aware, so to speak, of the great novelists, or has, at any rate, left the most extensive and valuable comment on technical method. The attempt is here made to approach from his analytical point of view the various problems of the story writer.

The method is that of the case book. A large number of novels of recognized merit are taken up and analyzed for various narrative principles and devices. Some of the novels are examined at length, others briefly. The fundamental principles of plot structure and point of view are first considered and from these the discussion proceeds to other technical considerations in an order of development which, the writer hopes, is intelligible and natural. There is no attempt to formulate "rules." There are no rules in story-telling; but there are the practices of skilful writers to be observed and studied. It is by the study of these and by his own experimental practice that the young writer learns his craft.

The book is designed primarily for the young writer who wishes to learn the tricks of his trade. But it aims also to interest those readers of fiction to whom a novel is more than an opiate or diversion of a moment and is a work of art. The keenest, the most discriminating, æsthetic appreciation is based upon technical knowledge, popular superstition to the contrary notwithstanding. Surely there has never been a more appreciative, more discerning reader of novels than Henry James, nor one better versed in the processes of their creation.

CONTENTS

CONTENTS

CONTENTS

INTRODUCTION

Between the artist and his audience lies always his form of expression, his medium, which is both barrier and bond. It is like a wall of semi-translucent glass through which are adumbrated his creative ideas; these more or less distorted as the medium is flawed and opaque; and softened in outline and inevitably colored in transmission. For it is impossible that the full force and body of the artist's conception should carry over and be exactly reproduced in the brain of another. Some loss, distortion, or discoloration there must inevitably be. The greater the skill of the artist, the greater his mastery of his tools, the more surely will he recreate in the mind of the percipient the precise image and emotion he intends. The study of technique is the analysis of the means whereby calculated effects are most swiftly and exactly realized.

The word "technique" has to most ears a forbidding connotation. It is loosely associated with "technicality" and suggests obscurities, confusions, and delays. Or if not so naïvely misunderstood and properly related to method—to the way of doing a thing—it is thought of, at least in the arts, as the dry and uninspired routine of composition, a kind of mechanical dexterity which the man of inspiration acquires without effort. The "movie" conception of the cowboy artist painting a masterpiece while lying in bed with a broken leg; of the bare-footed mountain girl singing before the impresario and a few months later taking the operatic world by storm; or of the girl slighted by the famous critic turning to her manuscripts and composing a best seller—these romantic fancies are no great exaggeration of the popular belief. Genius, we like to think, achieves its aims without plodding effort, obedient only to some mysterious instinct. The years devoted to scales, the bedaubed canvasses, the closet full of rejected manuscripts have no place in the easy conquests of genius. Only mediocrity, we assume, must endure these humiliations.

There is sufficient truth in this misconception to make it plausible. The precocity of a Mozart or a Chatterton seems to spring, like De Vries's primrose, inexplicably from its origins. These mutations, these divine bourgeonings, are disconcerting to the believer in scientific law, in slow adaptation and survival. But they are rare. Nor are they superior to many blooms of slower growth. In the field of the arts we look with justifiable misgiving upon the *Wunderkind.* Too seldom does he become an artist. In the slower mastery of the means to expression—of technique—lies a stabilizing moral discipline. It is not safe to be born too facile, to learn too early and too easily.

Yet whether the process be swift or slow, whether magical or laborious, the acquisition of technique, the mastery of tools, is much the same essentially for all, and presumably follows some such order as this: observation of methods already in use—study, that is, of models; experimentation with methods and the adoption of those which prove successful; and last, through habitual use, the instinctive choice of the right method—the stage of mastery attained by the finished craftsman. It is in this way that we learn all things requiring a technique, as, for instance, swimming. There can be, essentially, little difference between the mastery of the Australian crawl stroke and the acquisition of a narrative style. Not every one, to be sure, whatever his efforts, can become a good stylist; nor, for that matter, can every one be made a good swimmer. But the slight degree of the accomplishment does not negate the method of growth.

Beauty and wisdom, which are the substance of the arts, are conveyed to us by a process of selection and indirection. The definition if inadequate is at least suggestive. A simple analogy will illustrate what is meant by the term selection. A scene reflected in a mirror or in the finder of a camera is—and the fact is strange—more beautiful than the scene itself. The reason lies in this: the frame of the mirror or finder enables us to concentrate upon a small field. Out of the overwhelming universe, in which attention is forever distracted from a part by multitudinous assaults upon the senses from other parts, a selected group of sense appeals has been arbitrarily delimited. Within the field of the mirror or finder we perceive with more than our usual intensity. The frame is a device which enables us to concentrate, to focus our attention, and thus to apprehend.

If there be further some process of simplification, that is, of selection, our enjoyment of the scene is yet more enhanced. A mist which obscures some of the too numerous details of a landscape and throws the larger masses into relief appeals at once to our sense of beauty. Simplification is a kind of emphasis which, by eliminating some details, forces the attention upon others. However haphazard and undesigned, there is always in any such simplification a kind of beauty. But if the effect is premeditated, if, that is, the photographer in developing his negative, or the painter in composing his picture, eliminates certain details so that others constitute a kind of pattern, the result is even more beautiful. By his omissions he has called attention to a certain arrangement of lines, masses, and tones which he has found interesting. The simplification in itself constitutes a kind of beauty. If his pattern is one which we ourselves perceived, or are thus made to perceive, the beauty is doubled. Between artist and observer a bond of sympathy has been fashioned; and we enjoy twofold that which is shared by another.

Memory is a kind of mist which obscures some

details of experience and magnifies others. Therefore it is that remembered experience is almost always beautiful. In retrospect even pain and sorrow are enriched, are somehow elevated and made mysteriously significant. The more remote the memories, the more poignant the beauty. The old usually look back upon their youth as a time of happiness. Yet youth is, in fact, more often unhappy than age. It is the perspective of time, the unconscious selective processes of memory, which glorify childhood and youth.

There is, withal, in this simplification, whether of art or memory, an element of strangeness which, it has been held, is always an accompaniment of beauty. In the suppression of some details and consequent emphasis upon others, experience is altered—not so much as to be wholly unrecognizable but remaining similar in dissimilarity. A beloved face seen amid unusual circumstances or in the light of unusual emotion is perceived suddenly as though afresh, as endowed with a new and unfamiliar beauty. The memories of childhood are beautiful because they are both ours and not ours. The boy to whom these experiences happened is not wholly ourself. In this fact lie strangeness and beauty.

Selection, then, which simpifies and thereby achieves a certain emphasis accompanied by strangeness, may be thought of as in itself a means to indirection, the other term of our definition; for by selection the essence of the thing is expressed by a suppression of some of the parts. The term "indirection" has, however, other corollary meanings into which, briefly, we must look.

In the mirror or in the painting the scene depicted differs from reality in that the hues are less brilliant than those of life. In the mirror the light has, in reflection, lost something of its intensity or has changed somewhat in character; and the pigments of the artist are lower-keyed than the colors of nature. We are conscious of looking not upon the thing itself but upon something subtly different. Apprehension is sharpened by that difference; like the beloved face, the scene is new and fresh. "By indirections we find directions out." The grapes of Apelles if indistinguishable from real grapes were a poor work of art. It is not the function of the painter to reproduce life exactly but life with a difference. For in the difference lies the emphasis, the meaning which he wishes to convey. The degrees of approximation of the picture to the thing represented may be many and various, and a different pleasure may be derived from each, as from the conventional pattern of an oriental rug and the realistic portraiture of a Rembrandt. But the most realistic depiction must fall short of a simulacrum if it is to give pleasure or if, indeed, it is to possess meaning.[1]

Indirection is further significant of the artistic process in that it is an invitation to the observer to share in the work of creation. When, in a work

[1]See discussion of realism, Chapters III and IV.

of art, a meaning, however edifying, is too explicitly stated, it fails to draw from the observer the utmost contributive effort. A symbol is inviting in that it prompts us to interpret the idea symbolized. We do not like labels to our pictures or too explicit interpretations of our music. The greater our degree of sophistication the less we desire these aids and the more we endow the work of art with meanings of our own. Allegory and parable are forms of indirection pleasing to simple minds. As we grow in perception we ask that our allegory—and in a sense every piece of fiction is an allegory—imply its meaning subtly, not obviously. The more we interpret, and the greater our contributory effort, the more we share with the author his view of life and aid in its expression. The great novelists have always the air of respecting our intelligence and flattering our powers of perception. They do not stress the obvious. Meredith ennobles us with his deference, raising us to an equality with himself. The cruder novelist writes down to us; he explains too much. Charm and beauty are fugitive virtues to be won only by subtlety and craft.

These few casual paragraphs have ventured into the field of æsthetics, from which I hasten to withdraw. My particular concern is with the technique of the novelist, and whatever æsthetic theory I have yet to offer will relate more precisely to fiction and its aims and methods. Yet in defining the terms "selection" and "indirection" it seemed not amiss to indicate their importance in the field common to all the arts. Their pertinence to the art of fiction will, I trust, be made explicit in the following pages.

THE TECHNIQUE OF
THE NOVEL

The brain-stuff of fiction is internal history.

George Meredith.

The Novel remains still, under the right persuasion, the most independent, most elastic, most prodigious of literary forms.

Henry James.

CHAPTER I

PLOT

The simplest form of story is that which tells, in the order of their occurrence, the adventures of a single character. Such is *Robinson Crusoe*. It is in Robinson's experiences that we are interested; we identify ourselves with him, look through his eyes, take on his character. He is a simple soul, easy to comprehend. We accept him without question and without effort. We enjoy him because he is commonplace, because he is simpler than we; to enter into his life is to strip ourselves of many vexations and subtleties. But the adventures which befall Robinson, though easily comprehensible, are unusual and foreign to our experience. De Foe's problem was to invent sufficient and varied incident to maintain the illusion early established, that of a simple character moving in an exotic world and enjoying unusual experiences. When his invention flags, as it does in the latter half of the book after Robinson has left his island, and when the glamour of tropical seas, parrots, goats, and cannibals has been dispelled, the reader's interest wanes. Unusual things must happen to Robinson if we are to stay with him; his prosaic drab figure must stand out against a wild and colorful background.

There are occasional instances in *Robinson*

Crusoe when the story departs from the simple
chronology of Robinson's adventures. Such are
the brief narratives told him by minor personages;
and of these the chief is that of the Spaniard relating the adventures of the settlers during Robinson's absence. Though not uninteresting the story
quickly fades in recollection. And the reason for
this lack of memorableness is not the weaker quality of the incidents in themselves, their failure to
surprise by their novelty, nor, wholly, their lack of
unity and totality of effect, but chiefly their re-
moteness from us. Robinson's experiences we have
made ours; they happen to us. The Spaniard's
story, like the lives of those about us, is less vivid
than our own. We cannot identify ourselves with
him so vividly as with Robinson.

There is in this episode a further bar to complete imaginative surrender. Robinson's adventures have previously carried us with him to Portu-
gal. This is the vivid present of the story. The
Spaniard's story relates happenings during his absence from the island, and for us to depart from
the present to recreate that past as the *now* of our
immediate experience demands some mental effort,
some ponderable loss of emotional intensity and
story illusion. Interpolated narratives of minor
characters, retrospections which ask new identifi-
cations and a fresh sense of the immediate *now*, departures from the straight highroad of the action,
inevitably weaken the story illusion; they impose a
strain upon the reader's attention. *Tom Jones,*

though long, is, by reason of its excellent structure, almost wholly memorable. Yet the story told by the Man of the Hill, an interpolated and irrelevant episode, relating the past experiences of a character strange to us, is neither vivid in the reading nor memorable in retrospect.

Robinson Crusoe is of a low order in the zoology of fiction, one of the invertebrates, a mollusc. Structurally it is self-contained. De Foe has only to cast away his hero amid circumstances sufficiently plausible; the essential story lies in Robinson's experience thereafter until the arrival of the rescue ship. The story then ends; the circle is complete. The author, having achieved so excellent a hero, was, however, loth to part with him. Robinson is led through a variety of subsequent adventures which no one remembers. For these have only a chronological relationship; they do not in any sense constitute a plot. They do not even happen in one place. There is no complication, no particular suspense, no resolution. Robinson is not even altered by his experiences save that he grows old. He remains the same prosaic non-conformist trader and speculator that he has always been. The story might end at one point as well as another. There is no apparent goal. The author invents episodes until he is weary or until the book is sufficiently long and then abruptly stops.

It is the defect of the *picaresque* novel and those novels of incident, such as De Foe's, which derive therefrom, that they have no clearly defined ob-

jective, no complication, and consequently little
suspense. They consist, like a bamboo pole, of many
sections laid end to end and all virtually alike. If
the reader remembers them at all it is only as a
string of episodes. Upon Robinson's adventures
while cast away unity is imposed by geographical
conditions. These episodes constitute a story with
a beginning, an anticipated conclusion, and breathless suspense in its attainment. But of *Captain
Singleton*, in many respects a novel superior to
Robinson Crusoe, all that I can recall is certain of
the more outstanding incidents of the journey
across Africa. And these be it observed have also
a kind of unity lent them by geography. The plot,
so to speak, begins on one seacoast and ends on the
other.

The Tameness of Robinson Crusoe

Is it the dulness of human nature which makes
Robinson Crusoe immortal? Was De Foe merely
a stupid fellow with an eye for fact, or was he an
artist with an instinct for the selection of convincing incident? It is well known that the life of Alexander Selkirk was a much more dashing, romantic,
and improbable one than that of the fictional hero
whom he begot. Fact is frequently incredible, and
the inventions of romancers are tame beside it. De
Foe, it would seem, made his hero unduly prosy,
with never an idea but for his preservation in this
world and his well-being in the next. The contrast
of this dogged, canting, cowardly, avaricious crea-

ture and his gorgeous tropical island—which we must imagine for ourselves, for he does not describe it—is sublime. Yet I doubt if De Foe knew what he had done. His method is no different from that he employs elsewhere. His chief character is familiar: the sensible, material-minded, non-conformist London tradesman. By chance this method hit upon a setting and circumstances which imposed unity upon it. And by chance or instinct—for De Foe seems not aware of it—the contrast of his hero with his surroundings is indelible.

How far De Foe was the conscious artist, I cannot decide, though I am inclined to think him intuitive. Yet in some important respects he was undoubtedly deliberate, and the study of his method throws light upon the question, what is realism? and upon the profounder one, what is art? It was De Foe's ambition to make fiction pass for fact. The accidents of the world, he was well aware, are frequently too extraordinary for belief. He toned them down, made them commonplace, and supported them by a wealth of circumstantial detail. His *Apparition of Mrs. Veal* has seemingly all the veracity and scientific care for evidence of a case reported by the Society for Psychical Research. His method reveals, notably, two truths: first the power that lies in details (when Robinson describes the clothing of his shipmates tossed upon the beach including "two shoes that were not fellows," who can fail to believe?) ; and, second, the law of the average, the commonplace, or, if you choose to call it that, the universal. Those experiences which are in themselves obvious, natural, and commonplace—which are, in short, the usual experiences of mankind—constitute, for De Foe, the stuff of fiction. Realism to him is synonymous with the actual. It is the function of his art to dissemble fiction as fact. Yet his world is not truly a factual world, for it is more rational, more orderly, more intelligible than life. By imposing order upon life, by toning it down, he is to some degree an artist.

If, as I believe, the unity and memorableness of a part of *Robinson Crusoe* are more or less a happy accident born of geography, Stevenson's *Kidnapped*, which it resembles, is unquestionably the product of a "low cunning." *Kidnapped* is a spare book, spare to thinness, as much of Stevenson is; but I find that I remember it, even to its sequence, and several of its scenes. Such memorableness is certain proof either of great vividness in the writing or logic in the structure, perhaps both. In *Kidnapped* the vividness is less than the structure, which is utterly simple but sound and complete, based upon a theme as elemental as that of *Robinson Crusoe*.

After the briefest of openings the story begins with David's visit to his miserly uncle. The attempt upon the hero's life and, shortly, the kidnapping, mark the beginning of the circle which is both logical and geographical. The events of the story occur in the hero's travels by sea from the east coast around the end of Scotland, his escape upon a rugged western island, and his flight with Alan Breck to Edinburgh. With his arrival there, his identity established, and his uncle brought to book, the story ends. Two loose threads are left hanging: Alan Breck is still in danger of his life as a fugitive from justice; and the love affair of David and Catriona has been merely suggested. This incompleteness is designed. These threads are to bind the story to its sequel. Throughout the story the motivation has been simple and elemental, the characters few and not too subtle, and every incident essential to the logical sequence of the narrative. The conclusion, the scene in which the grasping uncle is worsted, has been anticipated from the outset, and all the trials and adventures of the hero have been steps to its attainment.

Treasure Island, like *Kidnapped*, is distinguished for simplicity of theme. Search for buried treasure is promised almost at the outset and the story ends with its capture and the return of the gold-seekers. In the incidents there occurs but one complication which to any degree confuses the narrative. When Jim Hawkins steals the brig we need also to know what occurred in camp during his absence, and we have, consequently, two overlapping narratives and an enlargement of the point of view. This is, I think, the sole structural defect, if it deserves to be so characterized. There is no clouding of the adventure theme by any love interest. Indeed the only women mentioned, as I recall, are Jim's mother and the black wife of John Silver. Stevenson appreciated what so few romancers have the wit to learn, the relative unimportance of love in stories of simple adventure. In this respect he is of the great tradition of Dumas, Melville, and George Borrow.

Masefield's *Sard Harker* is a fine instance of a thrilling story almost ruined by an extraneous love-theme, the conventional romantic element corrupting the very springs of action. The story opens excellently with a description of a romantic South American background, a well-drawn hero, and a finely conceived ship and crew. The reader is made a little uneasy by the intrusion of a mystical element in the hero's propensity to dream. The dreams are stressed as prophetic. They have to do with a particular woman and a particular house. And they justify themselves insofar as they lead to a discovery of a plot to kidnap the heroine. The hero warns her brother of the danger and the plot seems well under way. We anticipate dangers in which the hero shall play an important part; his warning, we suppose, will have its place in the subsequent developments even though seemingly futile at the time. None of these anticipations is justified in the event.

The warning has no result whatsoever. The heroine and her brother are in no essential way affected by it. And the hero, instead of remaining in touch with the action, is the victim of a chain of accidents which lead to a vivid but wholly irrelevant series of adventures. He is taken inland to a mining camp, is imprisoned, escapes, and makes his way after great difficulties and dangers through jungles and over mountains to the sea. On every page the reader expects word or clew which will tie these experiences to the main thread of the story, the kidnapping of the heroine. Not a hint does he find, for indeed these adventures, which are the heart of the book, have no relation to the theme. Merely, at the end, when he has survived these perils, the hero finds himself by chance in the city in which the heroine is imprisoned. By a series of wholly improbable accidents he learns her whereabouts, is thrown with her, and passively shares her fate until, by another series of accidents, both are rescued. His dreams, his heroism, his power to do have led to nothing but this chance encounter at the end. He is wholly the victim of destiny, whereas he is, or should be, designed as the effective agent in guiding the story to its goal.

A critic need ask no finer instance of a story which goes wrong because of a flaw in its logical structure. The essential story is the account of the hero's wanderings in a savage country amid dangers. All that is asked is some simple motivation which will lead him to do as he does and as a consequence bring him at the end to a logical conclusion, success in his enterprise. The author, instead, seeks to blend this with a wholly different story and in so doing has failed properly to motivate the action. The two stories are never united. They lie side by side, chronologically, not logically, related. The cause of this failure is no doubt a mistaken desire to lend romantic color, "heart interest," to a theme to which these are alien. There need be no more love interest in *Sard Harker* than in *Robinson Crusoe* or *Treasure Island*. Or at the worst there need be no more than in *Kidnapped*. A heroine to serve as a minor reward at the end of an adventurous and well spent day is no great matter.

Structure of Scott's Novels—"Guy Mannering"

Structurally the novels of Scott are more complex than those of De Foe and the others I have referred to. Many characters are introduced, of whom a number are usually of major importance, and the plots involving these frequently rival in interest the adventures of the hero. Scott entered light-heartedly upon his stories with no more than a vague idea of where he was to come out, as a man turns down an inviting by-path careless whither it leads. Occasionally he even apologizes for his haphazard methods, as in the preface to *Waverley:*

The tale of Waverley was put together with so little care that I cannot boast of having sketched any distinct plan of the work. The whole adventures of Waverley in his movements up and down the country with the Highland Cateran Bean Lean, are managed without much skill. It suited best, however, the road I wanted to travel, and permitted me to introduce some descriptions of scenery and manners to which the reality gave an interest which the powers of the author might have otherwise failed to attain for them. And though I have been in other instances a sinner of this sort, I do not recollect any of these novels in which I have transgressed so widely as in the first of the series.

There is in this no whole-hearted conviction of sin. Scott took his responsibilities as a novelist lightly. To him a novel was a trivial form of composition which existed for entertainment only and was without influence upon the minds and characters of its readers. Nor had he the artist's conscience which holds the writer to the utmost pains that the reader's course may be made easy. With the greatest insouciance he alters his stories in mid-career, making of them something quite other than they promised at the outset. *Guy Mannering* is an excellent instance. For his changes in this, its lack of design, Scott apologizes in the introduction, as before in *Waverley:*.

The scheme projected (the life of one doomed by a sinister astrological prophecy) may be traced in the three or four first chapters of the work, but further consideration induced the author to lay his purpose aside. . . . In changing his plan, however, which was done in the course of printing, the early sheets retained the vestiges of the original tenor of the story, although they now hang upon it as an unnecessary and unnatural incumbrance. The cause of such vestiges occurring is now explained, and apologized for.

From the title and early chapters it is evident that Guy Mannering was intended to be the hero.

After the twenty year interval he becomes a minor character and it is Bertram with whose fortunes we are concerned. The introductory chapters have, however, despite their false emphasis, a certain expository value. We learn of the baby who is to become the hero, of Meg Merrilees, and Hatteraick the smuggler. Scott effects his transition to subsequent events in this fashion:

> He [Mannering] must also disappear from that of our readers, for it is to another and later period of his life that the present narrative relates.

The chapters immediately following recount the dispossession of the gypsies, introduce Kennedy the excise man, and tell the story of his murder and the disappearance of Harry Bertram, aged five. The true story has thus far not been launched; all the incidents are of an expository nature, acquainting the reader with facts essential to an understanding of the later action. To this Scott carries us with the sentence:

> Our narrative is now about to make a large stride and omit a space of nearly seventeen years.

At the end of this period Guy Mannering, now Colonel Mannering, is reintroduced in Scotland as the estate of Ellangowan is about to be sold. The rascally lawyer, Glossin, secures it, Colonel Mannering's bid, by an accident convenient to the plot, not arriving in time. Mannering's life in

India is then recounted for the benefit of the reader in a letter to Mannering's friend Mervyn, who presumably already knows the facts:

Let me recall to you—but the task must be brief—the odd and wayward fates of my youth and the misfortunes of my manhood.

The letter makes reference to one Ensign Brown and Colonel Mannering's jealousy of him which resulted in a duel. These references call attention to Brown and explain the obstacle to Brown's suit for the hand of Julia, the Colonel's daughter—a contrived and wholly factitious obstacle as later appears.

The story then introduces one of the heroines, Lucy Bertram, sister of the lost heir, and Dominie Sampson, a "humorous" character. We learn also of the second heroine, Julia Mannering, and her mysterious suitor—these facts through the instrumentality of a letter from Mervyn to Colonel Mannering. More light is thrown upon this episode by quotations from the letters of Julia to a friend:

The perusal of a few short extracts from these may be necessary to render our story intelligible.

Brown, it appears, is the suitor, of whose past, again told in letters to a friend who has no other function in the story, we are informed after the following characteristic transition:

And having thus left the principal characters of our tale in a situation which, being sufficiently comfortable to themselves, is, of course utterly uninteresting to the reader, we take up the history of a person who has as yet only been named, and who has all the interest that uncertainty and misfortune can give.

In twenty-one chapters Scott has pretty well laid the scene of his story, informed us of the leading characters, and indicated the lines of the ensuing action.

In the next chapter Brown starts upon a walking tour in the course of which he makes the acquaintance of the farmer, Dinmont, destined to turn up repeatedly in the subsequent incidents though without any relation to the plot. He is one in whom the author delights and is his own excuse for being. Meg Merrilees is reintroduced in an incident which has plot significance; she is struck with the appearance of Brown—an obvious hint that he is the long-lost heir. Mention of a minor character, Gabriel the gypsy, is also pertinent to the action; but the greater part of several chapters merely depicts Scotch rural life and country sports, descriptions which, though picturesque, have no relevancy to the story.

The action of the story is resumed in chapter 27 when Brown, lost in his post-chaise, sets out on foot to find shelter. He comes upon a lonely hut in which is a dying man attended by Meg Merrilees; is hidden by her from the returning smugglers; and is aided to escape after promising to go with her whenever, at some unspecified time, she shall call upon him—in exacting which promise Meg seems possessed of an extraordinary prescience of subsequent events. Brown's adventures are resumed but through the medium of letters from Julia to her confidante. Therein we learn of her sudden meeting with Brown, his contest with Hazelwood, lover of Lucy Bertram, and the unfortunate accident to Hazelwood, an accident which increases the dangers besetting the hero and has no other purpose. For Glossin, the villain in league with Hatteraick, learns Brown's true identity and seeks, on the pretext of the assault, to destroy him. The plot has now thickened. This is the end of the first volume.

Subsequent developments have been forecast in the main. Brown, now clearly Bertram, must undergo further perils at the hands of the villains Glossin and Hatteraick; must be rescued and identified through the agency of Meg Merrilees and restored to his ancestral estates, receiving thereupon the hand of the heroine. Yet the end must not be too soon and too easily arrived at. Therefore in various situations the hero is peculiarly unfortunate. Misunderstandings and ill-luck pursue him until, of a sudden, fortune smiles and all circumstances work together in his behalf. Scott meanwhile has not been content to confine himself to Bertram's story. Several chapters conduct the reader to Edinburgh that he may witness the high jinks of advocate Pleydell and his cronies; Dinmont is reintroduced; and Scott lingers on scenes and characters dear to him, however irrelevant to the action. Then, having dallied as long as he dare, he suddenly winds up his story, pairs off the lovers in the fewest possible words, and dwells for a moment with satisfaction upon the rightful heir's resumption of his feudal estates and privileges.

Thus to analyze *Guy Mannering* is, though a little tedious, amusing also in the disclosure of structural defects. The false opening, with its emphasis upon Mannering, perplexes the action for long and it is only after repeated and clumsy efforts that Scott succeeds in getting his story upon the right track. The true hero, Brown or Bertram, does not assume his proper place until after many pages and much tedious exposition. This latter is introduced largely in the form of letters, a dull and uninteresting device which is thrice employed: in Colonel Mannering's correspondence with Mervyn, Julia's letters to her confidante, and Brown's to his friend. And in each instance characters are named who have not the slightest part in the story. They are merely repositories of information, lay-figures through whom the reader is made cognizant of essential facts.

These are not the only characters superfluous to the story. The farmer Dinmont, Dominie Sampson, the advocate Pleydell, the artist Dudley, friend of Brown—introduced casually for a moment and as casually dropping from sight—all are inessential to the plot. Scott brings them in—with the exception of Dudley, for whom I see no explanation—for the simple and, to him, sufficient reason, that he was interested in them and through them could introduce scenes and aspects of Scotch life which appealed to him. The story merely offers a convenient rack upon which to drape these extraneous materials. Yet they provide the most interesting passages of the book. About them Scott writes with the most enthusiasm. They are dear to him because characteristic of his beloved Scotland. In *Guy Mannering*, as in most of Scott's novels, it is evident that Scott is not primarily a novelist at all, not a maker of stories, but a social chronicler. A story was merely a convenient device wherewith to set forth his observations of men and manners and his descriptions of romantic and historic scenes.

To depict customs, characters, and romantic scenes is legitimate enough. But there is no reason save laziness or indifference why these should not be made more integral parts of his story. Only a little ingenuity need be expended and Dinmont and Dominie Sampson would be structurally significant to the action. Meg Merrilees is to be the instrument to the hero's recovery of his heritage, and inasmuch as, at the outset of the story, she utters a curse upon Ellangowan, she must specifically exempt, as she does, "little Harry and the babe about to be born." The motivation here is sacrificed to the needs of the plot. Conceivably a novel can be made a vehicle to any end. The history of the form shows it to be adaptable to many purposes. But if these ends are to be effectively achieved, characters must be plausible and necessary, and the parts must hang together; episodes must all be related to the action, and be not merely decorations to the story, but essential elements of it.

In addition Scott fails for me, and I think for most modern readers, to maintain the story illusion. The reader will overlook or ignore all manner of logical defects in a story provided he can lose himself in it emotionally, can identify himself with a character or characters and live their experiences. In Scott's novels it is often hard to do this. His explanations and his historical disquisitions are frequently not narrative at all but mere lumps of explanatory matter. And his transitions from one character to another and one scene to another are often such as that previously cited: "Our narrative is now about to make a large stride." These are chilling words. The reader is plucked forcibly from the fictitious life in which he has been absorbed and made aware that all is pretense. He wishes to think it real, to lose himself in it, to make its emotions his, but he is not permitted to do so. With each break in the narrative, each clumsy transition, he resumes less easily his identification with the story's characters.

Ivanhoe, like *Guy Mannering*, though less obviously, suffers from a change of plan midway in the story. Ivanhoe, in the introductory chapters, is designated, by the emphasis upon him, as the hero, and the development of the story is forecast:

Ivanhoe is to be reestablished in his father's favor
and rewarded with the fair Rowena. Up to the time
of the tournament Ivanhoe is indeed the chief figure
and it is with his fortunes we are concerned. With
the advent of Richard disguised, of Prince John,
De Bracy, and the rest, the plot changes. The
theme becomes the story of Richard's conflict with
his brother, a contest, moreover, which does not
accord with the professed purpose of the book, to
exemplify the rivalry of Saxon and Norman. The
hero, Ivanhoe, is wounded and shelved for the
greater part of the ensuing action and Rebecca
supplants Rowena as heroine. Midway in his fiction Scott evidently perceived new possibilities in
it and nonchalantly altered its trend. This divided
and uncertain purpose is evident and is the cause
of the dissatisfaction which is mingled with the
reader's enjoyment of the book.

The complexity of *Ivanhoe* and the large number of its characters necessitate many transitions;
interest centres now in Ivanhoe, again in Rebecca,
or King Richard. The action after advancing one
group of characters to a convenient halting place
turns back to bring up a laggard column. The
places of the action, too, are various. Only the time
covered is unified and compact. To manipulate an
action so complex great dexterity is obviously desirable, and this Scott exhibits only indifferently. His time transitions are usually well covered,
are sunk in the body of the narrative, and the
reader is taken from day to day without undue em-

phasis. "The sun rose in unclouded splendor"—
the author so introduces his chapter descriptive of
the tournament. The preceding chapter has closed
with a night scene. But this deftness is not always
manifest. "Our history must needs retrograde,"
says the author in one place and proceeds to pick
up a dropped thread. Or again, "Like old Ariosto
we do not pique ourselves upon continuing uniformly to keep company with any one personage
of our drama"—and so apologizes for a rude jolt
in the narrative. The story illusion, so fragile, so
hard to create, is in such transitions endangered
if not dispelled. The reader is recalled to himself
and is no longer a participant in the make-believe
of romance.

Overplotting—Instances in Dickens

The easy moral derivable from the study of fiction is that in simple adventure stories too few authors make the action severely plausible, consistent, and logical; and in more complicated stories,
such as *Guy Mannering,* avoid looseness. Overplotting is the other extreme, and Dickens, of
course, is the notorious instance of an author who
attempts too complicated and at the same time, too
tight a structure. His admiration for Wilkie Collins, an excellent builder of elaborate plots—which
are, however, suited to their type of mystery story
—and his innate passion for melodrama explain
this defect. That it is a defect any real lover of
Dickens will admit. The mysteries, the villains,

the hidden crimes, the unnatural persecutions and pursuits with which Dickens abounds lend to his amiable sunny genius a wholly false and theatrical air. Even in his greatest structural successes, such as *Bleak House,* he fails, as his best critic, Gissing, points out, by knitting all the complicated threads into too close and improbable a pattern.

An excellent and outstanding instance of Dickens' congenital weakness is the use made of Micawber in *David Copperfield* as the tool of Heep. Nothing is more improbable than Heep's employing Micawber unless it be Micawber's remaining for so long in the employ of Heep. Micawber as the agent of destiny in unmasking the villain is quite unbelievable. To give Micawber a part so important structurally is to make a flying buttress out of a gargoyle. It is incredible; Micawber, wholly delightful as a free character without obligations to the plot, is sacrificed to his function. Estella's relationship to the convict in *Great Expectations* is another instance of a too close weaving of incident. The author's purpose, no doubt, was not only to relate all his characters one to another, to achieve a certain false air of structural compactness, but also to find therein a means to humbling Estella's pride. She is put, so to speak, in the same boat with Pip. Some other means would better have sufficed.

Dickens exhibits always an exaggerated passion for suspense, and it is to this that his vague mysteries and horrors and his proneness to overplotting are due. From this no doubt arise also the flaws, illogicalities, and inconsequences of his plots. He seems at the outset of a story to have planned, vaguely, mysteries which subsequent alterations of the plot leave unexplained. Thus in the *Tale of Two Cities,* Lucie's testimony in Darnay's trial intimates a secret later to be cleared up. There is also the testimony of the spies as to Darnay's mysterious trips to France whose purpose Darnay "even for his life" might not disclose. What this mystery is, Dickens never discloses, though there are subsequent allusions to it in Darnay's interview with his uncle. Also in the first trial the De Farges withhold their evidence, for no purpose, apparently, save to heighten the suspense. There are, again, two reasons assigned for the proscription of the Evremonde family, the second obviously an afterthought. And what of Jerry Cruncher's mysterious errands, of Barsed and Cly, of the body-snatching episode? Nothing comes of these that I recall. They merely are stage thunder designed to create an ominous atmosphere. Serving their turn they are never explained. The reader is supposed to forget them in the grand finale when the characters make their stage bows.

All of Dickens' faults in overplotting and in creating a meretricious atmosphere of mystery and crime are well illustrated in one of his best novels, *Our Mutual Friend.* In the postscript he explains his purpose in using the Harmon mystery as a background and its close interweaving with the design of the book. That it is closely interwoven will be admitted. That it is also essentially extraneous and has nothing to do with the main story will be the opinion of most readers. And why the first alias of Mr. John Harmon, Julius Blandford? This is surely unjustified and falsely motivated. It is only a part of the stage fire. And the Hexam implication in the supposed murder, and the whole of Rogue Riderhood and his deviltries are merely gratuitous attempts to graft a crime and mystery melodrama upon a social satire.

When I devised this story, I foresaw the likelihood that a class of readers and commentators would suppose that I was at great pains to conceal exactly what I was at great pains to suggest: namely, that Mr. John Harmon was not slain, and that Mr. John Rokesmith was he. Pleasing myself with the idea that the supposition might in part arise out of some ingenuity in the story, and thinking it worth while, in the interest of art, to hint to an audience that an artist (of whatever denomination) may perhaps be trusted to know what he is about in his vocation, if they will concede him a little patience, I was not alarmed by the anticipation.

To keep for a long time unsuspected, yet always working itself out, another purpose originating in that leading incident, and turning it to a pleasant and useful account at last, was at once the most interesting and the most difficult part of my design. Its difficulty was much enhanced by the mode of publication; for, it would be very unreasonable to expect that many readers, pursuing a story in portions from month to month through nineteen months, will, until they have it before them complete, perceive the relations of its minor threads to the whole pattern which is always before the eyes of the weaver at his loom. Yet, that I hold the advantages of the mode of publication to outweigh its disadvantages may be easily believed of one who revived it in the *Pickwick Papers* after long disuse, and has pursued it ever since.

The way in which Dickens achieves his close texture by relating his characters to one another in various ways may be illustrated by the dramatis personæ of *Our Mutual Friend*. Hexam and Riderhood, hunters of drowned bodies, are both implicated in the supposed Harmon murder. Hexam is reputed to be the criminal. Riderhood is the murderer in intent. Riderhood claims the reward from Lightwood for informing upon the murderer. He hates Lightwood's friend, Wrayburn, and later is associated in that hatred with Bradley Headstone, rival of Wrayburn for Lizzie Hexam. Lizzie is a friend of Jenny Wren's and of Riah's. Riah is the incredible tool of Fledgeby, who is a distant relative of Twemlow. Fledgeby is the candidate of the Lammles for the hand of Georgiana Podsnap. Many of these characters meet at the home of the Veneerings, which serves as a kind of social clearing-house. Lizzie Hexam is related to Harmon in that through him her father's name is cleared. Also it is she who finds Betty Higden dying. Betty is robbed in her wanderings by Rogue Riderhood. Her grandchild has been adopted by the Boffins. To her funeral Lizzie summons the Boffins who are accompanied by Bella Wilfer. Lizzie and Bella thus become friends. One further instance will serve. Mr. Venus, for a time fellow conspirator of Silas Wegg, is also suitor for the hand of Pleasant Riderhood, the lady who refused to be regarded "in that bony light."

The English novel, like the Russian, is traditionally of loose epic structure, built on a vast scale, and able to digest widely diverse materials. The artistry with which it is put together is tremendously uneven, from the carefully planned novels of Fielding, to the loosely picaresque stories of Smollett, or the hastily extemporized romances of Scott. The short artistic novel, conscious of form and stringently selective in content, is largely a modern thing, owing its existence to *Madame Bovary* and the French school. Jane Austen is, of course, an exception, achieving without models almost impeccable form. George Moore and Frank Swinnerton are derivative.

Comparison of the two types for the purpose of establishing the preeminence of one over the other is not particularly illuminating. It may be said that the short novel, if well done, is more easily recalled as a fable, its sequence of scenes, as in *Kidnapped,* remaining distinct. The simple stories of *Nocturne* or *Esther Waters* come back to one entire after years, together with certain of the more poignant scenes and the mood which the novel, when first read, evoked. It is hard to recall any of Dickens' novels in its entirety, or of Balzac's, save, perhaps, *Père Goriot* and *Eugénie Grandet.* Yet in their aggregate the novels of

Dickens or of Balzac create unforgetable and complete worlds. The nineteenth century, said Oscar Wilde, was the creation of Balzac. If Dickens, Thackeray, and Tolstoy be added, the epigram is almost a truism.

The Russian novel, like the English, is built traditionally on a large scale. Nothing in human experience is alien to it. It is not easy to see in *War and Peace* why some of the incidents told are included. All do not seem essential to the plot. Yet in so epic a story minor irrelevancies become, in perspective, insignificant. The novel is like some panoramic canvas painted with a large brush. The roughness of workmanship, the inclusion of all sorts of details, are of no importance in the general effect, provided that the larger outlines be well massed, as in *War and Peace* they are. And in *Anna Karénina* and *Resurrection*, the former particularly, there is evident structure. Dostoievsky is far more inchoate, almost formless; yet his power is undeniable. His novels have the complexity and sweep of life itself. In Turgénev the Russian wealth of observation is disciplined, is subjected to exacting standards of form. Turgénev is a happy blending of the best qualities in both French and Russian tradition.[1]

Turgénev is a novelist for novelists. Henry James and Conrad, themselves two most excellent craftsmen, write of him with enthusiasm. For in Turgénev are combined that richness of content

[1]Dostoievsky and Turgénev are further discussed in Chapter III.

and the passion for form, which is the perfect formula for great fiction. Such novelists as Turgénev must necessarily be rare. He lies between the inchoate richness of Dostoievsky and Dickens and the somewhat thin artistry of Flaubert, or, less notably, George Moore. The mass of fiction more nearly resembles one or another of these extremes than it does his. Writers of the modern naturalistic school tend to formlessness; writers with a sense of artistry, too often to thinness. The critic is no doubt tempted to over-rate the latter, forgetting that though form is desirable, is even essential to a masterpiece, content is the vital thing. For a novel is more than a form of art. It is also a criticism of life, a social record.

Solid Plot Structure—"Middlemarch"

There are sufficient examples in English of great novels neither thin in content nor poor in form. *Tom Jones*, at the very beginning of modern English fiction, reveals a sound sense of structure. Fielding's experience as a dramatist was the precise thing necessary to one who was to invent a new form of narrative, the comic epic in prose. I choose, however, for a somewhat more detailed analysis, *Middlemarch* as an instance of a long complex novel, rich in characterization and comment on life, which, at the same time, is an admirable piece of simple structure. It bulks immensely; it has an air of solidarity and permanence.

Middlemarch is a cross section of English provincial life and really comprises four distinct stories. Related one to another, woven together as George Eliot succeeds in doing, they are immensely more weighty, richer in their social implications, than had they been written and published separately. They are like the wings of an admirably designed building, individually sufficing, but in their relations to each other taking on a majesty quite disproportionate to their individual excellences.

With but one exception, which I shall note, the interrelations of the parts in *Middlemarch* are fashioned without the employment of unnatural circumstances or forced plotting. George Eliot uses the simplest devices to unite her various social groups, the ties of blood and marriage. The Vincys, Bulstrodes, Garths, and Mr. Featherstone, as well as several minor characters, form a single family connection. Dorothea Brooke marries Mr. Casaubon, to whom Will Ladislaw is cousin. Lydgate marries Rosamond Vincy and, as a doctor, has professional connections with all the chief groups of story characters. He serves as a cord to bind them together. So, too, Mr. Farebrother, a friend of Lydgate and Fred Vincy, and lover of Mary Garth, is also a clergyman, related in his office to most of the characters; Dorothea Brooke presents him with a living. Only in one instance, I think, does George Eliot force her relationships, achieving thereby a rather theatrical effect. Ladislaw, as the grandson of Bulstrode's first wife and defrauded by him, is surely unnatural. The tie

serves no useful purpose save to make Ladislaw
reject the banker's money and thus show himself
to be the hero worthy of Dorothea. When George
Eliot goes wrong either in plot or characterization the cause is usually some young man cast as
the hero. It is with her admirable young men that
she wanders farthest from the paths of homely
plausibility.

The serial form of publication which Dickens
defends in *Our Mutual Friend* has undoubtedly
been responsible for much overplotting. The novelist has at the end of every instalment to pique the
reader's interest in the next. Mystery, false glamour, are almost inevitable. Moreover changes in
the plot mid-way in the story, as in *Martin
Chuzzlewit, The Tale of Two Cities*, and *Barnaby
Rudge*, result in inconsistencies and obscurities.
The Victorian novel in general suffers from too
heavy a structure. Charles Reade's novels are exciting enough but verge on melodrama. The con-
tagion is manifest in such a work as *Jane Eyre*.
De Morgan's novels were hailed as Victorian and
Dickensian largely because they returned to the
elaborate plotting of a former generation. The
practice of novelists had changed by De Morgan's time.

The modern novel for various reasons mini-
mizes the importance of plot. On the one hand it
follows the naturalistic[1] lead and considers the
elaboration of plot false to experience. On the

[1]See Chapter IV for discussion of naturalism.

other, with its emphasis upon character or whimsy, and its reliance upon charm and mannerism, it avoids the painful business of plot construction. To this it pretends superiority. The result in most instances is boredom. I speak for myself only. I find that half the novels I read, though interesting at the outset, do not hold me to the end. It is not wholly age or saturation that is responsible for this loss of interest. Plot, suspense, the weaving of a complication of whose end we are curious, are legitimate devices of the story teller. A reader is seldom so sophisticated that a well-built story will not intrigue him and hold his attention. But a well-built plot, not too complicated, but simple, logical, and consistent, into which each episode is built as definitely as a bit of stone in a pattern of mosaic is a hard thing to contrive. It involves fundamental brainwork, and this many novelists shirk. The story teller must be both able and artistically serious to force himself to it.

The Scène à Faire

In chief the careless novel neglects the *scène à faire* which is as inevitable a requisite in fiction as in the drama. The reader of fiction shares with the spectator at a play a sense of God-like omniscience. He knows more of the characters than they know of themselves. He anticipates their conflicts and the outcome of them. His pleasure consists very considerably in looking forward to the logical event. The delightful scene in *Pride and Prejudice* in which Darcy first proposes to Elizabeth has been prepared for. We know that Darcy is to be rejected and enjoy, prospectively, the blow to his pride. In *Lorna Doone*, John Ridd's fight with Carver Doone, though almost too long delayed, is highly satisfying when it comes. The sight of Carver sinking "joint by joint" into the bog is a grateful one. And that scene in *Vanity Fair* in which Rawdon Crawley confronts Becky and Lord Steyne is of the essence of drama, as, too, is the scene in *Henry Esmond* in which the hero renounces allegiance to the Pretender.

Henry James is masterly in his forecast, in his preparation for the inevitable scene; from the quietest incidents he can extract strong excitement. His novels are remarkable for suspense—a suspense too tardily relieved, no doubt, for the taste of many. So quiet a book as *The Ambassadors*, elsewhere[1] discussed, is an exciting story, although nothing more violent than a tea or a tête à tête occurs in the whole two volumes. The great scenes in James are always mental conflicts, are, even in words, but rarely scenes of passion. The scene at the end of *The Awkward Age* in which Nanda bursts into tears seems almost brutal in its violence, so quiet is the author's scale of values. It is wholly satisfying, and one could wish that James more often let himself go in this fashion. Too often in his books the *scène à faire*, if violent, is told retrospectively or at second-hand.

[1]See Chapter II.

It is a fault of Meredith, to my taste, that he denies us so often the *scène à faire* for which our expectation has been whetted. It is deliberate this avoidance, as of a thing too obvious; yet we are sometimes balked of our legitimate expectation. I find it disappointing that no one save Letitia in *The Egoist* speaks a few pointed words to Sir Willoughby at the last. My taste is no doubt crude. Other scenes in Meredith seem to demand physical violence. The violence, indeed, sometimes occurs, but off-stage and in a fashion unworthy of one who talks so admirably of the fistic art. I recall such instances in *Harry Richmond*, *One of Our Conquerors*, in *Evan Harrington*. In *Beauchamp's Career* we are primed for the duel in France. The incident is glossed over but there is rumor of Nevil's limping. Even retrospectively we could enjoy some account of the circumstance. Then, passingly, it is remarked that Nevil didn't fight at all, having, presumably, conscientious objections. George Eliot rises more nobly to her obligations in *Adam Bede*. The fight of Adam with Arthur must, it is true, be honored more for its intent than its execution. George Eliot was obviously no patron of the ring. Yet however inadequate in itself, the episode bears witness to the author's artistic conscience. The *scène à faire* is an obligation which, in the novel of plot, may not be denied.

CHAPTER II

THE POINT OF VIEW

Analysis of story structure can go but a little way without employing the term "point of view," thus introducing a structural principle of the widest implications. Various things are often meant by the term, but in this discussion it will be used only in its strict technical sense. It will imply, simply, Who is the teller of the story? By what convention is he possessed of the facts and empowered to narrate them? What may he tell, and what may he not? For there are several points of view open to the writer, each with its advantages and limitations. Each is in its very nature restricted; it must be consistent with itself on pain of destroying or impairing that illusion, to create which, as was earlier said, is the all-important object of the story. The reader desires to enter into and share the lives of the characters. He seeks vicarious experience. But this he can enjoy only as certain conventions are adhered to. For the novel, like the drama, like all art, is a game with certain rules which may not be violated without penalty. The penalty is a loss of convincingness, of story illusion.

In *Robinson Crusoe* the story is told by the chief participant. The point of view offers few narrative difficulties, for little of importance happens in which Robinson does not personally share, witness with his own eyes, and therefore convincingly put down for us. The story told him by the Spaniard upon his return to the island is the single noteworthy exception. And here there is no technical difficulty, for the incidents are narrated to Robinson in the most natural fashion and by him reported. There is some slight loss of vividness in telling a story thus at second-hand; that is all. But in stories of more complicated action, in which the narrator is not a participant in all the important episodes, the difficulties which arise are often insurmountable. The vicissitudes of an author employing this point of view in a story of complicated incident are agreeably demonstrated in *The Vicar of Wakefield*.

Point of View in "The Vicar of Wakefield"

It is very soon evident that the Vicar is no fit person to tell the story. The account of his sufferings, his Job-like resignation, or his philosophy of monogamy he tells affectingly or amusingly enough. But no sooner does he conduct a plot and recount the fortunes of his family than he is in difficulties. The story told by Mr. Burchell of Sir William Thornhill in which occurs the passage, "He now found that a man's own heart must be ever given to gain that of another. I now found that—that—I forget what I was going to observe: in short, sir, he resolved to respect himself . . ." indicates at once the nature of the difficulty. The Vicar must record but not note Mr. Burchell's slip. The slip is for the reader, that he may know Burchell's identity. The Vicar must be kept in ignorance and is stultified for that purpose to the end.

Through the same medium, the narrator, Burchell's character must be presented likewise in two contradictory aspects. He must be shown to the reader as honest, simple, just. To the Vicar who paints him thus he must, for the purposes of the plot, be made antipathetic. Such passages as these occur: "I began, for certain reasons, to be displeased with his return"; and in the next breath, "I know not how, but he every day seemed to become more amiable, his wit to improve, and his simplicity to assume the superior airs of wisdom." And in the scene in which Mrs. Primrose speaks of Burchell as "low-lived," the Vicar remarks, "He seems upon some occasions, the most finished gentleman I ever knew." A moment later he responds to Sophia's commendation of Burchell with, "such . . . is the cant of all the unfortunate or idle. But I hope you have been taught to judge properly of such men, and that it would be even madness to expect happiness from one who has been so very bad an economist of his own." The Vicar's inconsistency may be speciously defended on the pretense that the virtues of Burchell as a man may not necessarily recommend him as an impecunious son-in-law. But in the scene in which Burchell is confronted with the letter abstracted from his pocket book and indefensibly opened, the Vicar must be made an utter fool not to apprehend the character of his benefactor.

A like stultification is evident throughout in the episodes which concern young Thornhill. To the reader his villainy is evident from the first. The Vicar has only an occasional suspicion even in the face of the most open guilt and not until Olivia's disclosures does he see Thornhill for what he is. The plot, unfolded from the Vicar's point of view, asks this sacrifice; and though the plot is ridiculous enough, as will appear, the character inconsistency seems to me the greatest defect. For the story resides chiefly in the Vicar. He must charm and amuse. While we laugh at his simplicity we should love him. It is hard to love a character so wholly inconsistent and stupid, so impossible a mixture of folly and wisdom as he is made, for plot purposes, to be. If Goldsmith was unwilling to sacrifice plot to character consistency he had but the one alternative of telling his story from some other point of view.

While suffering all the inconveniences possible to his point of view the author does not, as a matter of fact, maintain it consistently. It merges inevitably now and then into the larger point of view of the author. The amusing chapter which tells of the town ladies at the home of neighbour Flamborough is told from the point of view of the observant author. It is with a start that we realize at the end the Vicar's supposed rôle as narrator. He has been wholly subordinated. And a little later when the Vicar's wife challenges Thornhill to avow his intentions the point of view is virtually omniscient. The two girls we understand were secreted in the next room. Of the Vicar no mention is made. But the interview is wholly related in dialogue and with description even of Thornhill's appearance and gestures. There is obviously here no pretense of consistency.

The Vicar's pursuit of the erring Olivia and the surprising experiences of his return journey are among the most entertaining chapters of the book, partly because of their content and partly because Goldsmith begins to give up the struggle with his point of view and rely upon coincidence to get him out of his difficulties. After his three weeks' illness necessary to the lapse of sufficient time for story developments, the Vicar encounters, by a series of accidents sufficiently extraordinary, the political-minded butler, the travelling players, Miss Wilmot, his son George—whose adventures comprise the most interesting chapter of the book—Thornhill, and last, the repentant Olivia. With her he returns home just in time to rescue his family from the flames.

It is evident that Goldsmith is now entertained by the absurdities of his plot and in the finale and resolution of the gaol episode pushes his comedy well into farce. The devices whereby all the characters are brought together in the prison and the repentant Mr. Jenkinson serves as official stage manager with his various messengers as assistants, constitute what is slangily known as a "riot." Even Miss Wilmot appears:

Her arrival was quite accidental. It happened that she and the old gentleman, her father, were passing through the town, on the way to her aunt's, who had insisted that her nuptials with Mr. Thornhill should be consummated at her house; but stopping for refreshment, they put up at an inn at the other end of the town. It was there, from the window, that the young lady happened to observe one of my little boys playing in the street, and instantly sending a footman to bring the child to her, she learned from him some account of our misfortunes; but was still kept ignorant of young Mr. Thornhill's being the cause. Though her father made several remonstrances on the impropriety of going to a prison to visit us, yet they were ineffectual; she desired the child to conduct her, which he did and it was thus she surprised us at a juncture so unexpected.

Goldsmith philosophizes gravely upon this happy coincidence:

Nor can I go on without a reflection on those accidental meetings, which, though they happen every day, seldom excite our surprise but upon some extraordinary occasion. To what a fortuitous concurrence do we not owe every pleasure and convenience of our lives! How many seeming accidents must unite before we can be clothed and fed! The peasant must be disposed to labour, the shower must fall, the wind fill the merchant's sail, or numbers must want the usual supply.

Whether as stylist or sophist Goldsmith is delightful and I can forgive him much in *The Vicar of Wakefield* for the fate to which he condemns the villain, Squire Thornhill:

His time is pretty much taken up in keeping his relation, who is a little melancholy, in spirits, and in learning to blow the French horn.

It is apparent that the author's story got out of hand and ran away with him. The original point of view proved inadequate to its control. And Goldsmith enjoys the thrill of the flight and the smash at the end. The conclusion is hilarious with a general breaking of glassware. Yet inasmuch as *The Vicar of Wakefield* is a classic and is gravely held up for the admiration of the young, it may be well to observe that not only as a story is it absurd, its plot a tangle of inconsistencies and coincidences, but also—and this a far more serious fault—it is not what it set out to be. The delicate humor and satire of the earlier chapters are not consistently maintained. Too melodramatic an action, too inadequate a point of view, transform pastoral comedy to farce. And worst of all, the Vicar himself, in whom Goldsmith had the germ of a delightful character, is likewise sacrificed. Only intermittently is he a person. Much of the time he is an inadequate cog in a poorly designed machine.

The point of view of the chief character is traditional in the English novel. A long and distinguished array of titles comes to mind—*Jane Eyre*, *Pendennis*, and *David Copperfield* among them;

as, too, *Lavengro, Romany Rye, Kidnapped, Moby Dick, The Purple Land, Green Mansions.* But it is in the latter group, I think, that the character of the narrator is most wholly identified with the story. Borrow's novels have all the charm and veracity of memoirs; how much of them is truth, how much fiction, we neither know nor care. The adventures of the hero as told by himself are completely absorbing; they create the perfect illusion in life. But these are simple stories, moving in a straight line, with few complications. The more elaborate stories employing this point of view inevitably share in greater or less degree the difficulties and failures of *The Vicar of Wakefield.* Illustrations could be cited from *Jane Eyre* or *The Newcomes;* but one from *David Copperfield* will suffice, being unsurpassed. David, who must be at the heart of the action which he is to record, goes on some pretext to Yarmouth where he is witness to the shipwreck in which Steerforth is drowned in the very sight of the home from which he seduced Little Emily. This is an appalling use of coincidence which springs, no doubt, partly from Dickens' fondness for lurid effects but no less from the exigencies of the point of view.

Composite Point of View

Occasional novels have employed a composite point of view, instances being *The Moonstone* of Wilkie Collins, and *The Master of Ballantrae* and

Dr. Jekyll and Mr. Hyde of Stevenson. *Treasure Island* in one place brings in the narrative of the Doctor to supplement that of Jim Hawkins. In *Bleak House* there is a curious shift in the point of view when Esther Summerson is made to tell her story in the midst of a narrative conducted by the author. The effect is not happy, for the two methods do not harmonize, employing as they do story conventions essentially different in kind. In *The Moonstone* or *The Master of Ballantrae* the method, though difficult and necessitating awkward shifts, has its compensations. In a story of unusual happenings the reports of eye-witnesses lend an air of plausibility; and in a mystery or crime story suspense may be created and sustained thereby. Subtle variations upon this point of view are to be found in *Chance*[1] and *The Turn of the Screw*.[1]

The letter form employed by Richardson is essentially that of the composite narrative save that the shifts from character to character are more frequent and are easier, perhaps, to accept imaginatively. Letter writing being a most familiar practice, a novel which adopts this method has an air of disarming ingenuousness. But novels in letter form are very difficult to write. Jane Austen, who began as a disciple of Richardson, soon developed the more flexible technique of the omniscient author. Letters involve inevitably many repetitions if an effect of naturalness is to be achieved.

[1] See detailed discussion in Chapter III.

Richardson's novels, though full of delicate and fine effects, are almost intolerably long. And the novelist is denied all comment upon his story and its characters. This limitation Richardson endeavored to overcome by explanatory footnotes here and there. These are out of harmony with the method, and the discord which they strike weakens the story illusion.

Inasmuch as all methods of telling a story are mere conventions, means whereby the story can be told, why do we ask consistency? Why should a point of view once adopted be maintained if a shift to another seems convenient? There is no moral nor even logical objection. The difficulty is imaginative only and inherent in the nature of story telling. At the outset the writer may adopt any method he likes, may choose any one of the several points of view which have been invented. The reader, whatever his individual preferences, cannot quarrel with the choice of conventions. It is his task to lend that "willing suspension of disbelief" of which Coleridge speaks. The author may tell his story as a participant or he may assume godlike omniscience. The reader is equally credulous, prepared to lose himself in the story, to surrender his identity and take on that of another. But the illusion established must be unbroken. Were the author to write as a participant and then of a sudden assume powers of insight no participant could possibly possess, the reader would be bewildered. He can take on the identity of a fictitious character, or, if the transitions are well contrived, the identities of several characters, but he cannot, at one and the same time, be both an actor in the story and the author surveying his creations omnisciently. To attempt to do so is to suffer a divided imagination. When Goldsmith in *The Vicar of Wakefield* endeavors virtually to do this, the result is the loss of the story illusion.

It is little, if any, more difficult for the imaginative reader to accept the point of view of an author conversant with the words and deeds of his characters or omniscient of their thoughts and unconscious motives than to believe the intimate adventures of Robinson Crusoe as told by himself. Yet the technical development of the point of view has an interesting history. Realistic fiction at the outset, in the picaresque novel and in the rogue story deriving from criminal records, endeavored to be no less actual than fact. De Foe in *Robinson Crusoe*, as was previously noted, made his fictive creation far less sensational than the actual life of the romantic Alexander Selkirk upon which it is based. De Foe apparently realized that the actual is frequently less convincing, harder to believe, than the imaginary, provided that the latter records the usual or average experiences of mankind. He made his fictions more sober than fact. And to give his inventions the air of life he puts them in the mouths of his characters. The hero tells his plain story with much corroborative detail. The aim is a disarming verisimilitude. Or if, rarely, the point of view is that of the author, it is, as in *The Apparition of Mrs. Veal,* a judicial editor who writes, examining the evidence, scrutinizing the documents, and reporting his findings with a fine air of caution. De Foe's aim in fiction was not so much to stir the imagination of his readers as to allay their incredulity.

The Omniscient Author—"The Scarlet Letter"

It is Fielding who first in realistic fiction assumes the point of view of the omniscient author without apology or explanation, relying upon his reader for the imaginative power necessary to its acceptance. In *Tom Jones* lie most of the seeds of the novel as it develops later into a serious art form. With the history of that fruitage I have not further to do. The novel which I next consider in detail is the product of a hundred years of experience and successful creation. In it are exhibited subtleties of method which Fielding could not guess. *The Scarlet Letter* is the work of a fully conscious artist manipulating his point of view with great skill to the attainment of an unique effect.

In his introduction, "The Custom House," Hawthorne explains the discovery of old papers and the scarlet token. Thereupon he makes the following statement:

The original papers, together with the scarlet letter itself—a most curious relic—are still in my possession, and shall be freely exhibited to whomsoever, induced by the great interest of the narrative, may desire a sight of them. I must not be understood as affirming that, in the dressing up of the tale, and imagining the motives and modes of passion that influenced the characters who figure in it, I have invariably confined myself within the limits of the old Surveyor's half-a-dozen sheets of foolscap. On the contrary, I have allowed myself, as to such points, nearly or altogether, as much license as if the facts had been entirely of my own invention. What I contend for is the authenticity of the outline.

Hawthorne, it is evident, while retaining the freedom of the author's point of view, seeks to enhance the plausibility of his tale by this fiction of documents in the background; and the reason therefor lies in the nature of the story itself, which, transcending the usual, verges constantly upon the supernatural. The suspension of the reader's disbelief is supposedly facilitated by this device. Yet I am not sure that in this respect it adds anything to the story, much less that it is essential. The imaginative reader needs no such sop to scepticism; he is willing to meet his author halfway. What the introduction more effectively does in Hawthorne's charming style is to set his story in its proper atmosphere, to establish its tone. The old decaying sea-port with its reminiscences and relics of a bye-gone greatness is exactly the setting in which to unfold this story of long ago. We are insensibly borne into the past. The gentle melancholy of ardent human passions stilled forever is evoked before we enter upon the record of their unfolding. The first chapters gain a little thereby, and yet so soon does Hawthorne establish his tone in the story itself, to maintain it unbroken throughout, that the tale may be read without its introduction and the reader suffer little loss.

In his first chapter Hawthorne describes his setting, the jail; and in his second, the crowd gathered before it. The severity of the judgment passed by the Puritan women upon the culprit arouses in us sympathy for the latter. When she first appears we view her at a distance, for we are among the crowd of onlookers. Then the point of view moves closer:

The unhappy culprit sustained herself as best a woman might under the heavy weight of a thousand unrelenting eyes, all fastened upon her, and concentrated at her bosom. It was almost intolerable to be borne. Of an impulsive and passionate nature, she had fortified herself. . . .

This is the point of view of the omniscient author. But our identification with the heroine is not yet complete. We do not wholly share her thoughts and emotions until, to what she sees and her emotional response thereto, are added memories which identify her with a past:

Yet there were intervals when the whole scene, in which she was the most conspicuous object, seemed to vanish from her eyes, or, at least, glimmered indistinctly before them, like a mass of imperfectly shaped and spectral images. Her mind, and especially her memory, was preternaturally active, and kept bringing up other scenes than this roughly hewn street. . . .

Therewith, in a casual and wholly natural way, the author gives us what we must know of antecedent circumstance.

In the record of her early life, the accented detail of the deformed scholar enables us at once to identify the stranger, whose questions further betray his interest in the criminal, and in the most natural fashion elicit responses informative to the reader. The method here is wholly objective. We see the questioner as though we stood by, a neighbor to him in the crowd and nothing more. Omniscience is not resumed until we turn again to Hester, and now it is not complete. "She seemed conscious . . ." says the author. Immediately thereafter, when the minister makes his appeal, we view both objectively, privy to the thoughts of neither. It is only when the deformed stranger speaks that the author is again for a moment slightly omniscient:

"Speak woman!" said another voice, coldly and sternly proceeding from the crowd about the scaffold. "Speak and give your child a father!"
"I will not speak!" answered Hester, turning pale as death, but responding to this voice, which she too surely recognized.

Hawthorne thus far has identified his chief characters, Hester, Dimmesdale, and Chillingworth; has intimated clearly that the physician is Hester's husband, and suggested some relation between Hester and the minister. Of the three Hester has received the most emphasis, because of the three she is the only one described with partial omniscience. The other two are subordinate to her. She is to be the central figure. And the author has defined his point of view, that of the narrator sparingly omniscient, telling us only what we must know, letting, as far as possible, speech and action reveal the thoughts and relations of his characters. Nor in the scene which immediately follows, that of the interview between Hester and Chillingworth, does he enlarge his method. He is almost wholly objective, giving now and then but an intimation of Hester's thought and emotion:

> She could not but tremble at these preparations; for she felt that—having now done all that humanity, or principle or, if so it were, a refined cruelty, impelled him to do for the relief of physical suffering—he was next to treat with her as the man she had most deeply and irreparably injured.

But of Chillingworth's thoughts we learn nothing from analysis. The phrase, "a smile of dark and self-relying intelligence," is the author's nearest approach to omniscience.

We enter now upon a general analysis of Hester's feelings upon her release from jail, an analysis which is made with reservations:

> It might be, too—doubtless it was so, although she hid the secret from herself, and grew pale whenever it

struggled out of her heart, like a serpent from its hole
—it might be that another feeling kept her within the
scene and pathway that had been so fatal.

and again:

Continually, and in a thousand other ways, did she
feel the innumerable throbs of anguish that had been
so cunningly contrived for her by the undying, the ever-
active sentence of the Puritan tribunal.

Thereafter although the author analyzes Hester's agony he gives her little individual character.
She might be any other woman similarly circum-
stanced. The personal secrets of her life are still
untold; we can only speculate as to them.

With the child, Pearl, Hawthorne's method is
almost wholly objective, for though he describes
her in part through Hester's eyes she is to Hester,
as to us, enigmatic:

The mother's impassioned state had been the medium through which were transmitted to the unborn
infant the rays of its mortal life. . . .

In his own person as author he describes the child's
deportment but little more. In this brief passage
he comes closest to omniscience:

Pearl felt the sentiment [the hatred of other children
for her] and requited it with the bitterest hatred.

The visit of Hester to the Governor, and
Dimmesdale's intercession in her behalf, are told

throughout objectively. We are left to guess from speech and action the motives of the characters. But in the chapters immediately following we move imperceptibly to a closer view of the Minister and the Leech, to whom a natural transition has been made through the interview at the Governor's mansion. The analysis of the two characters who are henceforth to occupy the chief place in the action is at first casual and superficial, no more than any acute observer might guess. The evil effect of the physician upon his patient is intimated largely through the "widely diffused opinion of the community," that "this diabolical agent had the Divine permission, for a season, to burrow into the clergyman's intimacy, and to plot against his soul."

Henceforth we are taken as intimately into the hearts of Chillingworth and Dimmesdale as the author's reservations permit, not quite so intimately as in the case of Hester, nor for long at a time. The method is curious, perhaps instinctive to the author, and the result highly effective. It may be likened to the glimpses of a volcanic crater as seen intermittently through the evil vapors which emanate from it. A horrible flash of reality pierces now and again, the more terrible because brief, suggestive of unplumbed fiery depths. And after such a revelation of the tortured souls of the sinner and his avenger, Hawthorne describes again little incidents, records the speech of his characters, or speculates upon the mysteries veiled for him as for us by evil mists. A few sentences will make clear what the figure intimates:

But as he proceeded, a terrible fascination, a kind of fierce, though still calm, necessity, seized the old man within its gripe, and never set him free again until he had done all its bidding.

When Roger has uncovered the breast of the sleeping minister, Hawthorne does not tell us what was revealed, but only that Roger turned away with "a wild look of wonder, joy, and horror."

Again, of Roger:

Calm, gentle, passionless, as he appeared, there was yet, we fear, a quiet depth of malice, hitherto latent, but active now, in this unfortunate old man, which led him to imagine a more intimate revenge than any mortal had ever wreaked upon an enemy.

The chapters which depict the sufferings of the minister exemplify the same method, analysis which is generalized, speculative; observant rather than omniscient; with only occasionally a swift thrust which is wholly personal and revealing. Hawthorne lectures to his class as though conducting a clinic. Only now and again does he seem to remember that his subject is an individual human being, not a pathological case. Therein lies the failure of *The Scarlet Letter* to interest the average reader. Its characters are too little personal; are typical, symbolical even. The story is almost an allegory, a subtle allegory, moreover, not so easy to grasp as *Everyman* or *Pilgrim's Progress*. We are not deeply concerned with the fates of the individual characters but with the mysteries of human destiny upon which they throw a brief and uncertain light.

The charm of the book lies very greatly in its mystery, in its massing of light and shade; in its occasional high lights, but more in its dim shadows suggesting so much but explicitly outlining so little. It reminds one of the masterpieces of Rembrandt, low-keyed, wonderfully massed, with a sure emphasis upon the face or figure which should command and hold the eye, and grouped around this focal point other figures less emphatic and subtly graduated. The art is highly selective. Out of the many figures only a few are identified; and yet the background is solid and populous. The æsthetic sense is gratified; these calculated and yet seemingly simple effects are art. The technical means to their creation in *The Scarlet Letter* is very largely the management of the point of view, which, as it bestows or withholds light, creates exactly the emphasis the author desires. No better instance could be asked of the all importance of technique. Only through his mastery of his tools is Hawthorne able to suggest to his reader that vision of life and of the nature of the human soul which is his. It is, if you like, a sermon, a piece of philosophy. But it is infinitely more moving than any rationalized exordium to virtue, or any philosophical analysis of the mind.

The Scarlet Letter, were it to be exhaustively analyzed, would afford material for varied technical discussion. Much could be made of its natural background, so seldom bright; nearly always the scenes are gray, autumnal, windless, as though to harmonize with the sombre human drama enacted amid them. Nature seems hushed, furtively expectant of tragedy; once only does the scene take on vivacity, when, in the forest, the sunlight dances on leaves and grass and the lovers declare their passion. There is symbolism, too, in the figure of Mistress Hibben, half mad, half preternatural. But the technique of background and symbolism will be elsewhere discussed and with illustrations from other books. Plot, only, demands here a further word.

The specific incidents of *The Scarlet Letter* are few. After the opening scenes the action drifts for a while; time passes without comment, without dramatic episodes to mark its progress, until the scene in the Governor's Mansion. Thereafter the incidents are again generalized, their sequence being without strict causative relation until the final, more dramatic revelation and denouement. The action quickens here and the articulation of parts becomes more definite. Yet on the whole the structure of *The Scarlet Letter* is rather invertebrate, a structure not unsuited to the effect sought, which is pictorial and static in quality rather than narrative. But for a theme less philosophical in tone and more concerned with the brisk action of everyday life, a firmer structure would be essential. The incidents would then be more numerous, more logically related, related that is as cause to effect, the second being the inevitable consequence of the first. And the progress of time would be more specifically noted.

Point of View in Jane Austen

Brisk movement, which would be out of place in the reflective tone sought in *The Scarlet Letter,* is characteristic of Jane Austen. The general effect of her books is of action which, though quiet, is never sluggish. Though the incidents are usually trivial they are so well articulated that the reader has an agreeable sense of progress. Suspense is admirably achieved. We are made to hang more breathlessly upon the momentous consequences of ball or tea than upon Scott's tournaments. There could be nowhere better found than in her novels illustrations of the great truth that, in a story, interest lies not in the intrinsic character of the incidents, in their uniqueness or violence, but in their emotional significance, their potential influence upon the destinies of the story's characters. It is so, also, in the drama. Iago's theft of the handkerchief moves the reader dramatically more than does the death of Ophelia, for the death of Ophelia is, in a sense, extraneous to the action, sufficing in its pathos but contributing nothing to suspense. Jane Austen has a fine instinct for the emotional values of incident and for the structural obligation of each to advance action and reveal character. Off-hand I should say that there is no incident in her novels which does not play its essential part. There is never too much and yet there is always enough. Her stories though spare are sinewy and well knit.

To create this air of briskness and pertinency Jane Austen employs a manner almost dramatic. In recollection her stories seem wholly to have told themselves; a closer scrutiny reveals her point of view to be, technically, omniscient. This assumption of omniscience is scarcely necessary. Her characters are quite competent to reveal themselves in word and deed, for their natures are not complex nor their emotions deep. Jane Austen avoids passion and the obscurities of human motive. Her stories are on the surface of life and, for this, analysis is not needed. If in *Persuasion* and *Mansfield Park* there is more of it than in the others it is because in these the heroines are more deeply felt and the tone is graver. Omniscience to Jane Austen is a technical convenience, merely, enabling her to inform her readers of necessary facts without burdening her dialogue. In the first chapters of *Pride and Prejudice* she tells in a few brisk sentences the constituency of the Bennet family, their place in society, the advent in the neighborhood of eligible young men, and something of the natures of Mr. and Mrs. Bennet. The scene is set, the characters are identified, and the story may now tell itself.

Thereafter she is occasionally omniscient to secure emphasis. Elizabeth is the heroine, and of her thoughts, more than of any other's, the author is cognizant. Darcy, as Elizabeth's feeling for him deepens, gradually shares with her the centre of interest, the emphasis being secured in part by telling Elizabeth's thoughts about him and in part by analysis of his character. Omniscience is confined almost wholly to these two. Mr. Bennet comes in for an occasional illuminating flash. Of Mrs. Bennet, Jane, Bingley, Wickham, and the rest she is almost wholly observant. Darcy's first proposal is told in detail, dramatically, with ironic effect. His second is not directly told but is summarized. The reason, I believe, is that the author had at this point achieved such intimacy with Elizabeth and Darcy that if the proposal were to be directly narrated she would be obliged to be omniscient of one or both of them. From so intimate a revelation of deep feeling she instinctively shrinks. She gives instead a rather hasty and self-conscious summary of the proposal and Elizabeth's acceptance.

Sense and Sensibility is a weaker book than *Pride and Prejudice* not because the theme is less interesting, for it is, rather, more significant. But the emphasis is never so clearly established and maintained. In the early chapters Mrs. Dashwood, Elinor, and Marianna divide the interest about equally. Later Mrs. Dashwood assumes a secondary place and the story emphasis is shared by

the two heroines. There is not here that deft subordination of one story to another which in *Pride
and Prejudice* is secured by restricting omniscience
to Elizabeth and portraying Jane through Elizabeth's eyes. Darcy, too, we see as Elizabeth sees
him until he divides with her the centre of interest.
Sense and Sensibility, though failing somewhat in
emphasis, employs, however, the same device in
characterization. The chief persons of the story
are largely portrayed as seen through the eyes of
others. Then as the characters change slowly to
these observers, they change also to us.

Point of View in Thackeray

The point of view in *Henry Esmond* is almost
unique in fiction. I can recall no other novel which
employs it, though *The Education of Henry
Adams* adapts the same device to autobiography.
The chief character tells his story in the third person. The center of interest is of necessity fixed in
the hero and he only is omnisciently observed.
Structurally the same effect could be attained by
the author omniscient of but one of his characters
and observant of the others, as in Bennett's *Clayhanger*. But the tone in such a case would be different. Thackeray achieves a certain formality
blent with intimacy which harmonizes with an age
of perukes and small swords, the prose of Addison
and the art of Watteau. This tone so perfectly established is undeviatingly maintained. Largely be-

cause of it the book is memorable. And it is the creation, technically, of the point of view.

Again in *Barry Lyndon* Thackeray is the artist that it was in him to be. The picaresque novel reaches no greater height as a work of art than in the cold self-portraiture of the rascally hero who tells the story of his life so composedly. In his other and reputedly greater novels Thackeray is content with a lower order of craftsmanship than in this and *Esmond*. Not only does his invention flag and he spar for time but he is careless in the mechanics of his tale. *The Newcomes* is ostensibly told by Pendennis but the narrator forever oversteps the point of view and assumes omniscience. For these artistic lapses Thackeray now and then makes a perfunctory apology. "If I did not hear these things," says Pendennis in effect, "they were, I fancy, much as I have recorded them." No doubt Thackeray discovered the limitations of his point of view when, in a story serially published, it was too late to change it. Dickens in a similar instance in *The Old Curiosity Shop* frankly drops one point of view after a few chapters and employs another.

The Intrusive Author

It is probably laziness which prompts Thackeray's intrusive comments upon his story characters. All the talk of puppets in *Vanity Fair,* despite its easy charm, is the second best of a writer who knew very well how hard it is to make characters reveal themselves in word and deed and how relatively easy it is to gossip about them. It asks the inspiration of a great situation to stir Thackeray from his sluggishness. When Rawdon Crawley surprises Becky and Lord Steyne the narrative takes on a dramatic swiftness all too rare in Thackeray. There is here no chatter of puppets. The story illusion is, for the moment, complete; we are wholly absorbed, forgetful of the storyteller, his medium, and his technique.

Your true Thackeray lover professes admiration for the chatty intrusiveness of the great sentimentalist. To me his gossip, his asides, his talk of puppets is irritating, so obviously does it gloss over his careless craftsmanship. Thackeray knows perfectly how the thing should be done and is usually content not to do it, cynical in his contempt for the great stupid public which does not distinguish good workmanship from bad. Nor do I like Thackeray's confidences. Fielding when he gossips —considerately, too, in interchapters which may be skipped—is to me far more entertaining. There is a heartiness and gusto in Fielding, a fine upstanding honesty and courage which I do not find in his professed follower. Thackeray as the heir to Fielding bears in his quarterings the bar sinister.

In her comments upon her characters and upon life George Eliot is the typical intrusive author, speculating freely, but, as a usual thing, impersonally. Her generalizations I usually like because of their shrewdness ("Diversity of taste in jokes is a strain on the affections") and because they are not designed to conceal a weakness in direct characterization. It is her practice after writing "window" upon the blackboard to polish her window with convincing thoroughness. Dramatically she is always competent to set forth the characters upon whom she has commented. Lydgate and Rosamond speak and act to the high level of their parts. Mr. Casaubon's speech and love letters are the perfect expression of the pedant. George Eliot at her worst is seldom more than redundant. The parentheses in the following passage are surely irksome:

> Mr. Casaubon was touched with an unknown delight (what man would not have been?) at this childlike unrestrained ardor: he was not surprised (what lover would have been?) that he should have been the object of it."

The philosophizing author I had begun to think old-fashioned until I happened upon it in so ultramodern a work as Mrs. Woolf's *Jacob's Room.*[1] The contemporary author in revolt against the heavy-handed Victorians is apt to generalize rarely, and if he has a moral or a philosophy, to suggest it by his symbolism. Yet symbolism can be made as offensive as author's comment. Mr. Galsworthy's fondness for embroidering his human *leit motif* with a canine counterpoint exasperates me. I judge his implication to be that of the cynic who

[1] See Chapter IV.

remarked, "The more I see of men the better I think of dogs." The epigram has savor, but Mr. Galsworthy's heavy implications frequently have not. Nor again do I like his lyrical descriptions of nature, so ostentatiously contrasting with the pettiness of man. A comparison too obviously made, a contrast too forcibly implied, may be worse than a moral explicitly stated. Thus, in *The Country House,* the two seamstresses perceived through the windows of the Stoics' Club:

One was in consumption, having neglected to earn enough to feed herself properly for some years past, and the other looked as if she would be in consumption shortly, for the same reason. They stood on the pavement, watching the cabs drive up. Some of the Stoics saw them and thought "Poor girls: they look awfully bad." Three or four said to themselves: "It oughtn't to be allowed. I mean it's so painful to see; and it's not as if one could do anything. They're not beggars, don't you know, and so what *can* one do?"

Besides the implications of its aggressive contrasts, *The Country House* is illustrative of a number of technical merits and defects. Galsworthy, it is obvious, is more a spinner of parables than a novelist content with life for its own sake. The abstract purpose of his books can seldom be forgotten as one reads. The characters are carefully selected to represent types, classes, and intellectual points of view. The method of portraiture is highly selective; over and beyond that trait which a character exemplifies there is little waywardness, little

unexpectedness, that incalculable margin which
makes a character wholly vital and convincing.
Yet as types and mouthpieces Galsworthy's characters are well-defined, and their freedom from
complexity makes them, as one reads, singularly
distinct. They create an immediate and exact impression, one which does not, however, grow with
further contacts. Few are memorable. Exception
should be made of several in the *Forsyte Saga,* a
work which transcends the author's usual limitations.

Yet though the characters in *The Country
House* are not individually memorable, they are
drawn with great rapidity and clarity in the initial
scene. The social atmosphere is, in a few paragraphs, unmistakably established, and within this
milieu individuals are differentiated. They are perhaps more sharply defined visually than tempera-
mentally, although mannerisms and prejudices are
intimated deftly enough. And in addition the relationships among the characters and hints of the
ensuing developments are all suggested, lightly and
swiftly; it is a piece of clean-cut workmanship.
That the remainder of the book does not fulfil the
promise of its opening is due largely to the author's
abstract manner. He has a thesis to establish, in
conformity with which his characters must do
certain prescribed things. Their parts, the reader
feels, are too neatly assigned. In the background
is the author pulling the strings, and, through the
lips of one of his puppets, likening mankind to a
shoal of fish.

That a great novel cannot be written around an abstract thesis is certainly untrue; that such a novel is in danger of becoming a tract is likewise obvious. It is a misfortune Galsworthy does not wholly escape. For instance, in *The Country House* the passages in which the lawyer expounds the English divorce law are too purely critical and expository to have narrative interest. They constitute an aside. Because the author thinks the English divorce law absurd he wishes to analyze it. The reader's interest in the passage is necessarily intellectual, not emotional. The whole discussion could be omitted without loss to the story. In *Silas Marner* or *Resurrection,* didactic as are both, the reader has not this sense of irrelevance. In them the moral springs directly from the human relationships of the characters. Moral lessons, moreover, which spring from the unchanging character of humanity are forever true; whereas the evils of a divorce law are temporary. Once the law is altered the point of the story is dulled. It is with transient aspects of life, the defects of particular laws and conventions, that Galsworthy is too often concerned, rather than with the eternal character of the human heart.

As in a drawing of Hogarth's, the parable of *The Country House* is sharply underscored. Upon one typical scene the author comments:

Just as around the hereditary principle are grouped the State, the Church, Law, and Philanthropy, so round the dining table at Worsted Skeynes sat the Squire, the Rector, Mr. Paramor, and Gregory Vigil.

Again in different vein but accenting his points so that the most stupid cannot fail to see:

> And the same brown owl that had hooted when Helen Bellew kissed George Pendyce in the conservatory hooted again now that Gregory walked grieving over the fruits of that kiss.

In such an emphasis the author may be as intrusive, may reveal the guiding hand quite as openly as though he commented in the first person; and the method is rather more irritating than one devoid of all pretense.

Galsworthy is the modern man of feeling brushing aside the furtive tear. Dickens in his death bed scenes strangles a sob. Many a reader is callous to the death of old Colonel Newcome and his *"adsum."* It does not necessarily argue lack of feeling to be indifferent to scenes which moved our grandparents. Styles change, and the children of science look less sentimentally but no less sensitively upon the tragedy of man. Facile emotions are easy enough; it asks a deeper sympathy with life than was common to the age of sensibility to make Madame Bovary and Anna Karénina themes for tragedy, and a more restrained artistry to depict them. Flaubert's sympathy is implicit in his emphasis, in the endless patience which created that limpid sequence of incidents whereby Madame Bovary is so completely revealed. If he has a moral he does not state it. As author he holds himself rigorously aloof. Comment is easy, overemphasis is easy. But restraint is not easy, nor that firmness of structure, that hard brain-work which makes all author's comment superfluous. The technical problem of the point of view merges here into the allied problems of plot construction, of selection and rejection of incidents, of emphasis inherent in the proportions of the parts. Restraint and memorableness are the product not of one but of all these.

Few novels both notable and complex have succeeded with the point of view of a minor character. The difficulties of such a point of view have been already indicated. Inevitably the author is led to transcend its limitations and become virtually the author observant or omniscient. Butler's *The Way of All Flesh* is a good instance in point. The narrator, as godfather to the hero and friend of the other chief characters, may plausibly enough tell most of the chief incidents from first hand observation. He does more than this in recording incidents in the lives of Ernest's parents which they could never reveal to any one. He even tells us Christina's thoughts and dreams, a clear assumption of omniscience. The inconsistency of the point of view springs from the desire to be both wholly informed and at the same time detached, to be a chorus to the action. It cannot be said that actual obscurity results, but the imaginative reader suffers a divided allegiance.

Conrad's Management of the Point of View

Conrad's singular use of the point of view may be illustrated by any one of half a dozen stories: by *Victory,* in which the unidentified "I" of the first chapters is lost afterward in the omniscient author; or by *Lord Jim,* in which Marlow, the narrator, becomes indistinguishable from other minor characters, with the result that the interest in the later chapters flags. It is in *Chance,* however, that the point of view is most baffling and the results, both for effectiveness and confusion, most debatable. *Chance* is an interesting novel, exhibiting all of Conrad's excellences as a painter of character and with one of his best heroines. Whether the peculiar point of view which he attempts is deliberate or unconscious is not easy to determine.

The story opens with "I" and Marlow meeting a retired seaman by the name of Powell who tells the circumstances of his first commission as second mate under Captain Anthony. Marlow, characteristically, knows much about Captain Anthony which the "I" of the story relates, explaining that "much of the above I elicited from Marlow." Marlow in person then takes the story for many subsequent pages, becoming so wholly the narrator that when, at infrequent intervals his auditor intrudes, as in the sentence, "I smiled incredulously at Marlow's ferocity," it is with a shock that we recall the existence of "I." For we have ceased to identify ourselves with the auditor and have become one with Marlow, seeing events through his eyes. The precise place of this shift in the point of view may be easily detected. On one page occurs the passage, " 'I sat down on a bank of grass,' Marlow went on." But the next paragraph drops all quotation marks, and thereafter save when "I" interrupts we have no recollection that the story is told to an auditor. The original point of view has been merged in another. The absence of the quotation marks points the transition. Why then recall the original narrator afterward?

Marlow then delves deeper into the lives of his characters. We learn of the heroine's father, even to his start in life. We learn what his father said to him on that occasion and later his wife's comments upon him. Marlow remarks "You may be surprised at my knowledge of these details. Well I had them ultimately from Mrs. Fyne." Mrs. Fyne we suspect had also her share of omniscience, though in no wise comparable to Marlow, who can spin an analysis and portray a character from broken details told him by another. He punctuates his narrative with "I am told (for I have not witnessed those scenes myself)," but he becomes actually more than a minor participant or even the observant author. He says of his character de Barral, "He had arrived to regard them as his own by a sort of mystical persuasion." This is clearly the omniscient point of view. "I" remarks, "You seem to have studied the man." To this Marlow replies: "No! Not studied. I had no opportunities. . . . But in such a case I verily believe that a little is as good as a feast—perhaps better. If one has a taste for that kind of thing the merest starting-point becomes a coign of vantage, and then by a series of deducted verisimilitudes one arrives at truth—or very near the truth."

It is characteristic of Conrad that twenty pages of ancient history recording so fully the life of a man Marlow had seen but once should interrupt a conversation. We return to the scene of that suspended dialogue in the following transition:

" 'You must not think,' went on Marlow after a pause, 'that on that morning with Fyne I went consciously in my mind over all this, let us call it information; no better say, this fund of knowledge which I had, or rather which existed in me in regard to de Barral. . . . No! I didn't reckon up carefully in my mind all this I have been telling you. How could I have done so, with Fyne right there in the room?' "

Most readers, I think, will in the interest of the twenty pages have wholly forgotten the point of departure and pick up the thread of the narrative with a slight sense of bewilderment. Occasions for such momentary confusion are frequent in Conrad. I have remarked elsewhere[1] that in *Nostromo* these departures from the time order, these huge parentheses, spoil wholly, for me, the pleasure of the story. In *The Rover,*[1] on the other hand, the method achieves without confusion a

[1]See Chapter III for further analysis.

rich complexity. The analogy of these retrospective digressions to Conrad's free handling of the point of view is this: The reader when he pauses to ask himself, Who is now telling the story? How can the narrator know all these things? loses for a moment the story illusion. So, too, when after a long retrospective passage the author resumes the thread of the narrative. In either case there is an awkward mental readjustment. The story ceases for a moment to be wholly convincing.

Marlow, in resuming his story of the de Barrals, enlarges in his customary manner upon the details told him by Fyne. These elaborations become in subsequent chapters actual omniscience, despite the occasional reappearance of the auditor with a comment or objections: "I couldn't refuse Marlow the tribute of a prolonged whistle." Marlow has been depicting the sensations and thoughts of the child Flora at the mercy òf the wicked governess. It is an imaginative and moving narrative, nor do I think the reader would begrudge Marlow his omniscience or indeed question it were it not for the interruptions. For Marlow, however interesting in himself, is less interesting than the characters of whom he tells. We wish to forget him and even more to forget his auditor. Marlow's frequent apologies for his fancies become a little stereotyped:

"You understand . . . that in order to be conservative in my relation of this affair I am telling you at once the details which I heard from Mrs. Fyne later in the day, as well as what little Fyne imparted to me with his usual solemnity during that morning call."

The point of view for the remainder of Book I is that of Marlow, who is sometimes an on-looker, a minor participant in the action, or again author omniscient. There is no hesitation in his assumption of omniscience when, for our clearer understanding, he tells us Captain Anthony's thoughts. The reader does not haggle at this en-largement, for the inquisitive auditor is almost completely forgotten. The story almost wholly sus-tains its illusion. But with Book II the auditor reappears to ask pertinently "How do you know all this?" To which Marlow replies, "You shall see by and by." We don't see with any conviction. Mr. Powell, the second officer, is, it seems, Mar-low's informant in these later episodes of the story and Marlow exercises his customary liberty to assume omniscience. It is largely Powell's story, but this enriched and elaborated by Marlow's in-terpretations and elucidations. He spins his yarn from Powell's hints. And at the end Marlow, Powell, Mrs. Anthony, and the auditor of the story, the narrator to whom all these things have been told, take their parts in rounding out the scene, concluding what, in the drama, would be called the enveloping action.

It is always difficult in a good novel to deter-mine how much of its excellence arises from what academically may be called its technical defects. Idiosyncrasies of method may be virtues or they may be weaknesses—however negligible as compared with the essential stuff of which the story is composed. Conrad has always the essential stuff. He creates illusion of character and scene. His people live for us. And it may be argued with some plausibility that the reality of his characters in *Chance* is due in part to his method. A certain authenticity is imparted by awkwardness, an authenticity kindred to that of *Wuthering Heights* in which defects in the point of view are even more striking.[1] Yet awkwardness is in itself surely a defect, and lapses from the story illusion, of which there are many in *Chance*, are a defect also. Truly, to see a story and characters indirectly through several personalities—the narrator's, Marlow's, Powell's—is like viewing a scene through several thicknesses of colored glass. A certain color and atmosphere are thereby achieved. Life is set off at a little distance or is, so to speak, framed as in a picture. This effect of distance, this indirection, and the attendant air of homely authenticity are virtues. Yet one asks, could they not be more directly attained and by simpler methods? Hawthorne, be it recalled, achieves his effects with no sacrifice of method, no awkwardness, no breaks in illusion.

[1]See Chapter III.

The Point of View Variously Illustrated

May Sinclair in *Mary Olivier* employs a technical device which I do not recall elsewhere, the use of all three persons in the introspection of a single character. Two citations will make the nature of the practice evident:

> She turned off the electric light and shut her eyes and lay thinking. The violent motion of the express prolonged itself in a ghostly vibration, rocking the bed. In still space, unshaken by this tremor, she could see the other rooms, the quiet beautiful rooms.
> I wonder how Mamma and Dorsy are getting on. . . . I'm not going to think about Mamma. It isn't fair to Richard. I shan't think about anything but Richard for this fortnight. One evening of it's gone already. It might have lasted quite another hour if he hadn't got up and gone away so suddenly. What a fool I was to let him think I was tired.
> There will be thirteen evenings more. Thirteen. You can stretch time out by doing a lot of things in it; doing something different every hour. When you're with Richard every minute's different from the last, and he brings you the next all bright and new.

Again:

> Forty-five. Yesterday she was forty-five, and today. Tomorrow she would be forty-six.
> If I were going mad I should have gone mad long ago. . . .
> In the cramped room where the high bed stuck out from the wall to within a yard of the window, Mamma went about, small and weak, in her wadded lavender Japanese dressing-gown, like a child that can't be still,

looking for something it wants that nobody can find. You couldn't think because of the soft pad-pad of the dreaming, sleep-walking feet in the lambs-wool slippers.

The employment of the first person in these instances does two things: it creates a sense of intimacy which the impersonal "she" does not convey, and implies, too, a formulated thought—as though the thinker had spoken aloud. The second person suggests, seemingly, an impersonal introspection, a thought of self carried over to a generalization and made a text for philosophizing. Mary Olivier is a philosophizing creature, endeavoring from her own inner life to fathom the nature of existence, and this employment of three persons of various degrees of intimacy serves the author's purpose. It creates, also, variety and makes the introspection, of which there is much, less formidable. Moreover the greater use of the first person toward the end of the story brings the reader to share the heroine's life with growing intimacy and intensity. The device has possibilities. Bojer in *The Great Hunger* employs a technique in part analogous when he conducts his hero's speculations from the personal case to impersonal generalization which, in this instance, however, seems to be the philosophy of the author, rather than of the hero, and virtually, therefore, an enlargement of the point of view.

In Walter de la Mare's *Memoirs of a Midget* so steadfast is the point of view that the reader seems throughout to see the world through the eyes of a being two feet high. The visual illusion is deftly created by a thousand little touches: in delicate perceptions of lowly flowers and leaves; in the shock of the great opened jaws of the greyhound —to the Midget as vast as a lion's; in the description of the postal order stretched upon her lap like a table covering; and in the daintiness of the Midget's appetite and her revulsion from the gross feeding of mortals. The purely physical virtuosity of the point of view, though unostentatious, is admirable. And this is made the means to a criticism of life. More subtly than *Gulliver* the book reveals the coarseness, cruelty, and stupidity of mankind. This arraignment of humanity is never explicit. It is built of a thousand little details, of unstressed comparisons; but it is cumulative, and after the death of little Mr. Anon, thrown from his horse in the circus ring, we are glad when the heroine vanishes, perhaps to that isle of the blessed which Mr. Anon had once pictured to her. She does not denounce humanity, finding for herself now and then a bit of understanding and sympathy. She even professes a liking for mortals. The indictment is all the more compelling because implicit; the grossness of life to the sensitive spirit is made almost unendurable.

A contrast of method is afforded in a comparison of Willa Cather's *My Ántonia* and Hémon's *Maria Chapdelaine*, both novels of frontier life, both with their central figure an heroic young woman, a daughter of the soil in whose life is expressed the unflinching mettle of the pioneer in his struggle with nature. Antonia is seen through the eyes of a contemporary, one who has known her from childhood. She is set before us partly through her words and acts as known to him, partly in her profound influence upon him, and in the admiration he professes for her. She is a genuine and appealing figure. The point of view suffices to portray the simple epical qualities of her nature. Glimpses into her thoughts are not essential. We see her, like the plow silhouetted against the prairie sunset, larger than life, a symbol. Nevertheless she becomes more remote and less dominant in the latter part of the book. The narrator then meets her but rarely. We have but rumors of her and few direct glimpses. Nor has the book any fable. Antonia is not memorable for her part in any incident. We remember her as a personality and a symbol, not as the central figure in any related series of events.

Maria Chapdelaine pursues a different method. The fable is a simple one but perfectly articulated. The incidents cover no more than two years, whereas the time covered in *My Àntonia* is thirty or forty years. Hémon employs the omniscient point of view but exercises it sparingly. Maria, too, like Àntonia, is largely an objective figure, though we have an occasional glimpse into her thoughts and feelings which immensely adds to our knowledge of her. In retrospect she is a defi-

nite personality recalled in several unforgettable
scenes: as she waits during the summer night for
her bread to bake, as she hears her lover's simple
proposal in the forest, and as she repeats a thousand times the prayer which, she has faith, will
bring him safely back to her. If in *My Àntonia*
the point of view and the lack of plot, together
with the long period of time covered, combine to
give the narrative an air of truth, a certain authenticity, *Maria Chapdelaine* declares the merits
of a method more consciously artistic. One forgets
soon the means which a writer employs and remembers only the results of it. These in *Maria
Chapdelaine* are sharper and more persistent than
in *My Àntonia*. Reality consists for the story
writer not in the skill with which he makes his
story pass for fact but in the impress which he
makes upon the imagination. The contrast in these
two novels lies partly in the point of view but
more, no doubt, in their relative looseness and
closeness of texture; in the presence in one of a
simple but definite plot covering but a short period
of time, whereas the other is but a casual string
of incidents and scenes spread over many years.

In Willa Cather's *A Lost Lady* the point of
view of the author whose omniscience is somewhat
restricted fails as notably as an analogous though
narrower point of view succeeds in *My Àntonia*.
The lady is seen almost wholly through the eyes of
her boyish admirer, Niel, or as she reveals herself
to one or two others in word and act. We have

no direct glimpses into her mind. It is reiterated that she has charm, has rare qualities wasted and perverted in the desert air of Nebraska. This charm is supposedly evident in the impression which she makes upon Niel, but which she singularly does not make upon the reader. Nowhere does she utter a word that is more than commonplace and her acts are not truly revelatory as are those of Antonia. Whether the failure lies then with the suggestive method—the author's inability, with this technique, to make her character come alive—or whether there was nothing really in the lady to reveal, the reader never knows. The suggestive method is excellent provided enough clews are provided to stimulate the imagination. If there are not, the character's effect upon others is not justified, is unreal—is, in short, sentimental. This sentimentality in *A Lost Lady* is enhanced by the author's thesis that the Nebraska pioneers were all noble, honorable, and chivalrous men of wide vision; whereas the second generation is almost wholly base and money-grubbing. No hard-minded realist can believe so romantic a fiction as that, nor condone the lady's taste for French brandy and vulgar lovers on the score of an environment unworthy of her.

Action stories, in which interest derives chiefly from incident, and in which character, background, and idea are of minor importance may be very well told by the hero. The English novel can boast a number of great stories which have em-

ployed this method, not without awkwardness and
strain but with so complete an illusion of life that
it is almost impossible to think of them as told
from any other point of view—*Pendennis, David
Copperfield, Lorna Doone* come at once to mind.
To hold that character is of secondary interest in
these may seem a labored criticism. But it is nevertheless, I think, true. The fortunes of the hero are
of prime importance; his character, in each instance, is sufficiently obvious, is not subjected to
elaborate introspections. And the other actors,
seen through his eyes, need not be profoundly
known. Their words and deeds suffice to portray
them.

Detachment is essential to the profoundest character portrayal. Self revelation is not enough, for
too elaborate introspection soon becomes tedious
and rings false. The impersonal author dissecting,
tracing motive to its source, and holding his characters against their background is master of this
genre. Ever since the novel has found itself in
a varied and adequate technique, the omniscient
method has been the one which has cut deepest and
upturned the greatest treasure. With its wider
employment have come certain refinements which
I have noted in the study of Hawthorne and of
James.[1] I wish to point out in Arnold Bennett's
Clayhanger a lesser but instructive instance.

In *Clayhanger* the author is omniscient almost
solely of the hero, Edwin. Why then should Ed-

[1]P. 81 *seq.*

win not tell his own story? We see most of the
action through Edwin's eyes, live in his emotions.
Why can he not reveal himself to us? Were he to
do so he would not then be the appealing figure
that he is, for the charm and the pathos lie in the
two-fold revelation of Edwin as he seems to himself and of Edwin as we perceive him against the
background of the Five Towns, and especially in
his conflict with old Darius. To Edwin his father
is harsh and unintelligible. The author lifts the
veil for us and extends his omniscience for a brief
space into the childhood of Darius who becomes
thereafter an appealing figure. Edwin's lack of
charity and understanding we can forgive. Though
we live Edwin's life we are also a spectator of it,
seeing it with something of the omniscience and
kindliness of God.

That Bennett might have contrived his glimpse
into the childhood of Darius without departing
from the method he otherwise employs is I think
true and argues a slight loss in technical effectiveness. But the instinct which led him to enlarge our
knowledge, to make us share the creator's omniscience, is a right one. A point of view restricted
wholly to the hero is narrow. Besides the technical
difficulties in the manipulation of incident it denies
the reader that large purview, that sense of God-
like knowledge which is half the pleasure of the
spectator at the play and of the reader of a story.
In the intense and restricted identification of the
reader with the participant narrator lies one vir-

tue; in omniscience another. The novel omniscient of one character and observant of others combines to a very large degree the merits of both methods.

Jane Eyre is an excellent illustration of a novel which struggles with an inadequate method. Jane's difficulties in spinning her incidents, in getting the situation of her story before us, are sufficiently obvious. Greater is the difficulty of self-portraiture. She must be perceptive but not too perceptive, must be naïve and yet wise, bold yet charming. She must analyze herself enough and not too much. Though Charlotte Brontë succeeds in her attempt, the effort of the struggle is written upon the pages of the book. Not so successfully as in *Wuthering Heights* does genius triumph here over the crudities of workmanship. Had the author written from a different point of view, omniscient of Jane and observant of the other characters, little vividness would be lost and much else would have been gained: swiftness, deftness, and, in the delineation of the heroine, a sharper, more triumphant portrait.

The Mill on the Floss, again, would be a better book, in my judgment, had the author been omniscient only of Maggie, making her thereby consistently the centre of interest. Tom is of importance only as he relates to her, and the chapters devoted to him have the effect of dividing and weakening the emphasis. In retrospect we think of Tom only as Maggie saw him, which fact proves the contention. We forget the chapters devoted to him alone, but these, as we read the book, threaten for a moment the true line of development. And in *Silas Marner* likewise, were Silas consistently the centre of interest, the effect of the whole would be more sustained. The transitions to Godfrey Cass are not always easily made, nor does he engage our interest as does Silas. It may be said in justification of George Eliot's method here that she is concerned with the two sides of the coin: the effects both of selfishness and unselfishness. But in so stressing her moral she sacrifices something in sheer story emphasis and æsthetic enjoyment.

Excellence of the Point of View in James's "The Ambassadors"

The point of view, it is apparent, is the fundamental principle of technique in novel structure. By the adoption of one or another point of view, plot, characterization, tone, description are all to some degree determined. The choice of his point of view is to an author contemplating a story the most vital question of method, the one most fraught with possibilities. The illustrations and analyses thus far have revealed this technical principle in its more obvious aspects. Discussion of it will be incident to many other novels later to be cited for other purposes. No better novel than James's *The Ambassadors* could be found to make the transition to this more complex study which I have entitled "The Conduct of Narrative." For it is a novel which handles a difficult point of view with great subtlety and is further prefaced by the author's analysis of his purpose and the reasons which led him to construct his novel as he did. The implications of the point of view, its basic determination of all story effects, are therein exhibited.

The preface to James's novels are a mine of technical criticism, for in the final edition of his work, reviewing and revising the labors of many years, his interest in the creative process itself led him to recall, insofar as he could, the inception of each story, the choice of a method, and the technical difficulties met and overcome. These admirable analyses are unfortunately in James's latest stylistic manner, which most readers detest. A little patience with it is well rewarded. There never has been in English a better critic of fiction, nor one combining great creative power with so singular an acuteness of analysis. From the preface to *The Ambassadors* I quote regretfully only so much of his comment as relates to the centre of interest and the point of view:

. . . Every question of form and pressure, I easily remember paled in the light of the major propriety, recognized as soon as really weighed: that of employing but one centre and keeping it all within my hero's compass. The thing was to be so much this worthy's intimate adventure that even the projection of his consciousness upon it from beginning to end without intermission or deviation would still leave a part of its value for him and *a fortiori* for ourselves, unexpressed. I might, however, express every grain of it that there would be room for—on condition of contriving a splendid particular economy. Other persons in no small number were to people the scene, and each with his or her axe to grind, his or her situation to treat, his or her coherency not to fail of, his or her relation to my leading motive, in a word, to establish and carry on. But Strether's sense of these things, and Strether's only, should avail me for showing them; I should know them but through his more or less groping knowledge of them, since his very gropings would figure among his most interesting motions, and a full observance of the rich rigour I speak of would give me more of the effect I should be most "after" than all possible observances together. It would give me a large unity, and that in turn would crown me with the grace to which the enlightened story-teller will at any time, for his interest, sacrifice if need be all other graces whatever. I refer of course to the grace of intensity, which there are ways of signally achieving and ways of signally missing—as we see it, all round us, helplessly and woefully missed.

Again of the point of view he remarks:

Had I, meanwhile, made him [Strether] at once hero and historian, endowed him with the romantic privilege of the "first person"—the darkest abyss of romance this, inveterately, when enjoyed on the grand scale—variety, and many other queer matters as well, might have been smuggled in by a back door. Suffice it, to be brief, that the first person, in the long piece, is a form foredoomed to looseness, and that looseness, never much my affair, had never been so little so as on this particular occasion.

The difficulties incident to his point of view, that of an author omniscient, or partly so, of a single character who must be consistently the centre of interest and through whose eyes we are to see the other characters, are numerous, especially if, as James further restricts it, exposition to set forth antecedent circumstances is explicity denied. We must infer from the speech of the hero and from thoughts naturally arising in the story circumstance what it is necessary for us to know of the hero's past. James remarks:

It may be asked why, if one so keeps to one's hero, one shouldn't make a single mouthful of "method," shouldn't throw the reins on his neck and, letting them flap as free as in *Gil Blas* or in *David Copperfield*, equip him with the double privilege of subject and object—a course that has at least the merit of brushing away questions at a sweep. The answer to which is, I think, that one makes that surrender only if one is prepared *not* to make certain precious discriminations. . . . Strether . . . encaged and provided for as *The Ambassadors* encages and provides, has to keep in view proprieties much stiffer and more salutary than any of our straight and credulous gape are likely to bring home to him, has exhibitional conditions to meet, in a word, that forbid the terrible *fluidity* of self-revelation.

Strether's revelations are largely to Maria Gostrey who serves the story in the form of confidante:

Thanks to it [her function] we have treated scenically, and scenically alone, the whole lumpish question of Strether's "past," which has seen us more happily on the way than anything else could have done . . .

More obviously then, if less subtly, the point of view, wilfully restricted, narrowed in its omniscience to the present and formulated thoughts of a single character, gives a deeper impression of reality, creates in this instance more completely the story illusion than any other which James could command. In the perfection of that illusion and in the artistic pleasure of difficulties overcome resides the story's charm.

That the charm is great, however frequently coquettish, and that the triumphs of method are notable, need not disarm criticism. James, it must be, lacks something or he would be more widely read. The smallness of his circle cannot be wholly due to human stupidity. And in such a book as *The Ambassadors*, so blent of excellence and failure, the technical approach reveals, I believe, both his strength and weakness. The choice of tools, when there are so many tools from which to select, and the craftsmanship displayed in their use, are significant of the man; James is not one to tackle his adversary with sabre and horse pistol. The most delicate of foils is his weapon. He wears gauntlet and mask. The chalk mark upon his opponent's breast suffices him; he has no taste for the brutality of blood.

An examination of the first chapter of *The Ambassadors* reveals beneath its casualness and its seeming verbosity the utmost definiteness and economy of method. It implies, conveys by indirections, a number of things. Strether is named as the chief character. We learn that he is about to meet an old friend at Chester and that, by reason of some elation, some new-found sense of freedom, he is not anxious for this meeting. The manner of his picking up by the clever Maria Gostrey suggests his attractiveness and also his willingness to be "picked up." The rigidity of his American standards, it is distinctly emphasized, has been relaxed in the soft English air. There is the further implication of some one in the background. Strether thinks of Miss Gostrey as "more thoroughly civilized. If 'more thoroughly than whom?' would not have been for him a sequel to this remark, that was just by reason of his deep consciousness of the bearing of his comparison."

This is our first intimation of Mrs. Newsome, who does not, in the flesh, enter upon any scene. Always she is in the background, the voice of America, the personification of Woollett and of unimaginative virtue. She is the force with which Paris struggles for the possession of Strether's soul. And she is quite as real as Paris; is, perhaps, the most distinct character in the book, a miracle of the indirect method. For we know of her only as she is present in Strether's thoughts, as she assumes the form of conscience when his moral dilemma becomes clear to him, and most as Maria Gostrey's questions elicit from him those details which with such swiftness create her portrait. She comes a step nearer to us when her daughter Sarah arrives with full credentials as her emissary. In Sarah her spirit lives, and in the words which Sarah quotes she visibly takes form:

"She has confided to my judgment and my tenderness the expression of her personal sense of everything, and the assertion of her personal dignity."

They were the very words of the lady of Woollett—he would have known them in a thousand; her parting charge to her child.

Maria Gostrey, James has confessed, plays the part of confidante. It is her function to put the leading question and to draw from Strether all those facts which we must know. And this, as James's characters "so wonderfully" say of each other and he of them, she "wonderfully" does. Indeed she passes credulity in the skill with which from slight hints she creates for us full-length portraits of Mrs. Newsome and the Pococks. But all of James's characters are too clever for life. It is a convention of his art, the means by which the story is expedited, that his people shall avoid the obvious word and strike at once to the root of the matter. Therein lies the "difficulty" which so many readers feel. Miss but one step in the game and the whole is meaningless. Yet it is not for her excessive cleverness that Miss Gostrey is reprehensible. She cannot be other than extraneous. She is too much the oracle, has too little an active part. The promise which she gives in her first scene with Strether is never realized. Of the other accessory characters, Miss Barrace, Little Bilham, and Waymarsh, who, to a lesser degree, serve as conversational targets, the same criticism holds, though Waymarsh is more pertinent than others —the comic understudy of American morality as personified in Mrs. Newsome and her daughter.

The lightness of the method, then, whereby the exposition is sunk in, made an integral part of, the narrative, has its attendant difficulties not wholly overcome. The admiration we feel for the skill and indirection is tempered with impatience. While the antecedent circumstances are being elicited the story stagnates; the tempo is so retarded that we seem to dwell infinitely upon a single protracted chord. And the dialogue employed has often too little the dramatic character, has too little the emphasis which dialogue should have and which in general James contrives to give it. Yet *The Ambassadors* has its swift moments, in which dialogue satisfies our whetted appetite. Strether's scene with Sarah is one of these. It is a *scène à faire* long discerned in the offing and our approach to it is infinitely slow, a series of tacks in light head winds. Once he has grappled with it James is pleasantly downright. The excitement of the scene, enhanced by this long delay, is an interesting instance of the suspense which his technique permits.[1]

Suspense is the very consequence of the point of view which James in *The Ambassadors* employs. We see the action almost wholly through Strether's eyes. Strether himself we see largely in his thoughts and utterances, in the words and impressions—these last intimated—of others, and ever so slightly in the comment of the author. James is chary of his omniscience, careful not to push it too far even in the instance of his hero, and this restraint goes to the root of his method. It is observable that in some instances James builds from

[1] See Chapter III.

his character's thoughts and memories impressions of the past needful to our knowledge. Even I think he pushes his method a little far in some cases so that we seem not wholly to identify ourselves with Strether but to look upon him through his creator's eyes. Strether's thoughts and impressions are, at any rate, ordered and directed for the story's purpose, and we do not in these instances feel any great emotional intimacy with them.

It is not emotional intimacy which James desires, but intellectual intimacy. We do not learn all that goes on in Strether but only that which takes form in utterance or in thoughts which are as explicit as though spoken. We do not, for instance, know precisely what Strether *feels* to be the relation of Chad to Madame de Vionnet. We perceive from his questions and from his declarations what he permits himself to *think*. And there are suggestions of his uneasiness, intimations that his formulated thoughts are not all. Thus when the true relation of the lovers is explicitly revealed in the scene by the river it has the effect of anticipated surprise. It is the high point of the action. But in attaining this effect James has sacrificed intimacy and emotional power. We share Strether's thoughts but never, deeply, his feeling. This restraint is inevitable to James's method, which springs instinctively from his reticence, from his constitutional avoidance of, his fear of, passion.

To consider for a moment the modern method of the psycho-analyst will be to point sharply the

differences in James's technique. The psycho-analyst would be more concerned with Strether's emotions, intuitions, the all but inexpressible nuances of
feeling; and the result no doubt would be incoherent
—incoherent but warm. The reader would more
wholly sink his consciousness in that of Strether,
would feel with Strether's nerves and guess his inarticulate attractions and repulsions. There would
be a loss of symmetry and clarity but a more immediate sense of life. There would be also a loss
—which in *The Ambassadors* could not be compensated for—of the suspense which is resolved
only when Strether intellectually accepts the fact
of which his feeling must long since have apprised
him. There are both loss and gain then in the restricted point of view which James adopts, and no
doubt this is always so in any choice of technique.
James follows his instinct and finds his triumphs.

Nevertheless the loss in such a book as *The
Ambassadors* cannot be blinked. It is most manifest in the instance of Madame de Vionnet. With
all his skill James does not, to my taste, succeed in
making her a passionate figure. She, too, is an "intellectual." Her conversation is a triumph of subtlety and indirection. He tells us that she is "hard
hit." The circumstances of her situation lead us
to believe this to be so. But she is cast for no action, is made to utter no word that cuts deep into
the abysses of feeling which lie beneath the suave
controlled social life. That she is "wonderful," we
have everybody's word, including the author's.

Yet she fails, to me, to live the part. James's method forbids. For this loss the book's triumphs cannot wholly compensate.

It is those triumphs, however, that constitute the greatness of James and make him, for all his limitations, one of the most intellectually satisfying of novelists. I can take space to point out only a few of his merits and these inherent in the point of view. The account which Strether gives to Maria Gostrey of the Pococks amusing themselves in Paris is far more biting and more humorous, because far swifter, than any "scenic" rendition, as James would express it, could possibly be. He does in a few paragraphs what, in the direct method, would ask as many chapters. The imagination of the reader is stimulated to fill out the meagre but deft suggestions—Waymarsh in his highly proper flirtation with Sarah; the "impossible" Jim being shown the wickedness of Paris by Madame de Vionnet. These are triumphs of the suggestive method, of indirection. They reveal James at his strongest, looking upon action retrospectively and extracting the rich essence of it.

There are excellent instances, too, of James's dictum that to the novelist description and narration are never separable, that they are so fused as to be one and the same. The truth of this statement is illustrated in the examples which I quote. It is to be noted, too, how in each the point of view is wholly maintained. Waymarsh is depicted as Strether sees him: Observe the introductory and concluding sentences, which hold the description as in brackets. And in the description of the Paris morning it is the effect of the scene upon Strether which is emphasized, Paris evoking memories and Paris, too, pressing upon his present mood, the mood of the particular situation, and insidiously modifying it.

Of Waymarsh:

There was yet an impression of minor discipline involved for our friend in the picture Waymarsh made as he sat in trousers and shirt on the edge of his couch. With his long legs extended and his large back much bent, he nursed alternately, for an almost incredible time, his elbows and his beard. He struck his visitor as extremely, as almost wilfully uncomfortable. . . . On their first going up together to the room Strether had selected for him Waymarsh had looked it over in silence and with a sigh that represented for his companion, if not the habit of disapprobation, at least the despair of felicity; and this look had recurred to Strether as the key of much he had since observed. "Europe," he had begun to gather from these things, had up to now rather failed of its message to him; he hadn't got into tune with it and had at the end of three months almost renounced any such expectation.

He really appeared at present to insist on that by just perching there with the gas in his eyes. This of itself somehow conveyed the futility of single rectifications in a multiform failure. He had a large handsome head and a large sallow seamed face—a striking significant physiognomic total, the upper range of which, the great political brow, the thick loose hair, the dark fuliginous eyes, recalled even to a generation whose standard had dreadfully deviated the impressive image, familiar by engravings and busts, of some great national worthy of the earlier part of the mid-century. He was of the personal type—and it was an element in the power and promise that in their early time Strether had found in him—of the American statesman, the statesman trained in "Congressional Halls," of an elder day. The legend had been in later years that as the lower part of his face, which was weak, and slightly crooked, spoiled the likeness, this was the real reason for the growth of his beard, which might have seemed to spoil it for those not in the secret. He shook his mane; he fixed with his admirable eyes, his auditor or his observer; he wore no glasses and had a way, partly formidable, yet also partly encouraging, as from a representative to a constituent, of looking very hard at those who approached him. He met you as if you had knocked and he had bidden you enter. Strether, who hadn't seen him for so long an interval, apprehended him now with a freshness of taste . . .

Of the Paris morning:

He knew he should recognize as soon as see it the best place of all for settling down with his chief correspondent. He had for the next hour an accidental air of looking for it in the windows of shops; he came down the Rue de la Paix in the sun and, passing across the Tuileries and the river, indulged more than once—as if on finding himself determined—in a sudden pause before the book stalls of the opposite quay. In the garden of the Tuileries he had lingered, on two or three spots, to look; it was as if the wonderful Paris spring had stayed him as he roamed. The prompt Paris morning struck its cheerful notes—in a soft breeze and a sprinkled smell, in the light flit, over the garden-floor, of bareheaded girls with the buckled strap of oblong boxes, in the type of anciently thrifty persons basking be-times where terrace-walls were warm, in the blue-frocked brass-labelled officialism of humble rakers and scrapers, in the deep references of a straight-pacing priest or the sharp ones of a white-gaitered red-legged soldier. He watched little brisk figures, figures whose movement was as the tick of the great Paris clock, take their smooth diagonal from point to point; the air had a taste of something mixed with art, something that presented nature as a white-capped master-chef. The palace was gone, Strether remembered the palace; and when he gazed into the irremediable void of its site the historic sense in him might have been freely at play—the play under which in Paris indeed it so often winces like a touched nerve. He filled out spaces with dim symbols of scenes; he caught the gleam of white statues at the base of which, with his letters out, he could tilt back a straw-bottomed chair.

CHAPTER III

THE CONDUCT OF NARRATIVE

The young novelist who looks with despair upon the finished works of the masters should study their first efforts and take heart. Therein he will perceive that technical skill is not a gift but an acquisition. More indispensable qualities to the writer may be largely innate, but technique, like the art of dancing, must be learned. There are writers, it is true, who display a discouraging proficiency almost from the first. No young novelist should be so clever as is Meredith in *The Ordeal of Richard Feverel.* Few of them are. On the other hand George Eliot in *Scenes from Clerical Life* is as awkward as a country girl at the opera. Dickens in *Oliver Twist* vainly seeks to disguise his clumsiness with a jest. Henry James though never, of course, crude even at the earliest, is decidedly thin and obvious, with a manner so evidently studied as to defeat its object.

Transitions reveal more clearly than any other technical device lack or acquisition of skill. They are not in themselves of the highest importance, though smoothness adds much to the ease and pleasure of the reader; but facility in transitions implies, usually, skill in selection. Once the young writer perceives that he need not laboriously count the milestones or itemize the calendar he rejoices in a sense of liberation. He is no longer the slave to time and space. Imagination will, in a moment, bear him wherever he wills. Ease of transition is the symbol of his release from a rigid actualism. He ceases to be a caterpillar and becomes a butterfly. The following transition from *Oliver Twist* is an instance of Dickens' early clumsiness, which he rapidly outgrew, though structural infelicities incident to the inclusion of too much matter, to the failure to omit, are to be found sometimes, perhaps always, even in his maturer work:

If so, let it be considered a delicate intimation on the part of the historian that he is going back, directly, to the town in which Oliver Twist was born; the reader taking it for granted that there are good and substantial reasons for making the journey or he would not be invited upon such an expedition on any account.

George Eliot displays a weight of metal from the first, but *Scenes from Clerical Life* and *Adam Bede* are bungling efforts as compared to her masterpieces; though even of her best work it may be said that it is massive, solid, and well-proportioned rather than graceful. She was eminently not a light-minded person and when she aims at a cosy effect of intimacy and takes her reader by the hand he quite justifiably quails. This from *Amos Barton:*

And now that we are snug and warm with this little tea-party, while it is freezing with February bitterness outside, we will listen to what they are talking about.

Again:

> We will not accompany him to the Clerical Meeting to-day, because we shall probably want to go thither some day when he will be absent. And just now I am bent on introducing you to Mr. Birdmain and the Countess Czerlaski, with whom Mr. and Mrs. Barton are invited to dine to-morrow.

It would seem to be a simple matter to effect transitions, to get one's characters from place to place without counting the steps. All the author need say is, "He resolved to go to Japan," and in the next paragraph or chapter to begin: "He found his first glimpse of Fuji Yama from the deck of the *Princess Alexandra* disappointing." This, though not subtle, obviates all the unpleasantness of a sea voyage and is at least swift. The most notable *tour de force* in transition that I recall is in George Moore's *Evelyn Innes*. The heroine goes to sleep in Paris having learned that day she is destined to become a great opera singer. She opens her eyes in the morning; the maid enters and draws the curtains, remarking, "Madame forgets that she told me to awaken her very early. Madame said she wanted to go for a long drive to the other end of London before she went to rehearsal." The reader is bewildered for a moment until he realizes that between the paragraphs, in the supposed interval of slumber, years have passed and that the heroine has achieved the success predicted of her. I think here that some break in the narrative, a chapter division perhaps, would obviate the momentary confusion. Yet essentially how deft the transition is, permitting the omission of so much time and so many incidents irrelevant to the author's purpose.

Many a novelist cannot get a character into a room without mentioning the door-knob, or let him depart without superfluous leave-taking. The following is a chance instance:

Gregg walked to the window, his head down; and slowly he came back. "Glad you told me," he said at last to Jim. "What direction are you going to-night?"

"South Shore Club."

"I thought it wasn't in the direction of Evanston. Have a good time, Jimmy."

"Night, Gregg."

Left alone in his room, Gregg stared at the wall.

Jimmy makes his physical exit decently enough, but the farewells and the mention of places have no more to do with the story than the snow on the roof. Jimmy is never to reappear. But the author has a momentary compunction at having introduced him to so little purpose. He pretends to an interest in him. He wishes to part with him courteously. Thereby the reader is put upon a false scent. The echo of that mistaken emphasis lingers for pages.

Worse, perhaps, than clumsy transitions are appeals to the reader for aid. I recall an instance from a "best seller." The author, choked with emotion at the pathetic situation of his heroine, exclaims, "Try to see the poor girl!" George Eliot is almost as crude in *Scenes from Clerical Life*. This from *Amos Barton*:

Reader! *did* you ever taste such a cup of tea as Miss Gibbs is at this moment handing to Mr. Pilgrim?

And the following instance, from *Mr. Gilfil's Love-Story* is, I believe, the worst page George Eliot ever wrote:

See how she rushes noiselessly, like a pale meteor, along the passages and up the gallery stairs! Those gleaming eyes, those bloodless lips, that swift silent tread, make her look like the incarnation of a fierce purpose, rather than a woman. . . . There is a dagger in that cabinet; she knows it well. . . . Poor child! poor child! she who used to cry to have the fish put back into the water. . . .
But what is that lying among the dank leaves on the path three yards before her?
Good God! it is he—lying motionless—his hat fallen off.

Apostrophes and appeals to the reader cease, in George Eliot's later works, to annoy. Yet she is to the end capable of infelicity and clumsiness. Structure, *Middlemarch* undeniably possesses; character drawing also, and bigness of design; but it is, at times, ponderous:

In watching effects, if only of an electric battery, it is often necessary to change our place and examine a particular mixture or group at some distance from the point where the movement we are interested in was set up. The group I am moving toward is at Caleb Garth's breakfast table.

Technical Dexterity of George Meredith

George Meredith among English novelists, if but one were to be singled out for study, would afford the young beginner the most instruction. For where, despite his mannerisms, will you find a novelist so full of meat and at the same time so much the artist? His lack of popularity—I believe the younger generation repudiates him—declares the vanity of all technical skill. What signifies virtuosity if the writer spurns the conventional baits of commercialized story-tellers? Meredith is not of these. Yet it is not his technical mastery, I think, which makes him caviar, but the racy and quintessential quality of his work. He is too solid a diet for weak stomachs. To understand him, both mind and imagination must bend in unison to the task.

A page of Meredith is like a close woven fabric, of intricate design, but thick and warm to the touch. There are no loose threads. Pull it and it remains firm. Compression, the sense of fulness running over, of meaning so rich and varied that only crowded metaphor can suggest it, is the "quality" of Meredith. Selection, only, among too copious materials, can give this effect. From the fully imagined lives of his characters he gives but a part; yet the background is there—suggested, invoked by allusion, and stimulating thought and fancy. There is in his novels the sense of a populous world, of a social structure complete from peasant to noble, and as varied and complex as the natures of men and women. Yet Meredith no doubt fails to simplify life sufficiently for the average novel reader. He bewilders with his complications and his insights.

The analytic method which Meredith almost invariably employs and his habit of apostrophe in the manner of Carlyle undoubtedly contribute to his "difficulty." Readers in general prefer the dramatic method unencumbered with analysis. Meredith, notwithstanding, is skilful in his dissection and comment. Either it is swift, not halting the flow of the scene, or, if extended, comes between dramatic passages and thus affords contrast and relief. Adequately to illustrate the point asks more space than is afforded here, but a casual examination of *The Egoist* will verify it. Sir Willoughby is at times subjected to the most minute analysis; the vanity of the male was never more fully revealed. Nevertheless the scenes in dialogue move briskly; there is nowhere the sense of narrative clogged and impeded by misplaced analysis.

Much of Meredith's skill lies in his easy transitions. In stories so complicated as his, with so many characters minutely observed, with scenes so various, and with so much retrospective narrative— narrative, that is, departing from the strict order of time—it is vital that the transitions be smooth and swift. The joints of the structure must be wholly concealed, the imagination of the reader be conducted from one incident to another as upon wings. In achieving so much Meredith perfects a device not alone his but which no one employs more deftly; his transitions are based not upon proximity in time or place but upon the association of ideas. Almost any page of Meredith's maturer work will supply an instance. This, from *Beauchamp's Career,* is typical. The scene described involves several characters at Mr. Romfrey's country seat. The transition is to Nevil at a distant place and to a time previous:

And what could there be to warrant Captain Baskelett's malicious derision, and Mr. Romfrey's nodding assent to it, in an article where all was truth?

The truth was mounted on an unusually high wind. It was indeed a leading article of a bannerlike bravery, and the unrolling of it was designed to stir emotions. Beauchamp was the theme. Nevil had it under his eyes earlier than Cecil. The paper was brought into his rooms with the beams of day, damp from the presses of the *Bevisham Gazette,* exactly opposite to him in the White Hart Hotel, and a glance at the paragraphs gave him a lively ardour to spring to his feet.

Transitions in *The Ordeal of Richard Feverel,* a much earlier work, are not so uniformly buried in the narrative nor achieved with so little emphasis:

And so ended the last act of the Bakewell comedy, on which the curtain closes with Sir Austin's pointing out to his friends the beneficial action of the System in it from beginning to end.

Again:

Let us go behind the scenes for a moment. . . . Farther behind the scenes we observe. . . . The atmosphere behind the scenes is not wholesome, so having laid the ghost, we will return and face the curtain.

In *Evan Harrington,* likewise, the author intrudes now and then self-consciously to direct his scene:

We will leave Evan Harrington to what fresh adventures may befall him. . . .
We left Rose and Evan on their way to Lady Jocelyn.

In his maturer works Meredith has gained tremendously in his mastery of indirection. Purely informative matter is so blent with narrative as to be indistinguishable from it:

The spell upon Nesta was not blown away upon English ground [intimating her return from the Continent].
The smell of the Channel brine inspirited her sufficiently. . . .
By the very earliest of the trains shot away to light and briny air from London's November gloom. . . .
Skipsey was hurried over. . . .

Meredith is always the intrusive author commenting upon his characters and drawing expressly the philosophic implication; but in this as in his management of transitions his growth in technical skill is evident upon a comparison of his earlier works and his later. The first citation is from *Richard Feverel:*

If immeasurable love were perfect wisdom, one human being might almost impersonate Providence to another. Alas! love, divine as it is, can do no more than lighten the house it inhabits—must take its shape, sometimes intensify its narrowness—can spiritualize, but not expel, the old life-long lodgers above-stairs and below.

In the next instance, from *One of Our Conquerors,* the author's comment is more closely knit with the narrative, is less personal and intrusive:

She was unjust, as Victor could feel, though he did not know how coldly unjust. For among the exorbitant requisitions upon their fellow creatures made by the young, is the demand that they be definite: no mercy is in them for the transitional. And Dudley—and it was under his influence, and painfully, not ignobly—was in the process of development: interesting to Philosophers if not to maidens.

The Ordeal of Richard Feverel is one of the most popular of Meredith's novels. Yet the qualities for which it is commonly most admired are those which, in his best work, he characteristically avoids. The description of Lucy plumping herself with berries, of Richard purified by the storm and moved to thoughts of home by the caress of the leveret, are passages which have evoked much applause. And they are, of course, fresh and ardent and moving. But they fail in the one great quality which Meredith later triumphantly exemplifies: they are not wholly knit into the story. In them description and narration are not completely fused. They are, in short, decorative, the scene describing Lucy the more notably so of the two. The author's interest is divided. Half is upon his story, half upon the "beauties of nature." In this division there is loss.

Passages less obviously lyric and therefore better narrative may be found in *Richard Feverel:*

> The shadow of the cypress was lessening on the lake. The moon was climbing high. As Richard rowed the boat, Lucy sang to him softly.

In *Evan Harrington:*

> He went to the window and threw it up, and feasted his sight on the moon standing on the downs.

In *Beauchamp's Career:*

> They had crossed the garden plot and were at the gate of the park leading to the Western wood. Beauchamp swung the gate open. He cast a look at the clouds coming up from the southwest in folds of gray and silver.

In *The Egoist* fusion of description and narration is so complete that scarcely a descriptive passage can be cut from its context. The background is almost wholly implicit, is touched upon in a phrase here and a sentence there. Yet it is perfectly distinct. The whole countryside and Sir Willoughby's estate are vivid and complete before the mind's eye.

Fusion of Exposition in Narrative

The illustrations, however various, point all to one fundamental principle of story technique: the obligation which rests upon the author to transmute the composite elements of his story to pure narrative. Henry James has declared that for the novelist distinctions between narration and description do not exist. He is concerned only with making his scene real. Characters and background are inseparable elements;[1] they blend to extort from the reader that complete surrender of the imagination which constitutes the story illusion. Informative matter may, as has been shown, be similarly fused and made narrative. Here, too, James's practice is in harmony with his theory. The following excerpt from *The Wings of the Dove* is characteristic. The matter is wholly retrospective and expository in essence but is given a narrative character by being recalled through the memories of Mrs. Stringham. Were the author impersonally to tell it, it would far less readily fuse with the story:

The woman in the world least formed by nature, as she was quite aware, for duplicities and labyrinths, she found herself dedicated to personal subtlety by a new

set of circumstances, above all by a new personal relation; had now in fact to recognize that an education in
the occult—she could scarcely say what to call it—had
begun for her the day she left New York with Mildred.
She had come on from Boston for that purpose; had
seen little of the girl—or rather had seen her but briefly,
for Mrs. Stringham, when she saw anything at all, saw
much, saw everything—before accepting her proposal;
and had accordingly placed herself, by her act, in a boat
that she more and more estimated as, humanly speaking, of the biggest, though likewise, no doubt, in many
ways, by reason of its size, of the safest.   In Boston
the winter before, the young lady in whom we are interested had, on the spot, deeply, yet almost tacitly, appealed to her, dropped into her mind the sly conceit of
some assistance, some devotion to render. Mrs. Stringham's little life had often been visited by sly conceits—
secret dreams that had fluttered their hour between its
narrow walls without, for any great part, so much as
mustering courage to look out of its rather dim windows.   But this imagination—the fancy of a possible
link with the remarkable young thing from New York
—*had* mustered courage: had perched, on the instant,
at the clearest look-out it could find, and might be said
to have remained there till, only a few months later, it
had caught, in surprise and joy, the unmistakable flash
of a signal.

Milly Theale had Boston friends, such as they were,
and of recent making; and it was understood that her
visit to them—a visit that was not to be meagre—had
been undertaken, after a series of bereavements, in the
interest of the particular peace that New York could
not give.   It was recognized, liberally enough, that
there were many things—perhaps even too many—New
York *could* give; but this was felt to make no difference
in the constant fact that what you had most to do, under the discipline of life, or of death, was really to feel

your situation as grave. Boston could help you to that as nothing else could, and it had extended to Milly, by every presumption, some such measure of assistance. Mrs. Stringham was never to forget—for the moment had not faded, nor the infinitely fine vibration it set up in any degree ceased—her own first sight of the striking apparition, then unheralded and unexplained; the slim, constantly pale, delicately haggard, anomalously, agreeably angular young person, of not more than two-and-twenty in spite of her marks, whose hair was somehow exceptionally red even for the real thing, which it innocently confessed to being, and whose clothes were remarkably black even for robes of mourning, which was the meaning they expressed. It was New York mourning, it was New York hair, it was a New York history, confused as yet, but multitudinous, of the loss of parents, brothers, sisters, almost every human appendage, all on a scale and with a sweep that had required the greater stage; it was a New York legend of affecting, of romantic isolation, and beyond everything, it was by most accounts, in respect to the mass of money so piled on the girl's back, a set of New York possibilities. She was alone, she was stricken, she was rich, and, in particular, she was strange—a combination in itself of a nature to engage Mrs. Stringham's attention.

Story Tone and Story Logic

Stevenson in a notable letter to Barrie upon *The Little Minister* commends his correspondent for having lied about the ending. Logically the story should have ended in tragedy; but the manner throughout has been light and a tragic ending would, therefore, be false to the story's tone and a defect in art. Stevenson criticises, by contrast, the ending of *Richard Feverel,* remarking that it might so have happened but need not, and that the tragedy therefore is a wanton blow to the feelings of the reader. The train of circumstances set in motion in *Richard Feverel* must, to be sure, lead to a demonstration of the fallacies of Sir Austin's system, but the tone of the story is not one to forewarn of tragedy. It is tragi-comic at the most. The death of Lucy seems forced to stress the moral.

This is not the sole instance in Meredith of the same defect, if it be a defect. *Beauchamp's Career* affords another. That Nevil should win fame and fortune and live ever after in peace and happiness is impossible. Such young men as Nevil are destined to defeat, for society, against which they war, is inevitably too strong for them. But Nevil has met defeat before the author summarily and without warning drowns him—largely, it would seem, to rub into his uncle Romfrey all that he has too lightly valued and lost. Certainly the reader is struck between the eyes. Nevil has before this escaped death for which we were in a sense prepared and we are now taken off our guard. That Meredith deemed the ending a better one than to condemn Nevil to a life of frustration and disappointment and drowned him out of sheer pity does not—if this was his purpose—wholly excuse him. The suspicion lingers that to drown Nevil was to expedite an ending not otherwise easy to compass.

The cause of Meredith's departure from the story's tone in *Richard Feverel*, and, in *Beauchamp's Career*, from the strict logic of his narrative, to achieve an ending not prepared for lies in the purpose back of his novels, the philosophy which he reads from life. His justification, if any, is there.[1] The question of story tone in its relation to the logic of the narrative is, however, a large one and it is needful to cite instances for specific examination. The practice of the forced tragic ending is rare; that of the forced happy ending is common.

Fielding's *Amelia* is one of the earliest examples of realistic fiction other than the picaresque. It is a sustained sound study of an amiable young man bringing disaster upon those he loves. The whole logic of the circumstances which the author sets in motion demands that the end be tragic. Fielding at the last, out of his love for the heroine, makes her inherit a fortune and assures us that the weak but attractive Captain Booth proved thereafter an exemplary husband. The reader hopes that it is so but secretly disbelieves it. The end is like that of one of Molière's plays, in which the hero is identified in the last ten lines as the long-lost heir. It is a convention of the seventeenth and eighteenth centuries, this type of ending, and is of no real validity in the tone of play or novel. It serves merely to bring the action to a full stop.

Eighteenth century novels abound in long-lost

[1]See Chapter IV.

uncles returning from America and India with fortunes and the desire to endow impecunious nephews. Parents turn up in that casual fashion which we must believe characteristic only of the eighteenth century. These are excellent aids to the novelist desirous of rounding out his story in happy fashion at whatever cost to plausibility. Conventional fiction of our day has also its own first aids. The hero, with no apparent effort, creates his masterpiece—novel, picture, opera—and at a bound attains fame and fortune. He strikes oil or gold, makes a lucky speculation in the stock-market, patents his invention. In fiction which owes little to life's realities, these devices are of small importance. But the greater the pretense to realism in the story the less can we believe in them. The *deus ex machina*, though it takes on a fresh disguise with every mode, in serious fiction is always an evasion of the novelist's duty.

In *Adam Bede* George Eliot succumbs to the temptation of the "happy ending" in solacing Adam with Dinah. The suggestion was not her own but an inspiration of Lewes's. She prepared for it, she tells us, from the fourth chapter. It nevertheless is a false note. The story really ends with the banishment of Hetty and the tragedy which she has caused in Adam's life. Wedding bells strike an incongruous note after tragedy sustained and achieved. There are authors who go to the other extreme. Henry James—in *The Bostonians* if I recall—after permitting his heroine to marry the hero describes her in tears and says something to the effect that in view of the far from brilliant marriage she had made these were probably not the last tears she shed. This is a needlessly nasty forecast.

To *Middlemarch* we have an epilogue telling summarily the after fortunes of the characters. Dorothea is reconciled to Celia; Dorothea's son inherits the estate of Mr. Brooke. I for one am glad to know these details, as also to see Lydgate once more. Probabilities are not forced in these instances and the reader's legitimate curiosity is satisfied. It is an old-fashioned method, no doubt, and it is to be said in defense of the modern fashion that to imply the course of future events and leave the details to the reader's imagination is a bit more stimulating. Dickens sins in too explicit finales. All the characters bow before the curtain. Micawber writes from the antipodes, and we are taken at some inconvenience upon a jail inspection in order to perceive Heep behind the bars. Dickens is, of course, incorrigibly theatric, and dispenses rewards and punishments with painstaking thoroughness. The recording angel himself could not be more exact.

A story is not life, however profound the illusion it creates, and to bring the reader back to earth, to break the transition to the lighted theatre and the departing audience, is justifiable enough. It is a merit of *Hamlet* that the play ends not with the shambles of the throne room but with Fortinbras "carrying on." The high-pitched drama is naturally resolved by the transition and comes to its close like a symphony. Few novels create so happy an effect. *The Scarlet Letter* is one, *Madame Bovary* another, *Wuthering Heights* a third. These are outstanding instances, in which, after an end logically inherent in the premises and plausibly achieved step by step, with the dominant tone struck at the outset perfectly sustained throughout, the story comes equably and harmoniously to a pause.

Technical Study of Hardy's "The Return of the Native"

Hardy's *The Return of the Native* offers so many points of technical interest that I hazard a rather long discussion of it. The concatenation of incidents in its plot, its deliberate employment of accident, its characterization and the method thereof, and, last, the relation of the background to the human drama, all are striking. Moreover the book enjoys a large reputation and is already famed as a classic. Its pretensions to so exalted a place justify a minute scrutiny of its method.

The opening description of Egdon Heath sets at once a melancholy tone and intimates the part which the Heath is to play in the lives of its inhabitants:

Fair prospects wed happily with fair times; but alas, if times be not fair. . . . The time seems near, if it has not yet actually arrived, when the chastened sublimity of a moor, a sea, or a mountain will be all of nature that is absolutely in keeping with the moods of the more thinking among mankind. And ultimately, to the commonest tourist, spots like Iceland may become what the vineyards and myrtle gardens of South Europe are to him now; and Heidelberg and Baden pass unheeded as he hastens from the Alps to the sand-dunes of Scheveningen. . . . It was . . . like man, slighted and enduring.

The description of which this is a part is long; its position gives it a further emphasis. We anticipate a tragic story, of human passions thwarted by destiny. It is a vast theatre which the author prepares for his drama. The story worthy of it must be simple, profound, universal.

The reader's attention is neatly focussed upon a single group within this vast setting. From a distance we descry a point of light, and, moving closer, discover it to be a furze fire around which several rustics are gathered. They gossip racily; from their talk we learn of several characters who are to play important parts in the story: Thomasin, Mrs. Yeobright, and Wildeve. Our curiosity is piqued as to the forbidden banns. Thomasin we readily identify as the girl whom the Reddleman in the brief initial episode has befriended. The jealous critic of method will discern in this dialogue evidence of contrivance. The talk, though amusing and characteristic, is clearly informative, directed at the reader. It tells rather too much. But the visual scene is admirable.

The rustics in their gossip have made casual mention of Captain Vye and his beautiful granddaughter living isolated in their house at Mistover. To Eustacia Vye we are shortly introduced as she stands beside her fire on the knoll before the house with her companion, a small boy. Her acts, her posture, and the physical description excite interest, especially when it is said, "It was as though side shadows from the features of Sappho and Mrs. Siddons had converged upward from the tomb to form an image like neither but suggesting both." The pool nearby is described, the pool into which Wildeve, for a signal, tosses a stone. This pool is frequently mentioned in the course of the story, and we anticipate that it is to be the scene of some episode important in the lives of the characters. Wildeve's coming and the ensuing dialogue clarify the plot and intimate Eustacia's curious power of introspection: "Damon, a strange warring takes place in my mind occasionally."

The detailed portraiture of Eustacia, "the raw material of a divinity," with "the passions and instincts which make a model goddess," predicts a character of heroic size. She is described and analyzed very fully. "Her high gods," we learn, were William the Conqueror, Strafford, and Napoleon Bonaparte. . . . At school she had used to side with the Philistines in several battles, and had wondered if Pontius Pilate were as handsome as he was frank and fair." "And so we see our Eustacia," in the author's words, handsome, passionate, unconventional and discontented, hating her environment and seeing no beauties in the heath on which fate has condemned her to live.

The child, Eustacia's attendant at the fire, is the medium through which the Reddleman learns of Eustacia's meeting with Wildeve; an important link in the plot, for the Reddleman is to be thereafter the chief instrument of the author in the complication of an elaborate action. The motivation here, the Reddleman's concern for the happiness of Thomasin, whom he loves, may be deemed adequate, no doubt, though the Reddleman in his meddling is ultimately carried far. He is led to eavesdrop in the next meeting of Eustacia and Wildeve; to offer to marry Thomasin; and to be used by Mrs. Yeobright as a threat wherewith to coerce Wildeve. In the course of an interview with Eustacia in which unavailingly he attempts to win her to his cause she is made to say of the heath, "There is a sort of beauty in the scenery, I know; but it is a jail for me." These expressions of discontent are frequent in the story.

Eustacia, in whom interest chiefly centres throughout the book is, to the time of Clym Yeobright's arrival on the scene, largely passive though depicted as a passionate character. Despite her former relations with Wildeve and her half-love for him, love which is depicted as born largely of unrest and discontent, she is not made to seem deeply emotional. Nor, indeed, is Wildeve, though he invites her to elope with him. In both is a power of self-analysis which defeats passion and which makes their love-making only half convincing. The truth of this criticism can best be illustrated in passages too long for citation, but will be indicated in the following excerpts:

Eustacia again remained in a sort of stupefied silence. What curious feeling was this coming over her? Was it really possible that her interest in Wildeve had been so entirely the result of antagonism that the glory and the dream departed from the man with the first sound that he was no longer coveted by her rival? She was, then, secure of him at last. Thomasin no longer required him. What a humiliating victory. . . . The sentiment which lurks more or less in all animate nature—that of not desiring the undesired of others—was lively as a passion in the supersubtle epicurean heart of Eustacia.

And again:

She placed her hand to her forehead and breathed heavily; and then her rich, romantic lips parted under that homely impulse—a yawn. She was immediately angry at having betrayed even to herself the possible evanescence of her passion for him. She would not admit at once that she might have over-estimated Wildeve, for to perceive his mediocrity now was to admit her own great folly heretofore. And the discovery that she was the owner of a disposition so purely that of the dog in the manger, had something in it which at first made her ashamed.

Eustacia learns of Clym Yeobright's return through the convenient device of eavesdropping so frequently employed throughout the story. The rustics whom she overhears speak much to the purpose, telling us of Clym's past and his character. It is even intimated that Clym and Eustacia would be well mated: " 'I say, Sam,' observed Humphrey when the old man was gone, 'she and Clym Yeobright would make a very pretty pigeon pair—hey?' " Later she dreams of Clym, a device suggestive of present-day experiments in psychoanalysis. "The perfervid woman was by this time half in love with a vision. The fantastic nature of her passion, which lowered her as an intellect, raised her as a soul." This passion, so swiftly conceived and not, I think, wholly credible, leads Eustacia to the adventure of the mumming so that she may see and talk with Clym.

Eustacia's infatuation, her final rejection of Wildeve, all in preparation for the promised affair with Clym, ask no comment, though, in passing, the author's improbable use of the eavesdropping device should be noted. The Reddleman, anticipating a meeting of Wildeve and Eustacia at Rainbarrow, lies in hiding nearby. Later Eustacia asks him:

"How do you know that Mr. Wildeve will come to Rainbarrow to-night?"
"I heard him say to himself that he would. He's in a regular temper."

Eustacia's appearance at Wildeve's wedding and her services as witness, though prepared for, are likewise theatrical and inherently improbable.

Clym Yeobright serves the author as a peg upon which to hang a philosophy of disillusionment:

In Clym Yeobright's face could be dimly seen the typical countenance of the future. . . . People already feel that a man who lives without disturbing a curve of feature, or setting a mark of mental concern anywhere upon himself, is too far removed from modern perceptiveness to be a modern type. . . . What the Greeks only suspected we know well; what their Æschylus imagined our nursery children feel. That old-fashioned revelling in the general situation grows less and less possible as we uncover the defects of natural laws, and see the quandary that man is in by their operation.

Clym is described as an altruist, willing to sacrifice himself for the good of his kind, as one before his time, one of the stuff of martyrs. He loves the heath, is "permeated with its scenes, with its substance, and with its odors. He might be said to be its product." The inevitable tragic outcome of his infatuation for Eustacia, who detests the heath, is thus prefigured.

It is to the author's attainment of his tragic end that technical scrutiny must be chiefly directed. The inevitable disharmony of the two lovers has been intimated. Eustacia's passion for cities, for Paris, to which she hopes to induce Clym to return, is sufficiently stressed. Mrs. Yeobright's hatred and fear of Eustacia are likewise early indicated, though the justification of her feeling is not wholly convincing, especially in the extreme to which it leads her, the virtual banishment of her son. Yet this defect, if it is such, may be waived for an examination of the incidents whereby the overt tragic denouement is manipulated.

The tragic sequence is begun with Thomasin's need of money and her Aunt's, Mrs. Yeobright's, determination to give her the half of the spade guineas which is her inheritance. The other half is to be Clym's. She sends the guineas in two bags to Thomasin and Clym, both of whom are at Mistover, but she does this only after refusing to entrust Thomasin's share to Wildeve. That Wildeve should know Mrs. Yeobright has something to give Thomasin is not plausibly accounted for. Wildeve says, "She casually dropped a remark about having arranged to fetch some article or other." That Thomasin should so remark in view of the need of secrecy is wholly unlikely, but Mrs. Yeobright's refusal serves to arouse Wildeve's suspicion and hostility and these are put to later use.

Mrs. Yeobright entrusts the money to Christian, the clown of the story, whose unfitness for any office demanding common sense has been fully demonstrated. Christian puts the guineas in his boots. On his way he meets a number of people going to Wildeve's inn to attend a raffle. He is prevailed upon to accompany them, pays his shilling at the raffle, throws dice and wins the prize. Christian is much impressed by his luck and the wonders of dice. He says to Wildeve:

"If I could only use this power that's in me of multiplying money I might do some good to a near relation

of yours, seeing what I've got about me of hers—eh?"
He tapped one of his money-laden boots upon the
floor.

Wildeve asks him what he means and where he is
going:

To Mistover Knap. I have to see Mrs. Thomasin
there—that's all."

"I am going there, too, to fetch Mrs. Wildeve. We
can walk together."

Wildeve became lost in thought, and a look of inward illumination came into his eyes. It was money for
his wife that Mrs. Yeobright could not trust him with.

It is to be noted in this passage that Christian,
who tells so much, does not mention Clym, to whom
half of the money belongs. This omission is essential to the later misadventures.

Christian before setting out with Wildeve wist-
fully asks if he may have the dice and box and is
given them. On the way Wildeve remarks:

"So you have money to carry to Mrs. Wildeve," said
Christian's companion after a silence. "Don't you think
it very odd that it shouldn't be given to me?"

To which Christian replies:

"But my strict documents was, to give the money
into Mrs. Wildeve's hand: and 'tis well to do things
right."

Again the natural opportunity to speak of Clym's
share in the money is passed by, and in the ensuing

game at dice into which Wildeve entices Christian, employing the dice and box so conveniently at hand, Wildeve is throughout under the impression that the money for which he plays is his wife's. Only at the end, when he has lost all, does Christian cry out: "Half the guineas are poor Mr. Clym's."

The Reddleman, who has been eavesdropping and who after the departure of Christian challenges Wildeve to play, conveniently misses this confession of Christian's, for he, too, is throughout convinced that all the money is Thomasin's and when he wins it back takes it all to Thomasin. The author explains:

His mistake had been based upon Wildeve's words at the opening of the game, when he indignantly denied that the guinea was not his own. It had not been comprehended by the reddleman that at half-way through the performance the game was continued with the money of another person; and it was an error which afterwards helped to cause more misfortune than treble the loss in money value could have done.

The importance of the episode is thus emphasized and the effort is made to lend plausibility to an extraordinary concatenation of accidents. But that the Reddleman, eavesdropping, must have heard Christian's confession is slurred over.

The next step in the developing tragedy is dependent upon the preceding. Thomasin acknowledging the money does not mention the amount. Christian in terror is silent. When later forced to confession he quotes Wildeve as saying: "He said you ought to have gied Mr. Clym's share to Eustacia, and that's perhaps what he'll do himself." Yeobright's words were: "Well, 'twould have been more graceful of her to have given them to his wife Eustacia." But Christian's perversion of the remark suffices to plant the suspicion, almost the certainty, in Mrs. Yeobright's mind. She sets out to see Eustacia and "to ask plainly if Wildeve had privately given her money which had been intended as a sacred gift to Clym."

After a cold exchange of greetings Mrs. Yeobright demands:

"Have you received a gift from Thomasin's husband?"

"A gift?"

"I mean money!"

"What—I myself?"

"Well, I meant yourself, privately—though I was not going to put it that way."

After this singularly blind and inept way of putting the case a bitter quarrel naturally ensues. Yet even here an opportunity for clearing the mistake is offered. Eustacia says:

"You ignored me before my marriage, and you have now suspected me of secretly favoring another man for money!"

This is so wide of Mrs. Yeobright's meaning, blundering as she is, that it would seem the words would bring her to a pause and an explanation ensue. Instead she ignores it as completely as though it had not been uttered. Eustacia and Clym's mother part as enemies. Too late is the mystery of the money cleared up. Mother and daughter-in-law have said things which cannot be unsaid.

The second series of accidents and coincidences springing from the first is scarcely less complicated. Mrs. Yeobright, determining at the Reddleman's exhortation to be reconciled with her son, sets out in the heat of the day for the long walk across the heath. She sees Clym in the garb of a furze cutter enter his cottage before her. Instead of following him she seats herself in a clump of fir trees nearby. There she rests for twenty minutes and sees another visitor, Wildeve, precede her. When at last she knocks she is not admitted, has a momentary glimpse of Eustacia's face at the window, and turns away heartbroken. The explanation is somewhat involved. Eustacia did not wish to be seen with Wildeve. In the next room, Clym lies asleep on the hearthrug. Eustacia conducts Wildeve to the back entrance after a second knock at the door. This is the passage:

"Her knocking will, in all likelihood, awaken him," continued Eustacia; "and then he will let her in himself. Ah—listen."

They could hear Clym moving in the other room, as if disturbed by the knocking, and he uttered the word "Mother."

"Yes—he is awake—he will go to the door," she said, with a breath of relief. "Come this way."

Eustacia on her return finds Clym asleep still and Mrs. Yeobright nowhere visible. Clym had cried out in his sleep.

The closely calculated timing of these misadventures need not be further dwelt upon, nor the all but incredible incident of Clym, as Eustacia listens for him to answer the knock, turning in his sleep and speaking the word "Mother" audibly and clearly. Nor shall I enumerate all the circumstances which constitute the third and fourth series of tragic coincidences. Suffice it that Mrs. Yeobright unburdens her heart to a small boy met by chance; and later, as Mrs. Yeobright lies dying of exhaustion and snake bite, her son beside her in the shed on the heath, and Eustacia and Wildeve in the darkness listen without, the small boy makes a dramatic entrance:

"I've got something to tell 'ee, Mother," he cried in a shrill tone. "That woman asleep there walked along with me to-day; and she said I was to say that I had seed her, and she was a broken-hearted woman and cast off by her son, and then I came on home."

Three or four weeks later when Clym has recovered from the illness into which his mother's death had cast him, the small boy "repeated the exact words he had used on entering the hut." Also upon cross-examination he reports the circumstances of Wildeve's coming, of Mrs. Yeobright knocking, and of Eustacia looking out of the window. He is a boy to delight the legal mind. Upon his perfect evidence Eustacia is convicted in her husband's eyes.

Wildeve's inheritance, coming patly upon Eustacia's rebellion against her unhappy life; the letter which would have reconciled Eustacia to Clym, and which miscarries by a little series of tragic accidents—these are among the later instances of mischance which the author employs. I wish only to note the scene of the catastrophe. The reader has, throughout the story, been prepared by repeated mention of the pool near Eustacia's home at Mistover for its employment in some tragic circumstance. But the drowning occurs in Shadwater Weir, never before, I believe, named. The river itself is passingly noted early in the story:

> The garden was at the back, and behind this ran a still, deep stream, forming the margin of the heath in this direction, meadow-land appearing beyond the stream. . . . The water at the back of the house could be heard, idly spinning whirlpools in its creep between the rows of dry feather-headed reeds which formed a stockade along each bank.

On the night of the catastrophe Wildeve waits "some quarter of a mile below the inn." He hears "the roaring of a ten-hatch-weir a few yards further on." The pool below the weir is, a little later, fully described. It is in this that Wildeve and Eustacia are drowned, the incidents of the catastrophe confusedly described as seen successively by Wildeve, Clym, Thomasin, and the Reddleman. It is apparent, I think, that the pool beside Mistover was, in the original design, intended as the place of the catastrophe and so emphasized, but that later the author improvised a wholly new setting from scant materials.

The extraordinary series of mischances by which Hardy in *The Return of the Native* brought his story to a foreseen tragic close has, in his use, not to be dismissed simply as an instance of overplotting but considered in the light of his philosophy. That philosophy is explicit in *Tess of the D'Urbervilles*. Tess is the victim of a malicious destiny, the sport of the President of the Immortals, and suffers tragic mischance. The letter to Angel Clare which, had it been received, would have altered the lives of several characters, slips under the carpet. From this unlucky accident springs disaster. Yet æsthetically *Tess* is, in this instance, far more effective than *The Return of the Native* for the reason that the chain of accidents is short. Among the casual mischances of the book the miscarriage of the letter is chief. It is emphasized. Hardy calls the world to note we are the sport of destiny manipulating chance, and that fate may hang upon the most trivial incident. Criticism, in this instance, must direct itself more to Hardy's philosophy than to his technique. In *The Return of the Native* accident is piled upon accident in a chain which grows weaker with each additional link. So vast a series of mischances exceeds human credulity. There is, indeed, something almost comic in ill-luck so monstrous as this.

Hardy's employment of accident, however in-effective in *The Return of the Native,* is deliberate; it is the means to the expression of his pessimistic philosophy. This is not the philosophy of Natural-ism,[1] nor is his technique that of the naturalist. The philosophy of the true naturalist is determinism. Men are the products of heredity and environment. The universe is a soulless concatenation of forces, which, in their uniform operation, are known as laws. There is, strictly speaking, no such thing as chance. Coincidence, accident, are to the naturalist mathematically calculable. Good and bad fortune, humanly speaking, would, when spread over broad areas, be equally distributed. Our rough-hewn ends are the product neither of cosmic benevolence nor malevolence. With Hardy it is otherwise. Back of his conception of the universe is an ingenious devil who delights in making sport of human lives, who spins cunning webs to entrap his victims. This is the inversion of the philosophy that all experience makes for good. Hardy is essentially a Calvinist who has substituted the Devil for God in a fatalis-tic universe. The coincidences upon which he de-pends are perverted miracles.

Hardy's philosophy of a malevolent destiny is characteristic of his later manner. In his earlier novels destiny is more impersonal, is not the chess-master beguiling the tedium of eternity as in *Tess* and *The Return of the Native* and, even more fiendishly, in *Jude the Obscure.* An instance will

[1]See Chapter IV.

point the generalization. In *The Woodlanders* the action at the climax requires that the heroine run along a certain path to meet her lover. In this path, with malicious intent, a man-trap has been set. We anticipate mutilation, perhaps death. Instead, the heroine's skirt catches in the trap but she is uninjured. The author here plays benevolent destiny. In other of his books he ceases to be such. Either his philosophy darkens or he becomes—as I believe is the case—the victim of his mannerisms. More and more he takes pleasure in the ingenious fabrication of unhappy accidents leading to tragedy. Yet the greater the ingenuity, I feel, the more he fails to portray life faithfully. A forced tragic sequence of incidents is æsthetically no more satisfying, nor philosophically more convincing, than the happy accidents by which novelists of another faith contrive, however unplausibly, to bring their heroes and heroines to more cheerful fates.

Characterization in *The Return of the Native* is likewise sacrificed to the exigencies of a tragic plot. As instances in proof of a criticism which cannot be proved but merely asserted, I should point to the scene in which Clym and Eustacia, a few weeks after their marriage, first quarrel. There is in this little hint of past tenderness; it is not passionate but cold. It is not slowly worked up to, but hurried. The author has contrived the steps in his plot with great, if unconvincing, ingenuity, but the motivation and the depiction of character are hastily done and in crucial scenes ring false.

Eustacia is described throughout as passionate but she is merely petulant in word and act. Clym, too, is oddly cold with her for a man whose passion has swept him to an ill-judged marriage. And Wildeve, supposedly passionate also, is like Eustacia coldly analytical of his own moods. Eustacia remains the most vivid character of the novel, but her vividness lies in the author's description of her, not in her own passionate speech and action. She does not come wholly alive. She is an intellectual conception. Hardy is an intellectual novelist, whose philosophy, whose generalizations upon life, are more interesting than the fable and the characters with which he sets these forth.

Hardy's philosophy and his method are neither the philosophy nor the method of the naturalistic writer. In his characterization he is feeling, likewise with a technique inadequate to his purpose, for the effects of modern psycho-analysis. In Eustacia, Clym, Mrs. Yeobright, and Wildeve he is endeavoring to portray unconscious motives, the passions of the blood in conflict with the conscious will. In Eustacia it is particularly needful that he succeed if his conception of her is to live. There are but two ways in which this conflict can be presented, either by delineating character through act and word and hinting at clews when these fail to correspond with professed motive; or by analyzing character and telling his readers both the purported motive and the deeper subconscious motive in conflict with it. If the characters are made, as Eustacia and Wildeve are made, to analyze themselves and speculate upon their peculiarities, they cease at once to convince. Eustacia is too conscious that, in her own words, a "strange warring takes place in my mind occasionally."

Background as an Essential Element of Structure

It remains to consider the use of background in *The Return of the Native*. In the theory of Zola and the naturalists man is the result of heredity as played upon by environment. Nature or background is a determining force, more than a scenic accessory to a story. Egdon Heath, it is clear, is cast for such a part in *The Return of the Native*. In Clym and Eustacia are antithetical characters, the one moved to contentment or resignation, the other to revolt, by the scene in which fate has cast them. Yet their fates are in no wise determined by that scene nor are their characters essentially modified. Clym, though he loves his birth-place, is depicted as a man in whom it is evident "that thought is a disease." He is not a child of the heath though content to live there. Happiness, Hardy believes, lies in unthinking acquiescence to nature. Clym is neither acquiescent nor happy. Eustacia hates the heath though admitting its beauty. Her hatred springs from what it denies her, the social life of cities, the civilized delights of Paris. Any surroundings which cramped her— a life of poverty, suburban life—would serve equally well to fan in her the spirit of discontent.

In the main action of the story, whose end is determined by the curious concatenation of accidents which has been noted, the heath serves merely as a magnificent backdrop. It is the scenery of the drama, beautiful in itself but not essential to the action.

In the lives of the peasants, on the other hand, the heath is a determining force. They are its true children as Eustacia and Clym are not. Unthinking, they live in harmony with it. They are as indigenous as the furze and holly. Amid the simple and convincing story of their lives, the too forced, too dramatic, story of the chief characters moves like an alien, an irrelevant thing. It is so, I think, of Hardy's novels in general. *Far from the Madding Crowd, Under the Greenwood Tree,* and *The Woodlanders* linger pleasantly in the memory. In them the operation of natural forces is unstressed, is felt rather than analyzed. Scenes and characters blend as they should do. But in *Tess, The Return of the Native,* and in *Jude the Obscure* background plays a more dramatic rôle, or is designed to do so. In them, as for instance *Jude,* the pressure of circumstance, of unhappy environment, is so emphasized as to seem disproportionate and unreal; or, as in *The Return of the Native,* background is nominally assigned a rôle which it cannot fill. One instance, though trivial, will serve to illustrate Hardy in his happiest vein, unincumbered by too weighty a philosophy. The heathmen are described in their Sunday clothes "walking leisurely among the turves and furze-faggots they had cut during the week, and kicking them critically as if their use were unknown." There is excellent observation in that. It is in the heathmen that lies the half-told story of Egdon Heath, not in Clym and Eustacia.

Maurice Hewlett, taking his thesis for a comment upon Stendhal from the words, "L'auteur dit tout, explique tout, ne laisse rien à faire à l'imagination du lecteur," comments as follows:

He tells everything, explains everything, leaves nothing to the reader's imagination: this is a way of speaking. What he tells are bare facts, what he explains are credible motives; but in so doing he leaves exactly everything to the reader's imagination, because he records, not describes. The whole secret of good romancing is there. If authors of imagination could only understand for how much facts, well-conceived, count and for how little descriptions. It is, to my mind, one of De Stendhal's chief claims to honour that he relied upon this romance of fact, and made no attempt to convince by description. Sometimes you may think that he carries his principle to excess, that he condescends to description deliberately jejune. It is true that there are passages whose flowers are the veriest frittering ornaments. A mountain has a majestic summit, a lake has a glassy surface, the forest of La Faggiola has "sombres et magnifiques ombrages." This is when he deigns to touch such affairs at all; the nearest he will ever go is: "C'etait au commencement d'un matin exquis d'Avril." But I think that he gains enormously by this austere handling; he knows so well that the true way of moving the imagination is to give the imagination room in which to move itself. Consider the Waterloo chapters of this book [*The Chartreuse of Parma*], for instance;

there is no pathetic fallacy here, no geography. A clump of willows, a little shot-torn wood, a muddy road, a bridge broken down, a field with mist hanging about its edge. You will find no less in a war bulletin of the day. Yet you know that massed men are moving over broad plains, or cuirassiers in flight; you hear the guns, the rattle of artillery taking up position; the very vagueness of assertion works the spell: this is the landscape of war on a grand scale. Not Livy himself can marshal the facts better, or know more surely when to sound the charge.

In Stendhal's *The Chartreuse of Parma* I do not find that power of characterization or that revelation of the human soul for which, I read, it is remarkable. Its portrayal of individuals is neither vivid nor profound. The hero is never quite alive and the women are no more than pretty, passionate, and illogical. Nor is the story well constructed. It has no mass, no certainty of emphasis; its tempo is very uneven, jerky in fact. Yet it has the great virtue, which Hewlett commends, of telling facts and to a great degree permitting the reader to supplement these for himself. More, it does what its author intended, which was not to construct a moving story but to create a panorama. Stendhal reveals himself as the successor of Voltaire and the Encyclopedists, one who thought of Napoleon as the destroyer of the relics of feudalism, the renovator of Europe. *The Chartreuse of Parma* depicts the period of reaction which followed upon Napoleon's overthrow, the time of the Holy Alliance. The absurdities of the little principalities of

Italy, in which the monarchical tradition is held up for ironic scrutiny, and the worldliness of the church are the themes of his satire. Its utter good temper, its indifference to the fate of its characters, the very subordination of story to a portrayal of the larger social scheme constitute its merit. The author is not too intimate with his story nor his characters. They are typical figures moving in typical complications. They constitute a comment upon life.

Scott's narrative method can have pleased Stendhal no more than his politics, and must partially explain the ironic gibes at the most popular novelist of the age. For Scott professedly made his stories adapt themselves to the scenes he wished to describe. His popular success with a method artistically so questionable, together with the whole school of Gothic novelists and their stage machinery, is no doubt the inspiration for that "word painting" and that exploitation of local color which has been a curse in both English and American fiction. The nonessential but decorative description was and is of a piece with bad architecture, with functionless battlements and all gingerbread work whatsoever. Happily the soundest writers have instinctively avoided its excesses. Jane Austen is an antidote for Scott, and Borrow for Harrison Ainsworth; and in America Herman Melville at last is coming into his own while Cooper and Prophets of the Great Smoky Mountain school gather dust. This is not to say that a sound writer will win success in his own lifetime. The history of literature bears witness to the contrary. But a sound tradition must ultimately make for the slow, very slow improvement of contemporary standards.

Why is it that untrained taste in fiction is almost always bad, like untrained taste in anything else? Even masterpieces, one suspects, when honestly admired are valued for their defects more than for their merits. Simplicity, directness, a sense of fact —all primary artistic virtues—are supposed to be common among the untrained and illiterate, are assumed to be attributes of the barbarian. They are not, it is plain, common to the semi-civilized, the basely literate who constitute the masses of our modern world. For these, exaggeration, false emphasis, the sentimental, and the gaudy are easy lures. Simplicity and directness are hardly won virtues either for the writer or his readers; and it is seldom given any literary generation to celebrate those works in which its fame ultimately resides. Thus the novel that is easily done, whose decorations are extrinsic not structural, with its Corinthian capitals "loafing around the outside" as was pertinently remarked of the old Chicago Courthouse, is the popular thing. And if it is forgotten in a year, a thousand others, made from the same recipe, can be as easily concocted.

Nature description is one of the easiest of false substitutes for sound action; a cheap filler which it asks of the writer a stern conscience and unflagging awareness to avoid. The Romanticists who rediscovered nature, who made the appreciation of nature a cult, have much to answer for. A profound feeling for the outdoors, a sense of kinship with all life, like love itself flourishes best when not too articulate. Indirection is its mode of expression. The old ballads show, often, a more genuine love of nature, a sense of closer union with it, than most of our modern nature poetry. Our very emphasis marks our separation, our effort to recapture something that is lost.

The pertinency of these generalizations to the technique of story-telling is immediate. Observe how little Jane Austen describes her scene and yet how complete a sense of background the reader has. So, too, with Fielding. In *Tom Jones* there is, after the initial description of Allworthy's house and its setting, almost no description of scene. Yet it is always present, suggesting itself in a word and phrase here and there, perfectly realized in the author's mind and almost unconsciously referred to. Borrow's novels, full of the outdoors as they are and transporting the reader to English woods and lanes, have little description. And yet they are as rustic as *As You Like It* in which all the forest is there, so to speak, by implication. In Hudson, of recent writers the most descriptive of nature, the greater emphasis upon scene is wholly unforced in that Hudson is a naturalist and that his scenes present essential facts, endowed incidentally with charm.

The technical test for fitness in the employment of background lies, then, in the relevancy of the scene to action and to the mental states of the characters. It is only rarely that we consciously observe a scene and then only briefly. We are concerned with our own immediate objects, with our preoccupations. There are moments when we come alive, forget ourselves, and see all our surroundings with a vivid awareness. Scene is indelibly associated with these flashes of emotion and the writer with an eye to truth records scene as powerfully as he can at such moments. Provided he lives consistently in the minds of his characters and sees always through their eyes, he cannot go wrong. The vast use of background in many of Conrad's stories—*Typhoon* and *Heart of Darkness* for instance—never seems forced because it is of the essence of the story, determining incident, moulding character. But in Galsworthy, as I remarked of *The Country House,* the descriptive passages are too often things apart. I do not think that Galsworthy puts them in because he finds them easy, as padding, but because in them he finds momentary relief from the futility of human action; he seeks even to justify them on the score of contrast, to give them a value as symbols. They are nevertheless not a structural necessity. I have in reading them the sense which an aria in a grand opera so often gives, of something which, beautiful in itself, interrupts the story.

Technical Characteristics of "Wuthering Heights"

Of *The Return of the Native* it was remarked that the heath, designed to be a motivating force in the story and determining the lives of the characters, does not, in reality, play so vital a part. It is no more than a picturesque accessory, a scene on which is enacted a story determined by malignant fate. Any other environment would, essentially, be equally congruous. It is only as nature is cast for a less dramatic, a less calculable, rôle than in *The Return of the Native* that it can be made to dominate a story. The more implicit its pressure, the more indirect its influence, the greater is its true force. If with *The Return of the Native* be compared *Wuthering Heights,* the truth of the criticism will be evident. *Wuthering Heights* is crude in many respects, its technique faulty; yet it is a profound and moving book. Its setting in the moors of Yorkshire is very like Egdon Heath, but its characters are far more deeply rooted in the soil.

Charlotte Brontë characterizes her sister's novel in these impressionistic but apt phrases:

Wuthering Heights was hewn in a wild workshop, with simple tools, out of homely materials. The statuary found a granite block on a solitary moor; gazing thereon, he saw how from the crag might be elicited a head, savage, swart, sinister; a form moulded with at least one element of grandeur—power. He wrought with a rude chisel, and from no model but the vision of his meditations. With time and labor, the crag took human shape: and there it stands colossal, dark, and frowning, half statue, half rock: in the former sense, terrible and goblin-like; in the latter, almost beautiful, for its coloring is of mellow gray, and moorland moss clothes it; and heath, with its blooming bells and balmy fragrance, grows faithfully close to the giant's foot.

The strokes of the rude chisel and something of the greatness of the figure can be traced in a technical analysis of the book's method.

The crudity of the book inheres wholly in the point of view, which involves almost all possible difficulties and is accompanied by few advantages. The story opens with the narrator's encounter with Heathcliff, his landlord. Shortly thereafter, in his convalescence from the illness brought on by exposure on the moors, his housekeeper, Ellen Dean, in order to entertain him, tells him in several long instalments the story of a number of persons, Heathcliff among them, and the incidents of twenty years. This story is broken occasionally by the trivial affairs of the auditor, with some loss to the story illusion. The auditor is indeed of no value to the book whatsoever and intrudes only to confuse. Happily we can forget him most of the time. It is with Ellen Dean that we identify ourselves and through her eyes see the incidents of the story.

But Ellen is herself beset with difficulties. She is a servant successively employed in the various households involved in the story and, as an on-looker, reports dramatically what she has seen, giving the exact words of the speakers and even surmising motive with all the freedom of the author-observant. Virtually she is that, and we usually forget her identity until some device to account for her presence in certain scenes is thrust before us. These devices are often thin. She is made to be present at scenes to which she cannot plausibly be a party, as, for instance, Heathcliff's interview with Catherine Linton shortly before the latter's death. Again when the narrator is not present upon the scene of action, incidents are dramatically related to her in a letter from one of the participants, whose narrative manner differs in no wise from Ellen's. As an instance of this we have Isabel's long letter telling of her life with Heathcliff.

The awkwardness of these devices is obvious and in a lesser book would be a great handicap. *Wuthering Heights* easily survives them, and of a deeper difficulty makes almost a virtue. Expressive as action is of the dominant personalities of the story there is much that action or even dramatic dialogue cannot reveal. For the motives of the characters are not obvious, do not dwell in the plane of the simpler emotions, nor are they, strictly, conscious to those who hold them. They are felt in the blood. It is with the inarticulate, the half conscious or the wholly subconscious, that the author is essentially concerned. How then can they be revealed? Her device is to have the characters speak that which can only be felt. Catherine Linton speaking of Heathcliff remarks: "He's more myself than I am. Whatever our souls are made of, his and mine are the same." And a little later, "My love for Heathcliff resembles the eternal rocks beneath: a source of little visible delight, but necessary." Heathcliff likewise, haunted by Catherine's presence, exclaims aloud, careless of auditors, "Oh God! It's a long fight, I wish it were over." And again, "By God! she's relentless. Oh, damn it. It's unutterably too much for flesh and blood to bear—even mine."

So great is the book's power that the reader in the heat of the story accepts implicitly the convention of these utterances. They are, like the soliloquies of Hamlet, revelations of unspoken thoughts; more even, of emotions which cannot be made wholly articulate. But they are essential to that inner drama of which we must catch a glimpse sufficient for the imagination to seize upon. Like Hawthorne's, Emily Brontë's drama is that of the subconscious. If not with his artistry, with no less native power of imagination, she comes to grips with her story. Hardy in *The Return of the Native* had, it seems to me, a theme similar in kind and in potential effectiveness, but I do not feel that the subconscious in Eustacia, Clym, and Wildeve ever comes to the surface. Eustacia, it is true, analyzes herself much as Catherine Linton soliloquizes. Plausibility in each instance is slight; but the soul stuff turned up by Emily Brontë is vastly more elemental than in Hardy. Moved by its revelation we disregard the improbability of the method.

Aside from the inadequacies of the point of view and the contortions of incident which derive therefrom, the story's greatest defects arise from forced plotting. Isabel's infatuation for Heathcliff and her elopement with its subsequent misery are a bit hard to accept, though possible. Their chief purpose is to provide Heathcliff with a son to be utilized later in the story. This sub-plot, the marriage of Cathy and Linton, is forced; nor does it serve any particular purpose save to illustrate Heathcliff's avarice and harshness, already vivid enough. The whole story marks time at this point and the effect is of anti-climax after the tense and vivid episodes which led to the death of Catherine Linton. It is indeed hard to account for the long period of time between the two high points of the story, Catherine's death and, at last, Heathcliff's. That Catherine should hound him so relentlessly all these years has, it is true, emotional weight. And to relax the tension for a moment before pitching it even higher than before is also dramatically effective. Yet so long an interval need not have been granted, nor interest diverted from the major characters to those of little importance.

The structural inadequacies of *Wuthering Heights*, though not negligible, are, however, insignificant when weighed with its great merits. The roughness of execution was to be expected in a first novel, especially of a genre which had no models to offer. Emily Brontë beat a new path from the high-road of English fiction, one that few have been able to follow. I can recall no novel prior to *Wuthering Heights* in which environment is so vital and determining a force in the destinies of its characters. They truly are rooted in the soil. Their passions are as racy and wild as the heather. The moor-fowl are no more native to this rugged scene than are Catherine Linton, Earnshaw, and Heathcliff.

Yet it is remarkable how little "set" description there is withal. There are few descriptive passages of any length. Catherine Linton in her delirium plays with the feathers from her pillow and babbles of the birds, the moor-fowl and lapwing, in a passage of lyrical beauty. Usually the scene is implicit in the narrative, is touched in with a word or two incident to the action, as in the opening scene, where brief phrases—"a few stunted firs"—"a range of gaunt thorns"—contribute the background to the house. And again in the snow scene which follows, it is the danger, the relation of the scene to action, which is stressed; the visual picture is incidental. This interweaving of description and narration, of action and setting is, no doubt, the outgrowth of an overmastering motive: to tell the story. With writers more consciously "literary" as, of Emily Brontë's predecessors, Mrs. Radcliffe and Scott, scene is decorative, extrinsic. Emily Brontë obeyed a sounder instinct.

It is the moors which at the outset establish the tone of the story and never are they absent from the mind's eye in picturing the story incidents. The unity of place is remarkable throughout. Towns are mentioned but they are never described, nor does any of the action take place within them. The two houses, that of the Earnshaws and that of the Lintons, demark the limits of the visual scene. Between lie the moors, changing only with the progress of the seasons, constant but ever-varied, like the sea. In the development of its theme, in the recurrence of motifs, *Wuthering Heights* is like a symphony, striking at the outset the proper note, announcing its subject, working to its stormy climax, and dying away at the last in a chord which perfectly resolves its complex harmonies:

I lingered round them [the graves] under that benign sky; watched the moths fluttering among the heath and harebells, listened to the soft wind breathing through the grass, and wondered how any one could ever imagine unquiet slumbers for the sleepers in that quiet earth.

The Nature of Emily Brontë is not the Nature of Hardy. To Hardy Nature is philosophically conceived, is something apart, a hostile force determining human destiny. To Emily Brontë, Nature is neither hostile nor friendly. It is not a thing apart from man but the very substance of his being. Her characters could not live elsewhere than on their native moors. The question of happiness does not enter, nor articulate love or hate of the scene in which their lot is cast. The moors to them are home, are the whole of the universe. Life without them is impossible and even after death they haunt the scenes which they have known. So profound a sense of identification with the forces of nature is a primitive thing, a sense that to modern beings is difficult to recapture. Speculation is inimical to it. Only poets possess it. Emily Brontë, more profoundly even than Wordsworth—for she does not formulate her creed—is at one with the force that "rolls through all things."

Wuthering Heights is otherwise remarkable, besides its masterly fusion of action and scene, for several technical triumphs. It touches upon the supernatural with the same unquestioning certainty as upon Nature. It assumes an attitude of belief in discarnate spirits. The narrator never questions their possibility. The theology is pagan, is as unquestioning as a child's belief in a folk tale. Catherine Linton, dying, declares:

"I'll not lie there by myself: they may bury me twelve feet deep, and throw the church down over me, but I won't rest until you are with me. I never will."

She keeps her promise. The broken utterances of Heathcliff, his rapt expression of mingled ecstacy and torture, the narrator's earlier dream of Catherine trying to force open the casement, suggest enough and not too much of the supernatural forces invisible but ever-present. The description of Heathcliff lying dead is a piece of hair-raising realism with just the right mingling of the natural and the supernatural:

"Mr. Heathcliff was there—laid on his back. His eyes met mine so keen and fierce, I started; and then he seemed to smile. I could not think him dead: but his face and throat were washed with rain; the bed-clothes dripped, and he was perfectly still. The lattice, flapping to and fro, had grazed one hand that rested on the sill; no blood trickled from the broken skin, and when I put my fingers to it, I could doubt no more: he was dead and stark.

"I hasped the window; I combed his black long hair from his forehead; I tried to close his eyes: to extinguish if possible, that frightful, life-like gaze of exultation before any one else beheld it. They would not shut: they seemed to sneer at my attempts, and his parted lips and sharp white teeth sneered too!"

Again at the end of the story the note of the supernatural is struck with the exact ambiguity which leaves us free to accept or to reject. Were the narrator himself to see the apparition, half its power would be lost. The force of the suggestion lies in its unsupported character. Yet who can sense the supernatural if it is not children and animals?

"What's the matter, my little man?" I asked.
"There's Heathcliff and a woman yonder, under t'nab," he blubbered, "un' I darnut pass 'em."
I saw nothing; but neither the sheep nor he would go on; so I bid him take the road lower down.

Indirection, suggestion, the swift mention of little incidents which contribute to the picture most effectively because they are unstressed seem to be Emily Brontë's instinctive method, so casual are they. The sentence, "I knocked over Hareton who was hanging a litter of puppies from a chair back in the doorway," contributes more to the brutality of the scene in its deliberate avoidance of emphasis than a paragraph of description. Death scenes likewise are not stressed but are told with as unemotional a casualness as Heathcliff's savageries:

"A fit of coughing took her—a very slight one—he raised her in his arms; she put her two hands about his neck, her face changed, and she was dead."

And even more without pause in the story's stride:

"But the poor dame had reason to repent of her kindness: she and her husband both took the fever, and died within a few days of each other."

In Emily Brontë dwelt a fierce spirit which scorned superficial and soft things. *Wuthering Heights* is worthy of that unconquerable will which on the day of her death enabled her to clothe herself, to walk about, and to die in the effort to stand. We are told that her family dared not remonstrate. In the creations of such a woman conventional actions are not to be expected, nor is the speech likely to be well mannered and concerned with trivialities. The characters of *Wuthering Heights* talk as they act, with breath-taking directness. "I shall make you swallow the carving-knife, Nelly," says Earnshaw in one of his fits of drunken madness. And again when Nelly remonstrates:

"Have mercy on your own soul! ..."
"Not I! On the contrary, I shall have great pleasure in sending it to perdition to publish its maker. Here's to its hearty damnation."

Heathcliff is no less direct:

"For shame, Heathcliff!" said I. "It is for God to punish wicked people; we should learn to forgive."
"No, God won't have the satisfaction that I shall," he returned.

Catherine, dying, says to Heathcliff:

"I wish I could hold you," she continued bitterly, "till we were both dead! I shouldn't care what you suffered. I care nothing for your sufferings."

And Heathcliff cries in anguish when she is dead:

"May she wake in torment! ... You said I killed you —haunt me then!"

It is quite impossible that any group of human beings ever talked with such uncompromising and brutal directness while, at the same time, they revealed the hidden tortures of their souls. Cruelty and sensitiveness so mingled could not be articulate. This is the speech of melodrama. It is the kind of thing Masefield has done in *The Everlasting*

Mercy, and in *The Widow in the By-Street,* or, in prose and more comparably, in *The Tragedy of Nan.* It is customary to speak of Masefield's "realism" in these instances, to compare the literalness of the character's speech with the idiom of *Enoch Arden*—to the disadvantage of one or the other as may be. It is not my desire at this point, if ever, to become entangled in a definition of "realism," but merely to point out, and to justify, this paradox: the characters in *Wuthering Heights* or in *The Tragedy of Nan* employ a speech of mixed colloquial literalness and of elevated, even poetic, diction and imagery; and this mixture untrue to any phonographic record of life is in the deepest sense true, because revelatory, of the characters who utter it.

Heathcliff certainly never employed these words:

"I have no pity! The more the worms writhe, the more I yearn to crush out their entrails!"

This is an expression of Heathcliff's soul, something to be guessed, in actuality, from his expression, from a blow, or from some coarse oath. Emily Brontë employs these words to convey him to the reader, and the artistic problem is this: Is Heathcliff clear to us, does he live, and do we read his words, in their context, without feeling them to be forced or unnatural? In this twofold question, not to be easily answered and permitting the widest range of illustration, lies the problem of dialogue. It is the point Stevenson has in mind when, in his letters, he writes of *The Ebb Tide* and speaks of the "key" of dialogue and the problem of harmonizing a third person narrator with the too colloquial and literal speech of the characters.

The Key of Dialogue

Almost at random I selected the following bit of dialogue from the sword and buckler romance nearest to my hand, a readable one at that:

Helpless in his arms she lay.
"You coward, you beast, you vileness!" she gasped. And then he stopped her mouth with kisses.
"Call me what you will, I hold you, I have you, and not all the power of England shall tear you from me now. Realize it, child,"—he fell to pleading. "Realize and accept, and you will find that I have but mastered you only so that I may become your slave."

Taken by itself it is incredible, and yet I do not recall that, as I read the story, I was distressed. My concern was with the incident; my imagination needed but coarse symbols to create a stirring picture. The unreal dialogue "registered" distress, and in the pitch of excitement to which the story had moved me I was not critical of the over emphasis which "got it across." The instance is simple but typical of what is meant by the "key" of dialogue. A story of highly wrought sentiment, intense emotion, and exciting scene can carry and even exact a diction and a tone of dialogue wholly "unreal," that is, not in accord with the probable facts. In the scene described the heroine actually no doubt panted and struggled and said no word, endeavoring to bite the villain in the wrist. And he, if he spoke, swore at her.

Yet though the reader accepts uncritically the unnatural speech of the tense situation, it has not the power of more restrained utterance, of speech which, though beyond the level of ordinary discourse, falls short of the theatrical. Thackeray understood this principle excellently well, and the much admired quarrel scene in *Henry Esmond*, in which Colonel Esmond renounces his allegiance to the Pretender, is a fine example of rightly pitched dialogue:

"You will please, sir, to remember," he continued, "that our family hath ruined itself by fidelity to yours: that my grandfather spent his estate, and gave his blood and his son to die for your service; that my dear lord's grandfather (for lord you are now, Frank, by right and title too) died for the same cause; that my poor kinswoman, my father's second wife, after giving away her honor to your wicked perjured race, sent all her wealth to the King: and got in return that precious title that lies in ashes, and this inestimable yard of blue ribbon. I lay this at your feet and stamp upon it: I draw this sword, and break it and deny you; and had you completed the wrong you designed us, by Heaven, I would have driven it through your heart, and no more pardoned you than your father pardoned Monmouth. Frank will do the same, won't you, cousin?"

It is with the last simple question that the high-pitched utterance is resolved and resumes a normal tone. And it is in that resolution that lies the greatest thrill of a fine passage.

The speech of Ring Lardner's characters is agreeable to my ear and inasmuch as it seems at first glance to violate all the principles of selection and of heightened effect which I have been at some pains to illustrate, room must somehow be made for it in an appreciation of good method. That Mr. Lardner is a selective artist is evident in these brief excerpts:

> "How much are your medium prayer-books?"
> "What denomination?" asked the clerk, whose name was Freda Swanson.

And again:

> "How about to-morrow night?" he inquired.
> "I can give you a lower to-morrow night on the six-thirty," replied Leslie Painter, that being the clerk's name.
> "I'll take it," said Tommy.
> He did so and the clerk took $10.05.
> "I'll see old Bill after all," said Tommy.
> Leslie Painter made no reply.

His stories seem transcripts of the actual, but they are more literal than life itself. In them literalness is intensified until it becomes art. Intensification here resides, however, not in a heightening of tone but in a deliberate lowering of it. His stories are keyed one half-tone below the actual, and in that shade of difference lies the effect which he seeks. An examination of his use of American speech would reveal many subtleties differentiating various classes of society and degrees of culture. I must content myself with one short example of his literal but condensed and accentuated speech:

"What was the bust-up over?" ast Nate. "Didn't he like you boxing?"

"He didn't care nothing about that," says the kid. "But they was a gal he wanted I should marry. And I give her the air. So he done the same to me."

"Why did you quit the gal?" ast Nate.

"I figured I could do better," he says.

Consistency with itself is as necessary to this style of speech as in elegant writing is the avoidance of vulgarity. An amateur story-teller reports his hero as speaking thus: "This is the niftiest party I have attended for ages. Everything is here to make the heart glad." So pleasing an incongruity is beyond the reach of art. It displays a complete lack of ear, and it is upon the ear that consistent and harmonious speech depends. Disraeli must have been in some such way deficient, for his novels induce the mood familiar to half slumber or light fever in which moments of sharp awareness are succeeded by lapses into semi-consciousness or delirium. Contrasted passages from *Venetia* illustrate very clearly one cause of this disharmony. The first is natural, pitched to the level, or but little above it, of ordinary discourse. It is amusing and real. The second, high-pitched and unnatural, is doubly incongruous by reason of the contrast:

"Plantagenet, my dear, speak. Have not I always told you, when you pay a visit, that you should open your mouth now and then? I don't like chattering children," added Mrs. Cadurcis, "but I like them to answer when they are spoken to."

"Nobody has spoken to me," said Lord Cadurcis, in a sullen tone.

"Plantagenet, my love!" said his mother in a solemn voice.

"Well, mother, what do you want?"

"Plantaganet, my love, you know you promised me to be good!"

"Well! what have I done?"

"Lord Cadurcis," said Lady Annabel, interfering, "do you like to look at pictures?"

"Thank you," replied the little lord, in a more courteous tone; "I like to be left alone."

"Did you ever know such an odd child!" said Mrs. Cadurcis; "and yet, Lady Annabel, you must not judge him by what you see. I do assure you he can behave, when he likes, as pretty as possible."

"Pretty!" muttered the little lord between his teeth.

"If you had only seen him at Morpeth sometimes at a little tea party," said Mrs. Cadurcis, "he really was quite the ornament of the company."

"No, I wasn't," said Lord Cadurcis.

"Plantagenet!" said his mother again in a solemn tone, "have I not always told you that you are never to contradict any one?"

The little lord indulged in a suppressed growl.

And the second illustration:

"Venetia, you know how I have doted upon you; you know how I have watched and tended you from your infancy. Have I had a thought, a wish, a hope, a plan? has there been the slightest action of my life, of which you have not been the object? All mothers feel, but none ever felt like me; you were my solitary joy."

Venetia leaned her face upon the table at which she was sitting and sobbed aloud.

"My love was baffled," Lady Annabel continued. "I fled, for both our sakes, from the world in which my family were honored; I sacrificed without a sigh, in the very prime of my youth, every pursuit which interests woman; but I had my child, I had my child!"

"And you have her still!" exclaimed the miserable Venetia. "Mother, you have her still!"

"I have schooled my mind," continued Lady Annabel, still pacing the room with agitated steps; "I have disciplined my emotions; I have felt at my heart the constant, the undying pang, and yet I have smiled that you might be happy. But I can struggle against my fate no longer. No longer can I suffer my unparalleled, yes, my unjust doom. What have I done to merit these afflictions? Now, then, let me struggle no more; let me die!"

Venetia tried to rise; her limbs refused their office; she tottered; she fell again into her seat with an hysteric cry.

"Alas! alas!" exclaimed Lady Annabel, "to a mother, a child is everything; but to a child, a parent is only a link in the chain of her existence. It was weakness, it was folly, it was madness to stake everything on a resource which must fail me. I feel it now, but I feel it too late."

Venetia held forth her arms; she could not speak; she was stifled with her emotion.

It is always a matter of surprise to discover how small a part of a good novel is, in most instances, told in dialogue. The proportion varies, of course, with the genre, but even in the novel of manners, in the hands of Jane Austen for instance, dialogue in actual bulk is relatively of small amount and often in novels memorable for excellent dramatic scenes is even less. I commented passingly on this fact when analyzing *The Ambassadors*. In that masterpiece of technique, conversation is never perfunctory, never given to exploit the obvious, but always to give point to a situation for which preparation in previous analysis has been made. Often James withholds the expected, the necessary, word so long that suspense passes almost over to irritation; the speed is retarded almost too much. At least such is my feeling. Nevertheless the technical point is excellently illustrated by this exaggeration of method. The anticipated, the clarifying speech, is like the resolution of a chord, like the action which finally breaks a momentary paralysis of will. Speech so accentuated by the position and paucity of its use is tremendously more effective than if more prodigally employed. The whole scene of Strether and Sarah Pocock in the tenth book of *The Ambassadors* illustrates the point, the emphasis which dialogue gives when used sparingly. I can cite only the concluding passage:

"I find in her more merits than you would probably have patience with my counting over. And do you know," he enquired, " the effect you produce on me by alluding to her in such terms? It's as if you had some motive in not recognizing all she has done for your brother, and so shut your eyes to each side of the matter, in order, whichever side comes up, to get rid of the other. I don't, you must allow me to say, see how you can with any pretense to candor get rid of the side nearest you."

"Near me—*that* sort of thing?" And Sarah gave a jerk back of her head that might have nullified any active proximity.

It kept her friend himself at his distance, and he respected for a moment the interval. Then with a last persuasive effort he bridged it. "You don't, on your honor, appreciate Chad's fortunate development?"

"Fortunate?" she echoed again. And indeed she was prepared. "I call it hideous."

. . . .

Strether, quite as an effect of it, breathed less bravely; he could acknowledge it, but simply enough. "Oh if you think *that*——!"

"Then all's at an end? So much the better. I do think that!" . . .

Nothing is easier for the writer than to set his characters to facile but pointless dialogue or to employ speech in duties to which it is not appropriate: to the purely mechanical exposition of past incidents, or the conduct of a debate whose interest lies not in character portrayal but in some issue extraneous to the emotional field of dialogue. James has criticised the use of dialogue for expository purposes, and any problem novel will exhibit the misuse of dialogue for the purposes of debate, the characters becoming mere mouthpieces of the author. The more skilful writer employs in these instances summaries of dialogue or a kind of indirect discourse in which summary is intermingled with quoted utterance. The effect is that of direct quotation; the tone and flavor of speech are retained but mechanical deadness is avoided and conciseness achieved.

Use of Indirect Discourse

The following rather long passage from the *Memoirs of a Midget* illustrates excellently this fusion of indirect discourse, or summary of speech, with comment and description to which the occasional and sparing employment of the actual spoken phrase gives color and emphasis. Expanded to the full the scene would be too long for its value to the story. The dialogue, much of it expository in character, would be thin. The technical object, then, is to thicken, by boiling down, the less essential parts but to retain in so far as possible the flavor of the original speech. This is apparent in Mr. Anon's diatribe directed against the human race, which is a semi-quotation or, as I have employed the term, "indirect discourse." Thus the passage, "battened on meat, stalked its puddled streets and vile, stifling towns."

. . . "I am going away soon," I said, "to the sea." The wren glided away out of sight among its thorns. I knew by his sudden stillness that this had been unwelcome news. "That will be very pleasant for me, won't it?" I said.

"The sea?" he returned coldly, with averted head. "Well, *I* am bound still farther."

The reply fretted me. I wanted bare facts just then. "Why are you so angry? What is your name? And where do you live?" It was my turn to ask questions, and I popped them out as if from a *Little by Little*.

And then, with his queer, croaking, yet captivating voice, he broke into a long, low monologue. He gave me his name—and "Mr. Anon" describes him no worse. He waved his hand vaguely in the direction of the house he lived in. But instead of apologizing for his ill-temper, he accused me of deceiving and humiliating him; of being, so I gathered, a toy of my landlady's, of betraying and soiling myself.

Why all this wild stuff only seemed to flatter me, I cannot say. I listened and laughed, pressing flat with both hands the sorry covers of my book, and laughed also low in my heart.

"Oh, contempt!" he cried. "I am used to that."

The words curdled on his tongue as he expressed his loathing of poor Mrs. Bowater and her kind—mere Humanity—that ate and drank in musty houses stuck up out of the happy earth like warts on the skin, that battened on meat, stalked its puddled streets and vile, stifling towns, spread its rank odors on the air, increased and multiplied. Monstrous in shape, automatic, blinded by habit, abandoned by instinct, monkey-like, degraded!

What an unjust tirade! He barked it all out at me as if the blame were mine; as if *I* had nibbled the apple. I turned my face away, smiling, but listening. Did I realize, he asked me, what a divine fortune it was to be so little, and in this to be All. On and on he raved: I breathed air "a dewdrop could chill"; I was as near lovely naught made visible as the passing of a flower;

the mere mattering of a dream. And when I died my body would be but a perishing flake of manna, and my bones. . . .

"Yes, a wren's picking," I rudely interrupted.

Dickens is skilful in the art of indirect discourse, frequently summarizing a speech in half quotation which employs the style of diction appropriate to the character; often, to be sure, relying on mechanical tags such as the "very 'umble" of Uriah Heep or Mrs. Micawber's repeated declaration that she would never desert Mr. Micawber. By these methods the novelist avoids the disharmony which Stevenson deplored in narratives of the third person, the clash of tone incident to two dissimilar styles, that of the narrator and of his characters. De Morgan, who learned much from Dickens, is adept in this device, as any of his novels will show. I must content myself here with but one illustration from *Joseph Vance:*

"I put it on the gridiron the minute I see you get past the Roebuck," said my Mother, who must have seen us coming some time before we reached the Roebuck. My father commented and my Mother said she would have put it down for that matter as soon as ever she see us, only she wasn't going to have it done to a cinder while he was a-soakin'. It would have been just exactly ready only for my Father's 'abits. My Father said with a sigh that his Roebucking days were over, but he hoped there was something on the shelf. My Mother said there was enough to go round. I then felt that progress ought to be made with what I considered the Bill before the House, and cut in to the effect that Miss Lossie she laughed and told the cook, and the cook she said go in the garden and pick pears. And my Mother said, "Whatever is the child lecturin' about, with his Miss Lossie and cooks? Go along in and cut the bread, and don't cut yourself."

An elaborate discussion of the problems of dialogue and an examination of its use in a wide range of fiction is beyond my present purpose. I have endeavored to touch only upon outstanding points and briefly to consider them. Excellent contrasts in effective and ineffective dialogue are to be had in Charlotte Brontë's *Jane Eyre*. May Sinclair in her work *The Three Brontës* discusses Charlotte's uncertain touch with critical discrimination. It may be said of the dialogue in *Jane Eyre*, however, that unnatural as some of it is, it is rightly felt; that it is in key with the somewhat swollen and passionate character of the theme. Structurally this is the essential problem of dialogue. Naturalness, though desirable, is secondary to unity and suitability of tone.

Fidelity of speech to the actual pitch of colloquial use has, indeed, little to do with its effectiveness or even its plausibility, for these depend rather upon the suitability of dialogue both to the general tone of the story and the emotional tension of a particular scene. The speech of story characters can never wholly correspond with that of actuality if for no other reason than that selection, condensation, and pertinency are requisite to its fictional use. Even Dreiser and Dorothy Richardson omit much that their characters say, though that which is quoted may be virtually indistinguishable from the most commonplace utterance. And at the other extreme in romantic fiction, or in realism such as that of Henry James in which the employment of dialogue is highly selective, the speech of characters may depart widely from the actual. The analogy of speech and story tone to the key in music is wholly sound. Any key is right if adapted to its particular end and if all of the composition is cast within it.

Distinction Between the Real and the Actual Suggested by Problem of Dialogue

The vexed question of realism, both as to its nature and its desirability, is, in the light of this discussion of dialogue, made more intelligible. Life as depicted in the novel can never, however great the effort, be wholly actual, wholly a literal transcript of incident, character, and speech. It is a more or less close analogy to the actual, though the range of divergence therefrom is obviously great. Every novel is symbolic of life rather than literally descriptive of it, and the scale of fiction is as wide as from the fairy tale, the romance, or the allegory at one extreme to the most prosaic naturalism at the other. It would be agreed, I think, that we may gain an insight into life alike from *The Ugly Duckling, Pilgrim's Progress, The Three Musketeers, David Copperfield,* and *Growth of the Soil.* These works are wholly various, yet

they are all universal. No one of them is all of life
and yet each is true to some aspect of life. Each is
real if not actual. In the common use of the term,
Growth of the Soil is obviously more 'realistic'
than *The Arabian Nights;* its incidents, characters, and speech are more credible and usual. Yet
the power and beauty of neither depends upon its
correspondence with or departure from actuality
but upon its consistency with itself in the terms or
key of its creation. That to me *Growth of the Soil*
seems rather more important than *The Arabian
Nights* is an ethical rather than an æsthetic judgment; though I should add that *Growth of the Soil,*
because in my belief more difficult to do, gives, in
its triumph over the difficulties of its material,
a warmer satisfaction. It stirs, too, a wider and
deeper range of emotions than the other.

The devotee of form, with faith that selection is
the root principle of all art, is brought up abruptly
before the works of Dostoievsky. All the great
Russians, with the notable exception of Turgénev,
are deficient in the sense of form as we, with the
best English and French works in mind, understand the term. In Tolstoy one has a sense of vast
canvases painted with a large brush, panoramas in
which complicated effects are achieved; in which
there is, truly, mass, but therewith an infinity of
detail in which one easily becomes lost. In Dostoievsky this confusion is even greater. His novels,
even more than those of the professed naturalists,
produce the illusion of actual life. In them is the

complexity of life. They are peopled with innumerable figures, vivid—startlingly vivid—but having, many of them, no purpose other than to be, lending, that is, nothing of importance to the conduct of the narrative and falling into no perceptible pattern. Life itself is like that to the vision of most—vivid but confused—and it is the conventional theory of art that it is the function of the novelist to bring some sort of order from this chaos, to impose a pattern upon the waywardness of life.

Dostoievsky does not do this. To depict the confusion of life is, I take it, his first preoccupation. A novel which lacked this would seem to him unreal. Life to him is madness, nightmare touched with spiritual meaning. It is in these spiritual revelations that sanity lies; they redeem life from stark madness. And it is true that in his work they stand out against their chaotic background. They give meaning to *The Idiot* and *The Brothers Karamazov*. In Dostoievsky is an appalling lack of that illusion through which, for the preservation of our reason, most of us regard existence. We do not see life as it is, but, more or less, as we choose to see it; without Dostoievsky's spiritual insight, which mitigates the all but intolerable reality of his vision, but spared also his glimpses into the abyss.

An æsthetic problem nevertheless remains. To dip into Dostoievsky is to be immersed in life. It is a poignant experience, not wholly, nor even largely, pleasant. In retrospect it is this general impression of actuality that we recall, not the story nor even the characters of the story. To these we have been brought too close clearly to distinguish and remember them. The details are too numerous, the conduct of the action is too complicated, and the end is too little of an elucidation. If distinctness, clear memorableness, be the test of a great novel, Dostoievsky's must be pronounced deficient. Yet it would be pedantic to insist upon the sole validity of such a test; it cannot, in the face of Dostoievsky's work, suffice. The easy escape is to say that novels may be written in a dozen different ways, all of which are good. There is undoubtedly truth in the evasion; and yet standards should not so easily be set aside. Surely if to its revelations, its profusion, its richness, its vividness there had, in Dostoievsky's work, been added a sharper sense of form, a more rigid principle of selection and greater consequent relevance, he would be a greater novelist than he is. *The Scarlet Letter* and *Madame Bovary* are slight works compared to his; in them the scene of the actual world is not so powerfully evoked; yet these are distinct and unforgetable as Dostoievsky's novels are not. They give also pleasure, an æsthetic satisfaction, which his, at least to me, do not give.

The Aim and Method of Balzac

Balzac's presence in a discussion of technique is, like that of Dostoievsky, as disconcerting as that

of a volcano in a formal garden. No less than the
volcano can he be ignored. Whether or no he is a
great artist he is undeniably a great writer and
has a method suited to his ends. These are somewhat different from those of the ordinary novelist,
for Balzac is not primarily, I believe, concerned
with a story as a thing rounded and complete in itself, nor even is he deeply concerned with character. His characters are pawns with which to play
his game. He is a social historian. The *Comédie
Humaine* is a history, in many volumes, of a civili-
zation. The individual stories are but chapters, frequently incomplete in themselves, but each contributing its part to the larger epic. Any discussion of one of them must be made, therefore, with
this contributory purpose in mind.

Lost Illusions will serve as well as another instance to illustrate Balzac's historical method. It
is a link between his scenes of provincial life and
those of Paris. Lucien de Rubempré, brother of
Eve and friend of David, is for a part of the story
in Paris and to Paris he returns at the end with
promise of further adventures there to be subsequently told. Of itself then the book lacks unity,
consists of two stories, related to be sure, but without that subordination of one to the other that in
a well-rounded novel would be deemed essential.
Our interest is divided between Lucien's story and
David's, and only one of the two comes to a definite denouement.

Balzac's method of simplification in character

portrayal, his repetitions for emphasis, his heaping up of materials to enforce his selected points, and his resemblance to Dickens in the employment of "tags"—mannerisms that is to say in speech and appearance—has been pointed out by one of his critics.[1] Simplification is evident in the characterizations of David and Eve—the one the highminded man of noble purpose, the other all wifely devotion; and in old Séchard, miser and tippler, one of Balzac's many pictures of avarice. Lucien is more complex but even he is little more than the talented young man corrupted by ambition who suggests Pendennis, or Pip of *Great Expectations*. There are, too, many other characters, all distinct but, manifestly, types accented to suggest individuals; characters moreover—and this is widely true of Balzac—visually more vivid, and depicted in more detail, than mentally.

Varied and distinct as these creations are they interest not so much as individuals whose fates and fortunes intrigue us as they do as minor actors of a scene operatic in its scale and emphasis. The careful description of each of the many guests at Madame de Bargeton's soiree has no other purpose than to characterize the provincial aristocracy. Enough is told of each to suggest the habits and beliefs of a conservative and tenacious order; their relationships create, by implication, the whole web of country society. The legal processes by

[1]E. Preston Dargan in Modern Philology, "Studies in Balzac, III. His General Method," vol. XVII, No. 3, p. 1, July 1919.

which David is involved to his ruin and the chicanery by which his patents are stolen are also a part of the social picture. In the tight-fisted, unscrupulous, money-worshipping world which Balzac depicts, the individual and his private fortunes are only a symbol, a test-case to illustrate the argument. Balzac does not hesitate to include long accounts of technical legal processes, to expatiate on the contrasted characters of the Parisian and the provincial attorney, nor to quote in detail an elaborate bill of costs. He supposes, and rightly, that we will be interested in these matters, but our interest is that of the reader of social history rather than of fiction.

The topography of a town, the structural details of house or shop, are set forth with the same scrupulous detail and factual verity as legal and commercial processes. Things, it is evident, are as important to Balzac as are his characters; and both are less important than society. He conceives life, apparently, as an organism, the leviathan of Hobbes, of which persons and property and landscape are constituent parts, but which has a larger identity, a life, of its own. His emphasis upon the conventions and traditions of society, his simplification of character, and his use of reappearing characters by which his various books are made to seem chapters of a social history, are devices whereby the individual actor is dwarfed. The scene is populous, frantic almost as a colony of ants, and like the ant-hill a social organism. Ants may be individual, each with its peculiar traits and idiosyncrasies, but to the human spectator looking down upon them they seem only mechanical toys such as delight the behaviorist.

Balzac is a behaviorist among novelists. Society is the fascinating interplay of forces moulding the individual destiny. And though a hero such as Rastignac sometimes achieves success and seems to dominate, it is always at a price. He is stamped in the process, is as much in the toils as David Séchard who struggles with the forces of commercialism and is worsted. David, indeed, achieves freedom in the end, in so far as any freedom can be had. With sufficient money to live his own life, he quietly withdraws from the contest and on his small estate pursues the study of entomology. Balzac thus rewards a character he admires by granting him such a destiny. There is no doubt a moral implicit here, an unstressed judgment upon the vanity of ambition. It is a moral implicit, too, in all his many pictures of the struggles of men and women to rise, whether in the world of fashion, or business, or letters.

It is the larger, the populous scene, then, that Balzac, in retrospect, recalls rather than the rounded episode of the individual story. His conception of the *Comédie Humaine* explains and justifies this impression. Yet it would be unfair to overlook certain of his stories which are self-sufficient and memorable, novels which, though contributing to the larger effect, are comparable to the masterpieces of novelists with a different, perhaps a narrower, artistic philosophy. In the elaborate tapestry which Balzac weaves certain groups of figures stand out as complete and beautiful episodes. *Eugénie Grandet* seems to me, in retrospect, the most perfect of these, though *Père Goriot,* and, to a lesser degree, *Cousin Pons* are likewise distinct. In these Balzac is a novelist in the conventional sense, one who contrives a unified fable and peoples it with adequate characters. Perhaps these stories will individually endure when the grandiose *Comédie Humaine* is no more than a source book for the historian and sociologist. For they possess a beauty and a memorableness which Balzac's work in the large, to my taste, lacks.

Figures so colossal as those of Balzac and Dostoievsky can, in our discussion, be only glanced at, and the characterizations of their method be little more than an impressionistic comment. I have yet to discuss in some detail typical works of Conrad, James, and Turgénev, artists all of them of great skill and, though differing in their craftsmanship, possessed also of points in common. Of Conrad, for reasons which will appear, I select for analysis *The Rover.*

Conrad's "The Rover" and Its Structural Method

The Rover displays none of the peculiarities in the management of the point of view which are so striking in *Chance* and *Lord Jim.* The point of

view is that of an author omniscient of his chief
character and, as occasion demands, of others. In
this centering of interest and in the transitions incident thereto there lies considerable technical
significance, which will be manifest in a more
detailed analysis. It is because *The Rover* is a
simple but characteristic instance of Conrad's
method of weaving past and present into one pattern that I select it here. The same peculiar craftsmanship is evident in many of his stories, both
short and long, the most striking instance, if not
artistically the most successful, being *Nostromo*.
The Rover's structure is easier to follow because
simpler; the complication of incidents is less elaborate and the cast of characters smaller.

The story opens with an incident, the landing of
the chief character from his ship. A single paragraph explains very lightly who Peyrol is and the
immediate circumstances of the incident. A few
pages later childhood recollections stirred by his
return to France afford opportunity for a swift
review of his life. The story resumes, telling us of
the canvas jacket quilted with gold coins; and two
pages later we have the explanation of it, learn
where Peyrol secured the gold, and how he means
to make away with it. The method of narration
here is characteristic of Conrad and innumerable
instances in kind may be remarked throughout the
book; by telling us without warning a startling incident, Conrad secures an agreeable surprise; by
arousing our interest in the explanation, he secures

suspense. This is a curious reversal of emphasis. Suspense we think of usually as hanging upon anticipated action. But to Conrad, interesting as action is, its chief value lies in its index to character. Deeds are the letters of the inscription whose meaning he seeks. To decipher the Rosetta stone may be as enthralling, as charged with suspense, as to capture a ship.

Something of the character and past of the Citizen Scaevola are brought out in the dialogue of Peyrol and the old fisherman; sufficient again to excite our curiosity, to sketch for us something of the domestic character of the household which Peyrol is to enter. To this picture, ominously suggestive of murder and madness, the author adds the sketch of the girl with "her restless eyes that roamed about the empty room as though Peyrol had come in attended by a mob of Shades." Peyrol is surprised neither at Scaevola nor the girl. Surprise is no longer an emotion he can feel; and we have further details of his past which explain his *sang froid*. We learn a little more of the death of the girl's parents, learn that in this Scaevola was implicated, that something in Scaevola's past "cost her father his life." Then we are told another picturesque detail of Peyrol's life, the story of his seaman's chest, and incidentally how he came by the wound, the scar of which he bears. This incident is in preparation for an important episode several chapters later.

It has taken three chapters to carry the story to

this point. These chapters have established the scene, roughly defined several of the chief characters, and have intimated something of the ensuing action, that which is to reveal the past of Scaevola and the girl. What part Peyrol is to play is not yet clear, but the hints of his character give promise of a stirring rôle. The fourth chapter, like the second act of a play, opens after an interval of years. The purpose of this interval is twofold: to bring the historic incidents well into the Napoleonic era and thus utilize Nelson's blockade of France; and to permit, during these years, the growth of Peyrol's influence upon the girl and her partial recovery from her madness. This last, to be wholly plausible, asks a long period of time. Yet incidents of importance have occurred during this period, and it is characteristic of Conrad that he should unfold these casually in the course of the ensuing narrative, weaving past and present incident into one colorful tissue. The incidents tell us of Peyrol's tartane, and its launching and of his crew of one; of Scaevola's return with the girl Arlette, after the massacre of her parents. These past incidents are retrospectively introduced while the complications of the action are unfolding: those which involve the French naval lieutenant Reál and his project for deceiving Nelson.

It is in conjunction with this last that Conrad transfers his scene to one of the ships in the English blockading fleet, characterizes her captain and one of her crew, and develops a completely new centre of interest. Structurally this shift is of debatable value. It is not essential to the story, for the English and their activities could be seen throughout as they affect the hero, Peyrol. Yet the characters so introduced are in themselves interesting, and the significance of the ensuing action is enhanced by being related to large moments of world history. The little activities of Reál and Peyrol are given their weight in the destinies of nations. The theme is made, thereby, more spacious. Technical difficulties are, however, stored up which are manifest in the concluding episodes of the story.

It would be, perhaps, too tedious to report with like minuteness of detail each subsequent turn of the narrative. Conrad's method as already outlined is throughout consistent. Thus we learn of the Englishman lost from the landing party, then of a prisoner upon the tartane, and finally the identification of these as one. We learn how the prisoner was taken, of Peyrol's identification of him. That he is an old comrade in arms, one who had befriended Peyrol long ago, is not at once revealed. When at last we learn, we are told also further incidents of Peyrol's wild past as a Brother of the Coast. The sequence of incident is not chronological but associative. If an incident or a reminiscence is pertinent it is introduced. It is as though chronology did not exist. In *The Rover* these excursions into the past, because brief, do not, I think, bewilder the reader. In *Nostromo* the vast asides and harkings back are, to me, confusing, and make the book difficult to read.

This intermingling of past and present is an inevitable part of Conrad's creative method. It is apparent even in so simple and factual a narrative as *A Personal Record*. In that, after telling something of the origins of *Almayer's Folly*, he is carried off for chapters into the story of his boyhood in Poland, and it is with a start that we return subsequently to the ship imprisoned in the ice and the manuscript of Conrad's first story. As his mind moves back and forth weaving past and present into one intricate pattern, whether the facts are either actual or imagined, he resembles in his method of work more the painter than the story teller. First he sketches roughly a chief figure, then perhaps a bit of background and a second figure, only to return to his first and delineate it in sharper outline. Back and forth he goes touching here and there, often putting in a bit of color whose relation to the rest of the picture is not for some time apparent. A relationship, however, it subsequently reveals. It is not the product of chance, nor of a sudden inspiration. Conrad's stories give always the impression of being wholly imagined before he begins to write. The indirection of his method is due to the very copiousness of his materials. What, out of such richness, he shall seize upon first, what second, constitutes, apparently, his problem.

However speculative these conclusions, it is certain that they are given weight by the uniformity of Conrad's method both in *The Rover* and elsewhere. Arlette's story, her gradual mastery of her past—so essential to the restoration of her future, to her sanity and happiness—is given to us just as Peyrol's has been. When she seeks confession with the priest we learn the last essential things and we know, too, that she has recovered. Yet further details come after this, the most important being Peyrol's part in her recovery. Again in portraying Reál the author employs the same device, filling in retrospectively enough of the man's past to give body to his present. Kindred episodes in the epic of Peyrol crop up from time to time to the very end. In few authors is a man's present character so consistently made the outcome of his past. The author is forever remembering little picturesque significant details and does not cease to retouch until his story is wholly completed.

If indirection of method be the test of artistic greatness Conrad has few rivals. And yet it is apparent that his methods have their defects. This picking up of one character and then another, this mingling of present and past episodes, is a little puzzling; it demands of the reader more alertness than he is sometimes willing to give and, at times, weakens the story illusion. For it is not easy to cast off one identity and with little warning take on another. Even when the transition is deftly made, the process, if too long continued, is fatiguing. A fine instance in proof is to be found in the exciting chase of the tartane by the man-of-war, the culminating episode of the story. Here in the space of seven or eight pages there are as many shifts in the centre of interest. First we are with Captain Vincent on the English ship, viewing the pursued through his eyes, entering into his stratagems. A moment later we are with Peyrol at the helm, calculating the possibilites and from a distance viewing the deck upon which we so lately stood. The transitions are made in good workmanlike fashion, embedded not too ostentatiously in the narrative, as thus:

> For more than half an hour Captain Vincent stood silent, elbow on rail, keeping his eye on the tartane, while on board the latter Peyrol steered silent and watchful but intensely conscious of the enemy ship holding on in her relentless pursuit.

The method involves no real obscurity and even contributes an air of excitement. Nevertheless, it is, I think, accompanied by some loss of intensity. It would be better to see the experience wholly through Peyrol's eyes.

The academic critic is always a little vexed with the author who refuses to abide by the "rules"—especially if the author plays the game well despite them. There is no doubt that Conrad plays the game exceedingly well. Because of his methods, or despite them, his stories live; they are unforgetable. His peculiar management of the point of view as noted in *Chance,* and his characteristic in-

terweaving of past and present, his harking back
from effect to cause, observable in *The Rover*, are
essential to his technique. There is some attendant
loss: his stories not only cease sometimes to progress but actually move backwards; his long retrospective circuits lead one to forget the point of departure. If his stories were thought of as action
stories, I should consider his methods more clumsy
than successful. But action is with him always secondary to character. It is not so much what his
people do as why they do it, their essential nature,
that grips us. Conrad is a Henry James, a psychological novelist who happens also to have been a
seaman. His apocalyptic method in which time is
unfolded for us like a scroll and in which there is
no past nor future but only the all comprehensive
present; and in which we are alternately this human being or that other as seen by the character
himself, by his companions, or by God—these devices cannot wholly fail because his people are so
completely "known."

Turgénev's "Fathers and Children" as a Typical Instance of His Method

The resemblance to James recalls a passage analyzing the methods of Turgénev (with whom Conrad has affinities) to be found in James's critical
memoir which prefaces the edition of Turgénev's
work. The passage is so much to the present purpose that I cite it verbatim:

The germ of a story, with him, was never an affair of plot—that was the last thing he thought of: it was the representation of certain persons. The first form in which a tale appeared to him was as the figure of an individual, or a combination of individuals, whom he wished to see in action, being sure that such people must do something very special and interesting. They stood before him definite, vivid, and he wished to know and to show, as much as possible of their nature. The first thing was to make clear to himself what he did know, to begin with; and to this end he wrote a sort of biography of each of his characters, and everything that they had done and had happened to them up to the opening of the story. He had their *dossier,* as the French say, and as the police has that of every conspicuous criminal. With this material in his hand he was able to proceed; the story all lay in the question, What shall I make them do? He always made them do things that showed them completely; but, as he said, the defect of his manner and the reproach that was made him was his want of "architecture"—in other words, of composition. The great thing, of course, is to have architecture as well as precious material, as Walter Scott had them, as Balzac had them. If one reads Turgénev's stories with the knowledge that they were composed—or rather that they came into being—in this way, one can trace the process in every line. Story, in the conventional sense of the word—a fable constructed, like Wordsworth's phantom, "to startle and waylay"—there is as little as possible. The thing consists of the motions of a group of selected creatures, which are not the result of a preconceived action, but a consequence of the qualities of the actors. Works of art are produced from every possible point of view, and stories, and very good ones, will continue to be written in which the evolution is that of a dance—a series of steps, the more complicated and lively the better, of course, determined from without and forming a figure. This figure will always, probably, find favor with many readers, because it reminds them enough, without reminding them too much, of life.

James raises the question "whether a novel had better be an excision from life or a structure built up of picture cards, for we have not made up our mind as to whether life in general may be described." To some, "The manner in which Turgénev worked will always seem the most fruitful. It has the immense recommendation that in relation to any human occurrence it begins, as it were, farther back. It lies in its power to tell us the most about men and women." Of Turgénev's stories James remarks that, on rereading them, "I was struck afresh with their combination of beauty and reality. . . . They give one the impression of life itself, and not of an arrangement, a *réchauffé* of life." Turgénev had observed of Homais, the notary in *Madame Bovary,* that the "great strength of such a portrait consisted in its being at once an individual, of the most concrete sort, and a type." And James employs the same expressions in praise of Turgénev's creations: "This is the great strength of his own representations of character: they are so strangely, fascinatingly particular, and yet they are so recognizably general."

From the preface to the *Portrait of a Lady* I cite another comment upon Turgénev, explaining, as it does, so clearly his methods of work:

. . . "I have always fondly remembered a remark that I heard fall years ago from the lips of Ivan Tur genieff in regard to his own experience of the usual origin of the fictive picture. It began for him almost always with the vision of some person or persons, who hovered before him, soliciting him, as the active or passive figures, interesting him and appealing to him just as they were and by what they were. He saw them, in that fashion, as *disponibles*, saw them subject to the chances, the complications of existence, and saw them vividly, but then had to find for them the right relations, those that would most bring them out; to imagine, to invent and select and piece together the situations most useful and favorable to the sense of the creatures themselves, the complications they would be most likely to produce and to feel.

"To arrive at these things is to arrive at my 'story'," he said, "and that's the way I look for it. The result is that I'm often accused of not having 'story' enough. I seem to myself to have as much as I need—to show my people, to exhibit their relations with each other; for that is all my measure. If I watch them long enough I see them come together, I see them *placed*, I see them engaged in this or that act and in this or that difficulty. How they look and move and speak and behave, always in the setting I have found for them, is my account of them—of which I dare say, alas, *que cela manque souvent d'architecture*. But I would rather, I think, have too little architecture than too much—when there's danger of its interfering with my measure of the truth. The French of course like more of it than I give—having by their own genius such a hand for it; and indeed one must give all one can. As for the origin of one's wind-blown germs themselves, who shall say, as you ask, where they come from? We have to go too far back, too far behind, to say. Isn't it all we can say that they come from every quarter of heaven, that they are *there* at almost any turn of the road? They accumulate, and we are always picking them over, selecting among them. They are the breath of life—by which I mean that life, in its own way, breathes them upon us. They are so, in a manner prescribed and imposed—floated into our minds by the current of life. That reduces to imbecility the vain critic's quarrel, so often, with one's subject, when he hasn't the wit to accept it. Will he point out then which other it should properly have been? —his office being, essentially *to* point out. *Il en serait bien embarrassé!* Ah, when he points out what I've done or failed to do I give him up my 'architecture'," my distinguished friend concluded, "as much as he will."

Turgénev's *Fathers and Children* bears out all that Henry James and others have said in commendation of his methods. The author tells in his *Literary Reminiscences* the origin of his theme. "At the foundation of the principal figure, Bazároff, lay a personality which had greatly impressed me—that of a young country physician." This remarkable character he endeavored to understand, perceiving in him a type new to literature. The work of writing was taken up some weeks later—"the fable," says Turgénev, "had gradually assumed concrete form in my mind." The actual process of the story's growth would be interesting to know. To judge from the novel itself it was the invention of simple incidents casually but naturally related and designed to exhibit the characters which the writer desired to portray.

For the plot, the *fable*, of *Fathers and Children* is very simple. The chief character, Bazároff, upon his graduation from the university goes with his friend Arkády Kirsánoff to visit the latter's father in the country. The scenes in this setting are designed to reveal the characteristics of the older and younger generation. The two friends subsequently visit at the home of Madame Odíntzoff with whom Bazároff falls in love. They then make a short visit to the home of Bazároff's parents, call again upon Madame Odíntzoff, and return to the home of Arkády's father. In the absence of Arkády, who has returned to Madame Odíntzoff because of his love for her younger sister, Kátya, Bazároff is forced into a duel with Pável Petróvitch, Arkády's uncle. This is the most exciting, or at any rate, violent, scene in a quiet narrative. Bazároff returns to the home of his parents and shortly dies of an infection contracted in a post-mortem dissection—for he is a medical student and scientist. The few remaining events are summarized in a concluding chapter.

No novel could be simpler in outline. The changes of scene are infrequent, the time is very short—only a few weeks. The incidents are natural, designed wholly to set forth the characters. These number perhaps a dozen or more—not many as compared to those of most novels of equal weight, few indeed as compared to any novel of Tolstoy's or Dostoievsky's; but they are realized with that sharpness and fulness for which Turgénev is unsurpassed. This sharpness is manifest both in external and internal characterization, appearance and manner very largely suggesting character, and speech and significant action completing the picture. There are occasional bits of analysis but these are few and usually short. The characters are able to portray themselves. They walk bodily from the page, coming to life in a sentence. The following is typical:

. . . At that moment there entered the drawing-room a man of medium stature, dressed in a dark English suit, a fashionable, low necktie, and low, patent-leather shoes,—Pável Petróvitch Kirsánoff. In appearance, he was about forty-five years of age: his closely-clipped gray hair shaded dark in certain lights, like new silver; his face sallow, but devoid of wrinkles, remarkably regular and pure in outline, as though carved out with a light, delicate chisel, displayed traces of remarkable beauty: especially fine were his brilliant, black, almond-shaped eyes. The whole person of Arkády's uncle, elegant and high-bred, preserved its youthful grace, and that aspiration, upward, away from the earth, which generally disappears after the twentieth year. Pável Petróvitch drew from the pocket of his trousers his beautiful hand with its long, rosy nails, which seemed still more beautiful from the snowy-whiteness of his cuff buttoned with a single large opal, and gave it to his nephew. Having accomplished the preliminary European "shake-hands," he exchanged three kisses with him, in Russian fashion,—that is to say, he thrice touched his cheek with his perfumed moustache,—and said: "Welcome!"

The next passage, a description of Bazároff's mother, though rather long, must be quoted in its entirety to be fully enjoyed. Anna is both a type and an individual. Turgénev heaps upon her an astonishing wealth of detail but from it she emerges with perfect distinctness. The remarkable quality of Turgénev's descriptions, both of persons and of landscapes, is his easy clarity. Most writers get lost amid much descriptive detail; the outlines are blurred. This is never the case with Turgénev:

Arína Vlásievna was a genuine Russian gentlewoman of the petty nobility of days gone by; she ought to have lived a couple of hundred years earlier in the times of Ancient Moscow. She was very devout and sentimental, she believed in all sorts of omens, divinations, spells, dreams; she believed in holy simpletons, in house-demons, in forest demons, in evil encounters, in the evil eye, in popular remedies, in salt prepared in a special manner on Great Thursday, in the speedy end of the world; she believed that if the tapers did not go out at the Vigil Service at Easter the buckwheat would bear a heavy crop, and that a mushroom will not grow any more if a human eye descries it; she believed that the devil is fond of being where there is water, and that every Jew has a bloody spot on his breast; she was afraid of mice, snakes, sparrows, leeches, thunder, cold water, draughts, horses, goats, red-haired people, and black cats, and regarded crickets and dogs as unclean animals; she ate neither veal, nor pigeons, nor crabs, nor cheese, nor asparagus, nor artichokes, nor water-melons, because a water-melon when it is cut reminds one of the head of John the Baptist; and she never mentioned oysters otherwise than with a shudder; she was fond of eating—and fasted strictly; she slept ten hours a day—and never went to bed at all if Vasíly Ivánitch had a headache; she had never read a single book, except *Alexis, or the Cottage in the Forest*; she wrote one letter, at the most two letters, a year; but she was an expert in dried and preserved fruits, although she never put her own hand to anything, and, in general, was reluctant to move from one spot. Arína Vlásievna was very good-natured, and, in her own way, not at all stupid. She knew that there are in the world gentlemen whose duty it is to command, and common people whose duty it is to obey,—and therefore she did not disdain either obsequiousness or lowly reverences to the earth; but she treated her inferiors graciously and gently; she never let a beggar pass without a gift, and she never condemned any one, although she did occasionally indulge in gossip. In her youth she had been very pretty, had played on the clavichord, and had spoken a little French; but in the course of wanderings over many years, with her husband, whom she had married against her will, she had deteriorated and had forgotten her music and her French. She loved and feared her son unspeakably; she allowed Vasíly Ivánitch to manage her estate,—and never required an accounting for anything: she groaned, waved the subject away with her handkerchief and kept raising her eyebrows higher and higher, as soon as Vasíly Ivánitch began to explain impending reforms and his plans. She was given to forebodings, was constantly expecting some great catastrophe, and fell to weeping the moment she called to mind anything mournful. . . . Such women are now becoming extinct. God knows whether we ought to rejoice at it!

Turgénev in creating a scene evidently felt it essential not only to have all the background and accessories clear in his own mind but also, like a painter, to set them forth. His work in this respect affords an interesting contrast with that of Meredith who, in his later work especially, is content to suggest background with swift details and figures of speech and seldom gives the reader an elaborate description. All that can be said is that both methods are successful if skilfully employed. Turgénev's, I think, is the more difficult when the scene is long. Few writers avoid, as does he, confusion or heaviness. The following is an instance of short description:

Midday arrived. The sun blazed from behind a thin veil of continuous, whitish clouds. Silence reigned; only the cocks crowed provokingly at each other in the village, arousing in every one who heard them a strange sensation of drowsiness and weariness; and somewhere aloft in the crests of the trees resounded like a wailing call the unintermitting squeak of a young hawk.

This is highly selective. The details are mostly of sound and are chosen for their power of suggestion. They create, as is desired, an emotional atmosphere in harmony with the incident which they prelude. In longer descriptions, with many details, he achieves unity likewise by saturating the scene with emotion. In the following excerpt it is the changing mood of Arkády through whose eyes the scene is viewed that holds the details together and gives them narrative meaning. Only as they affect him are they closely woven into the story, although they are immensely useful in making the whole Russian scene intelligible to one unacquainted with it:

The localities through which they were passing could not be called picturesque. Fields, nothing but fields, stretched away to the very horizon, now rising gently, again sinking; here and there small patches of forest were visible, and here and there ravines, overgrown with sparse, low bushes, wound in and out, recalling to the eye the representations of them on ancient plans of the time of Katherine II. Here and there, also, small streams were to be encountered, with washed-out banks, and tiny ponds with wretched dams, and little hamlets with low cottages under dark roofs, which often had been half swept away, and lop-sided threshing-sheds with mottled walls of brushwood, and churches, now of brick with the stucco peeled off in places, now of wood, with slanting crosses and ruined graveyards. Arkády's heart gradually contracted. As though expressly, they kept meeting peasants in clothing which was too tight with long wear, on wretched nags; like beggars in rags stood the roadside willows, with tattered bark and broken branches; thin, scabby, apparently famished cows were greedily nibbling at the grass along the ditches. They seemed to have just succeeded in tearing themselves from some menacing, death-dealing talons,—and evoked by the pitiful aspect of the debilitated beasts, amid the fine spring day, there arose the white wraith of the cheerless endless winter, with its blizzards, frosts, and snows. . . . "No,"—thought Arkády, "this is not a rich land; it does not strike the beholder with its abundance or its industry; it is impossible, impossible for it to remain like this; reforms are indispensable . . . but how are they to be brought about, how is one to set to work? . . ."

Thus did Arkády meditate . . . and while he was meditating, the spring asserted its rights. Everything round about was ringing with a golden sound, everything was stirring with broad, soft agitation and shining beneath the tranquil breath of the warm breeze,—everything,—trees, bushes, and grass; everywhere the larks were carolling in unending, sonorous floods; the lapwings were alternately shrilling, as they soared in circles above the low-lying meadows, and silently hopping over the hillocks; the daws stalked about, handsomely black against the tender green of the spring rye, which was still low of growth; they preached sermons in the rye, which was already turning slightly whitish, only now and then showing their heads amid its smoke-like billows. Arkády gazed, and gàzed, and his meditations gradually faded away, then vanished altogether. . . . He flung off his uniform coat, and looked at his father so merrily, so much like a young boy, that the latter embraced him once more.

I must content myself with but one instance, out of many, illustrating the singular felicity of Turgénev's methods in blending description and characterization with incident so that the story tells itself without author's analysis or comment. The method is doubly effective in this case because the scene is a highly emotional one, and, told as it is in this objective fashion, it has a power of suggestion and restraint which a more subjective method would lack. An author as closely observant as Turgénev in the sentence—so simple that it is easy to miss its full significance—"his glances constantly slipped past his son"—has no need to analyze. He need tell only what he sees:

Bazároff and Arkády went away on the following day. From early morning everything in the house grew melancholy; the dishes tumbled out of Anfisuska's hands; even Fédka was surprised, and ended by pulling off his boots. Vasíly Ivánitch bustled about more than ever: he was evidently keeping up his courage; he talked in a loud voice and clumped with his feet, but his face was haggard and his glances constantly slipped past his son. Arína Vlásievna wept quietly; she was thoroughly distraught, and would not have been able to control herself if her husband had not argued with her for two, whole hours early in the morning. But when Bazároff, after repeated promises to return not later than a month hence, tore himself at last from the restraining embraces, and took his seat in the tarantás; when the horses started and the bell began to jingle and the wheels began to revolve,—and there was no longer any use in staring after him, and the dust had subsided, and Timoféitch, all bowed and reeling as he walked, dragged himself back to his kennel; when the old folks were left alone in their house, which also seemed suddenly to have shrunk together and grown decrepit: Vasíly Ivánitch, who only a few moments before had been bravely waving his handkerchief from the porch, dropped into a chair and drooped his head upon his breast. "He has abandoned, abandoned us,"—he stammered,—"abandoned us; he found it tiresome with us. Alone, solitary as a finger now, alone!" he repeated several times, and every time he thrust out his hand in front of him with the forefinger standing apart. Then Arína Vlásievna went up to him, and leaning her gray head against his gray head, she said: "What is to be done, Vásya? A son is a slice cut off. He is like the falcon: when he would he flew hither, when he would he flew away; thou and I are like mushrooms on a hollow tree; we sit in a row and never stir from our places. Only I shall remain forever inalterable to thee, as thou wilt to me."

Vasíly Ivánitch removed his hands from his face and embraced his wife, his friend, as closely as he had embraced her in their youth: she had comforted him in his grief.

No doubt it is because he explains so little and does not explicitly state his purpose in the story that *Fathers and Children* was so misunderstood even by Turgénev's countrymen at the time the novel was published. He was accused of flattering the nobility and of satirizing, in the person of Bazároff, the younger generation of revolutionists. Quite the contrary was his intent. He says in a letter:

Bazároff crushes all the characters in the romance. . . . The qualities ascribed to him are not accidental. I wished to make him a tragic personage—there was no place for tenderness there. He is honest, upright, and a democrat to the very tips of his fingernails. . . . The duel with Pável Petróvitch is introduced precisely for the purpose of demonstrating, at a glance, the triviality of elegantly noble chivalry, which is set forth in an almost exaggeratedly comic manner . . . *my whole novel is directed against the nobility as the leading class.* . . . The æsthetic sense made me select precisely good representatives of the nobility, in order that I might the more surely prove my point: if the cream is bad, what about the milk? . . . If the reader does not fall in love with Bazároff with all his roughness, heartlessness, pitiless aridity and harshness—if the reader does not fall in love with him, I repeat,—I am to blame, and have not attained my aim.

In his *Literary Reminiscences* Turgénev has more to say to the same effect. After describing how the novel was misunderstood he remarks:

I knew that I had borne myself honorably, and not only without prejudice but even with sympathetic interest, toward the type which I had set forth; I had too much respect for the profession of artist, of literary man, to act against my conscience in such a matter. The word respect is even not quite appropriate here. I simply could not work otherwise, I did not know how. . . . Critics will not believe that an author's highest purpose is to set forth the truth, the reality of life, powerfully and accurately, even when that truth does not coincide with his own sympathies.

Bazároff, with whom the author is much in sympathy, is depicted, nevertheless, as without æsthetic sense, because in him, the author felt "life moulded itself in this way. My personal inclinations had nothing to do with the matter." And he concludes with the following pertinent observation:

The reader always feels awkward, he is easily seized with perplexity, even vexation, if the author behaves with the character depicted as with a living being, that is to say, perceives and sets forth his bad and his good sides, and most of all, if he does not display manifest sympathy or antipathy to his own offspring.

Not only do readers wish their heroes and villains clearly labeled, but of the artistic conscience of which Turgénev speaks, the novelist's obligation to be true to life, few have any conception whatsoever. To the novel reader as to many novelists, as, for instance, Walter Scott, a story is only a makebelieve which may beguile an hour. That it can be a serious, a profound, and in the deepest sense a moral creation they do not hold. Yet the justice of Turgénev's belief and his faithfulness to his creed is manifest in the permanence of his work. *Fathers and Children,* misunderstood and reviled in its generation, is a living creation. Bazároff is more than a young revolutionist of 1860. He is the type of youth in revolt against outworn custom and tradition. He is an individual and yet universal. Nearly contemporary with *Fathers and Children* is *Uncle Tom's Cabin,* also a novel of idea, a novel with a purpose. Tremendously effective in its generation, *Uncle Tom's Cabin* is no more now than an historical document. It is too obvious, possesses too little enduring æsthetic value, to be read with interest to-day.

Uncle Tom's Cabin served its turn, did its work, and is dead without regrets. Its fate is the usual fate of the reform novel, or the novel which exploits a passing phase of social development. Such will be the fate, I have no doubt, of many of H. G. Wells's interesting novels. Only rarely I think does he, so to speak, assimilate æsthetically, turn into art, his sociology, philosophy, and suggestions for reform. Yet his novels have had a vast influence and so have justified themselves. A novel may be many things—entertainment merely, an historical record, an engine for reform—a tract—and, rarely, while all or some of these, also a work of art. As the latter it endures, and perhaps in the long run, even as propaganda, does more and better practical work than the novel of a day. But to weigh such values is impossible.

It was Oscar Wilde who remarked that the concern of the modern dramatist and novelist was no longer with types; that his aim was not universality but particularity. It is noticeable, I think, in modern fiction that singular characters and the oddity of character in general have been to a great degree its game. Perhaps it is to this cause that is due the slight bewilderment, the sense of moving in a world a bit "touched," which seizes upon the reader educated to the older fiction when he turns to the new. And as the greater part of the world is, no doubt, abnormal, the fiction which presents it as such may lay claim to a kind of realism, or, better perhaps, 'actualism.' The implications of the problem are too many to be pursued at this point.[1] I am not, for the moment, concerned with the æsthetic or ethical aspects of it but with those more narrowly technical: How, in typical instances, have the great novelists gone about the creation of character?

Methods of Characterization Employed by Representative Novelists

James, in the essay upon Turgénev, remarks:

If Dickens fail to live long, it will be because his figures are particular without being general; because they are individuals without being types; because we do not feel their continuity with the rest of humanity—see the matching of the pattern with the piece out of

[1]For a fuller discussion of modern tendencies see Chapter IV.

which all the creations of the novelist and the dramatist are cut.

That his Micawbers, Heeps, and Weggs are too literal, that Dickens had in each instance a human model, is a theory which will strike most readers with surprise, for these creations have an air of the fantastic. Mr. Pickwick is, as Chesterton remarks, a fairy. It has been said, also, that Dickens seldom if ever drew a convincing woman. But Gissing, knowing at a somewhat later period the London classes of which Dickens wrote, is of the opinion that the sharp shrewish female, in whose delineation Dickens excels, is most faithfully portrayed from life. Facts of experience are here evidently in dispute, but more than these, technique, and, fundamentally, the imaginative process of character creation.

Whatever their truth to fact, their virtual identity with human originals, there is no question, I think, that Dickens by his methods of portraiture contrives to give many of his characters an air of exaggeration. If drawn from life they are nevertheless caricatures, and this for the reason that Dickens in each instance stresses one or two particular traits, often no more than mannerisms of speech or appearance. The incessant reiteration of these peculiarities seems, in effect, to give his characters the quality of personified abstractions like the Allworthys and Millamants of the eighteenth century. Micawber is forever waiting for something to turn up. Heep is forever 'umble.

These are mere tags. They are the anticipated kick and stumble of the clown entering the ring; and they "get" the calculated "laughs." No doubt, too, they become often a bit wearisome. The device is overplayed.

Yet there are innumerable characters in Dickens not so over-simplified and over-mannered. The exaggerations do not vitiate the essential soundness of his work; indeed the true Dickens lover finds in them a part of that variety which constitutes the charm of their creator. Whatever strictures one may pass upon Dickens and his methods of work the fact remains that he creates a whole world of his own—like Balzac, Meredith, Thackeray. It is a world either too unlike reality or too like, as you choose, but there it is and not to be disregarded. I do not by the same token care in Fielding for Allworthy, Blifil, Thwackum, and Square. These smack too openly of allegory. They are personified abstractions. Yet in the very real world of Fielding they do not greatly matter. Squire Western outweighs a thousand of them.

Of Meredith's characters it may be said, also, that "they are strangely, fascinatingly particular and yet they are so recognizably general." Meredith's world is likewise complete, is wholly peopled, but unlike that of Dickens is without caricatures, without creations too wholly actual. This, at least, is my feeling with regard to them. In his greatest successes Meredith achieves that identification of the individual and the universal which used once to be, if it no longer is, the aspiration of the novelist. Sir Willoughby Patterne moves and breathes. He is an individual man. He is, more, the incarnation of male egotism, so that one should blush for one's sex when reading of his antics. In what other novelist can one find so many male characters created with such fidelity and complexity and yet withal such universality?

Of Meredith's women, the heroines at least, I am not so sure, despite the praise which they have evoked. It may, perhaps, be said of them that they are in essence pure womanly. Yet they inhabit a more ideal world than ours, the world of Shakespeare's heroines, and are sisters to Portia, Imogene, Desdemona, Perdita, and Miranda. Their charm is that they satisfy the masculine desire; but surely they never existed. Such surpassing combinations of beauty, virtue, and intelligence do not bloom on poor earth. And so young! Diana's repartee, when still in her teens, makes the weak spirit fail. To be sure Meredith does not, after the fashion of Mrs. Humphry Ward, declare his heroines to be witty and then fail to prove his assertion. He more than satisfies with a chapter of excerpts. They are women, nevertheless, such as God would have made had he been George Meredith.

It is in Jane Austen, George Eliot, Anthony Trollope, and Henry James that I find, among English novelists, women characters most wholly credible. They are not mere paragons of beauty and virtue, like the heroines of Scott, nor are they the super-women of Meredith. They are of this world. It is easy to see why they were desired and when married proved not too impossible wives. I should not say that Trollope's heroines equalled those of the others, but Eleanor Bold and Lily Dale are well enough. George Eliot and James strike the deepest note, are less reticent, less afraid of seeming ungallant. Rosamond Vincy has been widely and justly admired. And James has equalled if he has not surpassed her. Mrs. Brookenham of *The Awkward Age* is surely a magnificent study of worldliness and cruelty; and Nanda, her daughter, is one of the most charming, if pathetic, of heroines, perfectly realized and touching the emotions as James's heroines do not always do.

Beyond all questions of technique in characterization—of universality, simplification, particularity—lies the question of the imaginative process itself. As to this only guesses can be hazarded. Yet it is probable that in his creation of characters the good novelist works very freely from whatsoever models he employs. The point was anticipated in the discussion of Dickens, who too often fails, it was said, because he drew too faithfully the portraits of real people he had known. The novelist must, to be sure, make use of what life brings him. Into his consciousness pours an unending stream of impressions. All humanity sits for him as a model. The point lies precisely in that—waiving, for a moment, the theory of Oscar Wilde. Humanity, which is the artist's model, is a composite portrait. Even in the differentiation of men and women, of youth and age, it is from the human *mean* that he draws the chief part of his stock in trade. His art consists in playing infinite variations upon the one theme; in innumerable departures, not too great, from the one original.

Could the creative process, the working of the imagination, be, in particular instances, traced from its inception to its consequence, light would be thrown upon the question as it cannot, otherwise, be. There are, in general, only hints. George Eliot, we know, had her father in mind in the creation of Adam Bede—no outstanding success it may be noted. Caleb Garth, drawn no doubt from the same model, is vastly more real, suggesting the same type, but more freely, more imaginatively, handled. Mr. Casaubon it is said derives from Mark Pattison, a charge which, not liking Mark Pattison, I hope is true. Yet I very much doubt the fidelity of the portrait. Tom Tulliver is supposedly George Eliot's brother. No doubt essentially he is, but in that 'essentially' rather than in any irrelevant particularity of detail, lies the point. It is as Tom suggests the type of all selfish brothers that he becomes real to us.

Meredith's characters, it is known, are many of them drawn from living models. The original of Diana was a celebrated Mrs. Norton; Nevil Beauchamp is Captain Maxse, Meredith's close friend; many of the characters in *Evan Harrington* suggest Meredith's relatives; old Doctor Middleton is apparently a sketchy portrait of Thomas Love Peacock, Meredith's father-in-law. If the latter surmise is correct, the author's general method is revealed. For Doctor Middleton suggests both Peacock and those worldly table-loving clergymen he so delighted to portray in his clever novels. It is no literal portrait of Peacock; something in the spirit of the man is caught and serves to individualize what in Doctor Middleton would be otherwise scarcely more than a type or "humor." Only the free-working imagination without obligation of fidelity to particular fact could so seize upon the essential something that identifies character and dress it out in an external guise of incident, speech, and manner suited to an imagined fable. Character must be plastic, malleable, if it is to serve the purposes of the novelist.

Real persons as depicted in historical novels should be most convincing as they are remote in time and place and the facts known about them few. The more legendary the data, the freer the play of the writer's imagination. The theory fails a little in that historical characters in fiction, of whatever age, near or remote, seldom come very wholly to life. That Scott's King Richard is rather more of a person than the caricatured "Jamie fat-breeks" is due to greater romantic interest and greater zest in the author. Queen Elizabeth, Mary Stuart, and all the rest live no more vividly in Scott than in the pages of any reputable historian.

The old astrologer king in *Quentin Durward* remains, of all this pageantry, the most vivid to me. It is a novel in Scott's happiest manner, with little of the tediousness and slovenliness which characterizes most of his work.

George Eliot is in general head and shoulders above Charles Reade; as serious novelists they are usually not in the same class. Nevertheless *Cloister and Hearth* is a great book, compared with which *Romola* is a laborious failure. The terms of comparison are in many respects on all fours: the historical epoch is almost the same; so, too, is the setting, the social background; and in each fictitious characters mingle with historical figures. Nor is Reade less handicapped with knowledge. He, too, had "crammed" for his novel, had read a library full of books. Yet *Cloister and Hearth* lives and *Romola* does not. The characters, while not profoundly realized, are nevertheless vital; they carry the story with them. And the reason is, I think, that Reade wished only to tell a story as true to the life of the Renaissance as he could make it. *Cloister and Hearth* is alive and sturdy. But *Romola* is a conscientious modern thing; the characters are not mediæval but are cursed with the morality of a later age. For George Eliot is not content to make them live but must preach, also, her gospel of unselfishness. Too exigent an ethical sense is here the foe of the imagination.

Kingsley's historical novels also afford some interesting comparisons. *Westward Ho*, though a

stirring yarn, is almost spoiled and its characterization rendered unconvincing by its religious
theme. *Hereward*, of a remoter epoch, almost pagan, is free from the religious complex; is free,
too, of almost all obligation to historical fact. Of
the two, neither of which I have read for years,
Hereward stands out for me as having the greater
imaginative reality, far more, surely, than the well
documented *Hypatia*, which, though of a period
even more remote, is cramped by a religious purpose. The point I would make in all these instances
is that the more the imagination is hampered by
obligations of one kind and another—to historical
fact, to an ethical purpose, to the lineaments of an
actual model—the less vital, the less 'real' in the
sense true to art, will the result be.

Disraeli apparently drew his characters almost
wholly from living models. We are furnished keys
to his *dramatis personæ* identifying them with
this and another contemporary. Yet for whatever
reason we nowadays read his novels, and they are
not without shrewdness and tawdry charm, it is
surely not for their convincing characterization.
Whereas Trollope, working in a radically different
method, peopling his cathedral towns wholly from
his imagination, created types which, as he tells
us, the clergy of his day identified as individuals
drawn to the life. Greater gifts in Trollope do not
wholly explain the dissimilarity, for Disraeli, too,
was a man of parts. Their creative methods are
utterly different and Trollope's is the sounder. Ex-

perience was, for him, transformed by the imagination. He knew that to the novelist imaginative reality, imaginative truth, is all in all.

It is a generalization which may be endlessly proved in the specific instance, but I must content myself with one further comparison drawn from the work of Theodore Dreiser. The figure of Cowperwood is sketched from the traction pirate, Yerkes. The novels in which he appears are documented to the hilt, are as factual as the morning newspaper. Yet Cowperwood is less real a figure than John Silver in *Treasure Island*, of whom Stevenson remarked that for the purposes of the story he need be no more than a pair of loose breeches and a belt stuck full of pistols. Cowperwood is a dreary collector of women and art objects. He is stuffed with sawdust. Hurstwood in *Sister Carrie* is, on the other hand, a real person. If suggested by some man the author has known, he has, it is evident, been handled with such freedom that he is imaginatively realized. He is both an individual and a type; he is universalized, and haunts the memory. In him life is caught up and reflected. Cowperwood as an individual is wholly meaningless, not a personality at all, but a symposium of appetites.

The Technique of James's "The Turn of the Screw"

I turn now to a novel different in kind from any I have previously considered, one which is a triumph of artistic skill and which admirably illustrates a rather subtle but far-reaching principle in novel writing. The story is Henry James's *The Turn of the Screw*, which is, in my judgment, the most powerful and moving ghost story in English. It is surprising that James should have written it, for the thrills which he commands are usually those of the drawing-room. Scenes of deep passion he characteristically avoids. He prepares for them and analyzes their consequences, but his battles and alarms are usually reported by messengers. In a ghost story no such avoidance of the direct manner is possible. The ghostly thrill must be imparted by the straightforward depiction of ghostly happenings. An analysis of the story reveals James to be wholly adequate to the technical demands which it imposes on him.

The account which James gives, in the preface, of the suggestion for his story and of the problems which he confronted in its working out, is essential to an understanding of his method. The hint, he tells us, was given him by an anecdote told at a country house:

The story would have been thrilling could she have found herself in better possession of it, dealing as it did with a couple of small children in an out-of-the-way place, to whom the spirits of certain "bad" servants, dead in the employ of the house, were believed to have appeared with the design of "getting hold" of them. This was all, but there had been more, which my friend's old converser had lost the thread of : she could only assure him of the wonder of the allegations as she had anciently heard them made. He himself could give us but this shadow of a shadow—my own appreciation of which, I need scarcely say, was exactly wrapped up in that thinness. . . .

The thing had for me the immense merit of allowing the imagination absolute freedom of hand, of inviting it to act on a perfectly clear field. . . . I find here a perfect example of an exercise of the imagination unassisted, unassociated. . . . The exercise strikes me now, I confess, as the interesting thing, the imaginative faculty acting with the *whole* of the case on its hands.

James goes on to say that the story is an exercise on the order of the fairy-tale, which is of two types, the short "with the compactness of anecdote" and "the long and loose, the copious . . . where dramatically speaking, roundness is quite sacrificed—sacrificed to fulness, sacrificed to exuberance, if one will."

Improvisation is easy, "but the great effect it so loses is that of keeping on terms with itself. This is ever, I intimate, the hard thing for the fairy-tale; but by just so much as it struck me as hard did it in *The Turn of the Screw* affect me as irresistibly prescribed." It was his design, James says, "to aim at absolute singleness, clearness, and roundness." The story "is a piece of ingenuity pure and simple, of cold artistic calculation. . . . Otherwise expressed, the study is of a conceived 'tone' . . . the tone of tragic yet of exquisite mystification." Artistic awareness could not be more complete; that uncertain thing "inspiration" less in

evidence. And yet the result, however coolly calculated, is emotionally gripping.

The ghosts produced by the Society for Psychical Research James found inadequate to his
purpose, "inconceivable figures in action." He was
forced to decide, "between having my apparitions
correct and having my story good—that is pro-
ducing my impression of dreadful, my designed
horror. . . . Peter Quint and Miss Jessel are not
'ghosts' at all, as we now know the ghost, but gob-
lins, elves, imps, demons as loosely constructed as
those of the old trials for witchcraft."

Portentous evil—how was I to save that, as an inten-
tion on the part of my demon-spirits, from the drop,
the comparative vulgarity, inevitably attending, throughout the whole range of possible brief illustration, the
offered example, the imputed vice, the cited act, the
limited deplorable presentable instance?

Often in fiction, James observes, grand wrong-
doing or wrong-being is imputed, and "then all
lamentably shrinks to the compass of some particular brutality, some particular immorality, some
particular infamy portrayed: with the result, alas,
of the demonstration's falling sadly short." The
evil spirits must be capable of everything bad. But
precisely what? "Only make the reader's general
vision of evil intense enough . . . and his own experience, his own imagination, his own sympathy
and horror will supply him quite sufficiently with
all the particulars. Make him *think* the evil, make

him think it for himself, and you are released from weak specifications." So successful is the method that the author has been charged with "a monstrous emphasis . . . of all indecently expatiating" whereas "there is not an inch of expatiation, my values are positively all blanks."

The purpose of the enveloping narrative is to establish a point of view which will both excite the reader's credulity and whet his appetite for the horrors to come. The grave possessor of the manuscript who professes to know something of the author and of her innocent love-story is a kind of notary sealing the sworn statements of witnesses. But when he speaks of the "dreadful dreadfulness" of the story, its "general uncanny ugliness and horror and pain" he throws down a challenge. These are boastful words. Few stories can realize such pretensions. It is our expectation, I think, that the author will fail, that his protestations do but supplement an inadequate method. How much greater, then, his triumph, his ultimate effectiveness, if he makes good his promise.

The story, unlike so many stories of the supernatural, opens pianissimo with but the faintest single note of the unusual in the excessive pleasure which the housekeeper takes in the coming of the new governess. The setting is that of a beautiful old country house. The time is early summer. Yet the place is insulated and remains so throughout the story but for one or two slight contacts, later, with the outside world. A perfect unity of place is maintained. And the characters are few. Of the household only Mrs. Grose is named and characterized. At the outset the story directs itself, then, to a narrow channel; it aims at intensity.

The second intimation of the unusual, a note struck with slightly greater emphasis, comes two pages later. "There had been a moment when I believed I recognized, faint and far, the cry of a child; there had been another when I found myself just consciously starting as at the passage, before my door, of a light footstep." This slight uneasiness is dispelled by the charm of little Flora and the promise of greater charm in her brother, Miles, who is on his way home from school. His delightful manners and seeming innocence make his dismissal from school, for some cause untold, inexplicable. The dismissal is, again, an ominous note, preparation for incidents to be developed later. There need now only be references, sufficiently ambiguous, to the former governess who went away and shortly after died, and to some one as yet unidentified who "liked them young and pretty." The entrances for the characters completing the cast have been prepared.

The first apparition is in the late afternoon, the figure of a man on top of the tower against the evening sky, remote and somehow sinister. The description is slow and detailed, moving from the natural to the uncanny:

The place moreover, in the strangest way in the

world, had on the instant and by the fact of its [the apparition's] appearance become a solitude. . . . It was as if, while I took in, what I did take in, all the rest of the scene had been stricken with death. I can hear again, as I write, the intense hush in which the sounds of evening dropped. The rooks stopped cawing in the golden sky and the friendly hour lost for the unspeakable minute all its voice.

Yet the figure is represented as that of a man; there is not, save in the inexplicable note of horror that it strikes, any suggestion of the supernatural.

In this episode the story has gathered to its first minor climax, the first of the successive waves which, with increasing power and frequency, are to create the story's rhythm. The wave ebbs. The tone of naturalness is re-established. The innocence and beauty of the children are again stressed, and an explanation for the appearance of the man on the tower is ostensibly sought. Then the mysterious visitant again appears, this time near at hand, peering through a window. The actual circumstance is not wholly described as it occurs but as the Governess tells it later to Mrs. Grose: "He's a horror"; and with increasing detail: "He has red hair, very red, close curling, and a pale face. . . . He gives me a sort of sense of looking like an actor." Mrs. Grose cannot fail to identify him. She gives his name, Peter Quint. The sentence drops, "He died."

" 'Died?' I almost shrieked."

It is an inimitable example of suspense cut by a dramatic finale.

It remains now to divine the purpose of this apparition, for it is evident to the Governess that Peter Quint was looking not for herself but for Miles. Oddly Miles has never spoken of Quint, a suspicious circumstance; doubly so when we learn through Mrs. Grose, the housekeeper, that Peter Quint had had much influence with the children. The circumstances of Quint's death are revealed, intensifying the suggestion of his wickedness. And hard upon these comes the second apparition, that of Miss Jessel, the former governess. The horror of the fact is, however, subordinated to Flora's duplicity. Flora, it is certain, perceives the apparition and endeavors to hide the fact from the Governess. We learn more of Miss Jessel's past, but in vague terms only. It suffices that "she was infamous." Then it is slowly extorted from Mrs. Grose, with deepening implications of evil, that Miles knew of the relations of Quint and Miss Jessel.

This is the second wave, more powerful than the first, and it too is succeeded by a brief lull. Then the Governess suddenly confronts Quint on the stair at night.

He was absolutely, on this occasion, a living detestable dangerous presence. . . . It was the dead silence of our long gaze at such close quarters that gave the whole horror, huge as it was, its only note of the unnatural.

Again we have contrasting episodes with the children, but the relief which they afford is now only an intensification of horror, for the seeming innocence is more and more stripped from them and we guess them to be little monsters of depravity. The purpose of the discarnate demons comes home to the Governess with unanswerable conviction: "For the love of all the evil that, in those dreadful days, the pair put into them. And to ply them with that evil still, to keep up the work of demons, is what brings the others back."

Events mount with growing rapidity to the close. There is no other appreciable lull. The struggle of the Governess for the souls of the obsessed children will permit no intermission. The horror, it must be noted, has shifted from the merely uncanny, the horror of discarnate devils, to a horror infinitely deeper, the moral horror of the conflict of good and evil. The successive apparitions of Miss Jessel, "dishonored and tragic," "the terrible miserable woman" seeking mitigation of her torture, powerful as they are and nicely varied and graduated in effect, are accessory to that. No imaginative reader can, I think, at this time have failed to accept wholly the story illusion. These horrible presences are real as evil is real. It is with the sense of moral victory that we accept the final scene in which little Miles, finding salvation in his confession of theft, turns unseeing eyes to Quint's "white face of damnation":

"Peter Quint—you devil!—Where?"
We were alone with the quiet day, and his little heart, dispossessed, had stopped.

The lessons which this little masterpiece can teach the student of technique are many. I shall mention but a few and without much comment, for there is one point, perhaps less obvious, which is my chief concern, and which opens up a topic of wide implications. James's excellent management of his apparitions, the variations in the place of their appearance, their growing closeness and deepening horror, their sufficient but not over use, must be obvious. So, too, his employment of moral horror as infinitely surpassing the physical. Again, the perfect assurance of the close, ending upon the top note with never a hint of anti-climax. And last, his power of suggestion, which, as he perceived, must create in the mind of the reader a horror greater than the revelation of any explicit finite evil could possibly evoke.

These are admirable instances of technical dexterity but they are less, perhaps, than the absolute certainty of the tempo whereby the story is made to gather momentum until it rushes to its appalling close. I remarked in the course of the analysis upon the successive waves of the action and the ensuing lulls which offered emotional respite and in which the next crescendo prepared itself. The timing of these intervals, the selection of detail, both in amount and character, whereby each high point is made to overtop its predecessor, never disappointing the reader but more than surpassing his expectations, is analogous to the performance of a symphony, whose complexities, whose intermediate progressions and recessions, are all timed and graduated to the ultimate supreme effect.

Tempo, Its Importance in the Novel and Its Technical Method

The basic problem of tempo is a purely mechanical one, the adjustment of the story's pace to the visual speed of reading. Readers no doubt vary greatly in this respect, and a story which seems to some unduly swift in its development may, to others, seem unduly protracted. The speed of writing itself must, however, in any instance, be vastly slower than any reading speed whatsoever. A story which required, as Fielding tells us of *Tom Jones,* "some thousands of hours" for its composition may be read by a few readers in ten. There is herein a tremendous disparity. The author, dwelling upon the circumstance of his story, selecting among many details only a handful, takes up his residence among his characters. With them he may live the better part of his daily life for a year or two, or even more. How difficult then to adjust the speed of his story to the careless eye of his reader, to prepare for his intended climax with the proper weight and volume of detail. The problem is analogous to that of the painter who, working but a few inches from his picture, must step back from it at frequent intervals to judge from a distance of its effect.

The traditional English novel, that of loose

structure involving the fortunes of several groups
of characters, has in this matter of tempo one very
great merit. When the story shifts from one sub-
plot to another, the characters abandoned pursue
an unrecorded existence which, when we again re-
cur to them, has endowed them with greater actuality, as if, indeed, we had passed the interval in
their society though thinking of something else.
Middlemarch furnishes good illustrations of this
unchronicled growth. Dorothea's story after her
marriage to Mr. Casaubon is, for a time, interrupted, and the Lydgate and Rosamond story begun. Yet when we return to her at Rome it is with
a distinctly greater sense of intimacy than before.
And likewise in the Lydgate story. The actual
scenes marking the steps of his disillusionment are
few, but, detached as they are, and given at long
intervals, we have a sense of slow and inevitable
development. It does not need the mention of the
changing seasons to give the effect of time passed.

The psychology of the transition from one action to another in its power to suggest time intervals is well illustrated in Shakespeare's plays. In
Antony and Cleopatra, for instance, when Antony
appears in one scene at Alexandria about to depart
for Rome, there would be no sense of time elapsed
were he in the next to have made his journey and
appear with Cæsar. If, however, between the two
some scene, however short, is inserted, with other
characters speaking, we have upon Antony's re-
entrance the effect of a long interval passed. The

complete shift in interest suffices, however short the scene, to break the continuity. Story time is a record of impressions, not of counted hours, and the author's concern is with these. His parenthetical allusions to the calendar are but supplementary. Whether the story covers a day or ten years is a minor matter. His solicitude is for the desired effect, whether of acceleration, retardation, or of the normal speed of actuality. In attaining this, calendar time is secondary, in its emotional effect, to proportion—the relative emphasis accorded incidents—and to the continuity or lack of continuity among those incidents.

The unity of time, if considered in any literal sense, is, even in the drama, an academic principle. The old practice of limiting the action to twenty-four hours aimed at intensity of effect; but intensity of effect does not lie in any arbitrary restriction of time, nor, for that matter, of place, though an unchanged scene and a limited time period serve to facilitate intensity. Intensity resides in the cogency of the incident, that close weaving of cause and effect which carries the mind forward to the anticipated event; in this and in the close identification of the spectator or reader with the characters of the piece. The more wholly the story illusion is established, and the more completely the spectator lives vicariously the lives of others, the more wholly does time cease to be. A hundred years becomes in his sight but as a day; *emotionally* that is, for he may, at the same time, make intellectual note of the passage of days and years. The process is like that of the moving picture, in which the pace of action is quickened; but it is far more illusory and compelling than the mechanical action of the screen.

In *Antony and Cleopatra* the interposition of a brief scene suffices to separate two sequential incidents to whatever degree the imagination requires. Yet the play, for all its variety and complexity, its historical time of a dozen years or more, seems to occupy as a whole but a few weeks or months. In many of Shakespeare's plays, a more striking dual time scheme, logically a paradox but emotionally effective, can be remarked. *Othello,* as "Christopher North" pointed out, is a notable instance. It can be demonstrated from the rapid and causative sequence of the incident that the action occupies no more than a day. It can be shown likewise from time allusions that weeks or months are taken up. The seeming breathless pace of the incident creates suspense and that intensity of effect which is the most potent of the "unities." The retardation of time, intellectually perceived, allows for the plausible growth of Othello's jealousy and revenge. Two effects are achieved, logically incompatible, but emotionally triumphant.

Though the technique of the novel and that of the play necessarily differ, the two have the same simple end of seducing the spectator to the loss of his identity in the fictitious action. For each, time is an elastic medium to be manipulated at will. The

characteristic theme of fiction is the alteration of
human personality under the pressure of circumstance. For this, experience tells us, time is required. We must have the sense of slow change.
Yet if we are to be held to the story, there must
be also a brisk sequence of incident. That which is
irrelevant must be excluded. There must be selection, and an enhanced logic in the articulation of
events. In the adjustment of these two requisites
lies the technical problem of time.

In *Middlemarch* it was noted that the illusion of
growth and change was secured largely by shift-
ing the story interest first from one group of characters to another. Each of these separate actions
moves with sufficient celerity, stirs sufficient anticipation in the inevitable event, to charm the
reader's interest. There is not, to my feeling, any
sense of sluggishness. Nor, on the other hand, is
there undue acceleration. The effect, the illusion,
is that of life itself. In a novel such as *Clarissa
Harlowe* the pace of life is retarded. The number
of actual weeks or months which the action ostensibly occupies has little relevance to this emotional
effect. The sense of exceeding slowness is achieved
in part by the actual bulk of the narrative, the time
it takes to read it, but more by the constant shift-
ing of the centre of interest which the letter form
necessitates. The reader identifies himself first
with one character and then another, and each
shift brings with it the sense of elapsed time.
Moreover, every incident is viewed from innu-

merable angles, and in this repetition time ceases
almost wholly to progress. The common factor in
these effects is emotional fatigue. It is as though
the story occupied an eternity, that it went on forever, while at the same time it didn't get on at all.
I exaggerate somewhat its effect, and no doubt the
inevitable tragedy gains by the appalling slowness
with which we approach it. Yet surely Richardson pushes his method to the limit of human en-
durance.

Of how secondary an importance is calendar
time to psychological time in the conduct of a story
can well be illustrated by the comparison with
Clarissa of such a novel as Joyce's *Ulysses*. In its
many hundreds of pages are told the experiences
of a small group of characters in the course of a
single uneventful day, whereas in *Clarissa* the time
required is months. Yet in both alike the effect is
of time infinitely protracted. For in Joyce's novel
are many changes in the centre of interest comparable to the shifts of the epistolary manner.
Joyce employs, too, methods of portraying states
of consciousness such as Dorothy Richardson has
made familiar:[1] the incoherency of a mental state
is accurately conveyed and with it, inevitably, the
sense of getting nowhere, temporally speaking.
There are likewise recorded, as in *Clarissa*, innumerable little details of experience which serve only
to create a sense of actuality and which have little
emotional value. In the reading and in retrospect

[1] See Chapter IV.

one has, consequently, fully as vivid a sense in
Ulysses as in *Clarissa* of time elapsed. In the latter, despite its slow movement, there are, after all,
plot, suspense, and logical sequence. One does,
however tardily, get on. In *Ulysses,* as in a nightmare, one scarcely gets on at all, but stands forever
rooted to one spot. Calendar time can have little
meaning in a story employing such a method.

In *The Turn of the Screw* James, it was said,
manipulates his tempo to the utmost effect, raising
suspense to the greatest tolerable pitch without
ever protracting it too far. He is not always so
happy. In some of his novels the sense of movement is so greatly retarded as to be maddening.
The Ambassadors, for all its exquisite artistry, is
a good instance of tardy movement. Here again
the actual period of time which the story purports
to cover is of no importance. The effect would be
the same did the incidents happen ostensibly in a
few days instead of weeks or months. Our impatience lies in the paucity of incidents partly, for
these are few and far from stirring, but more in
the microscopic examination of the hero's thoughts.
Time stands still while retrospectively he dissects
each incident and extracts from it the utmost
meaning. The effect is extremely exasperating, is
provocative of unseemly violence. The reader
would like to break something, to intrude upon
these refinements of conduct and motive with some
rude apostrophe, some word or act distinctly
"low." Such at least is my response; and the same

irritation, less extravagantly conceived, is sometimes the effect on me of other analytical novels.
To pitch the tempo to the exact speed of life is
seemingly a very difficult thing; of the two alterna-
tives, acceleration, rather than retardation, seems
to me preferable.

Yet acceleration connotes, too often, thinness.
Bojer's *The Great Hunger,* excellent book that it
is, and justified in its method by its purpose, is open
to this criticism. In retrospect the reader recalls
the book's motive, its philosophy, rather than those
incidents and characters wherewith that philosophy
is realized. The "great hunger" is the hero's search
for faith. The episodes recount the various dissat-
isfactions of his life, and his final achievement,
after all his worldly successes and misfortunes, of
that which he seeks. The book is essentially a morality, like *Everyman,* but the characters are less
abstractions than *Good Deeds* and *Friendship.* To
the modern taste allegory is a bit thin and quaint
and to be effective must be disguised as life.

That the disguise in *The Great Hunger* is not
complete is due to several causes, chief of which,
I think, are the variety of scene and the number of
characters depicted in rather short space. That a
considerable period of years, the greater part of a
man's life-time, is covered, is of minor importance.
Other books no longer than this have covered an
equal time with greater solidity. Compare, for instance, Hamsun's *Growth of the Soil,* longer to be
sure, but achieving its effect of slow growth largely

through the nature and paucity of its incidents, its single setting, and the limited number of its characters, but these held to throughout. In *The Great Hunger* there are many settings; characters, with the exception of the hero, are seldom carried continuously throughout, and the consequent effect is to accelerate the tempo of life very greatly. It is life foreshortened, as an old man might review his past, the events so slow in their actual occurrence, seeming, in retrospect, fleeting. And as in retrospect the experiences of childhood occupy a disproportionate place because of the particularity and vividness with which they are recalled, so in *The Great Hunger* the youth of the hero is told with more detail than his subsequent life, and the pace is, consequently, less hurried than in later chapters.

Bojer deliberately accentuates his time intervals, to enhance the transitoriness of life, for to the moralist life is characteristically brief, its value lying not so much in experiences as in the teaching of experience. Thus:

For the next few years Peer managed his estate and his workshop.

.   .   .   .

And time passed.

.   .   .   .

Some years had passed—a good many years.

So to slip over, unremarked, large portions of the lives of characters in whom our interest has been asked is to dampen our concern for them. And when, moreover, the group is not constant, when the friends of youth do not remain those of middle life, or the sharers of affluence the consolers of adversity, the effect is rather like that of turning over the family photograph album. We wish to dwell longer with these people. Either we should have less of them or more.

There is no question, however, that Bojer's technique is conscious, that it is designed to secure the effect he desires of the swift flow of human experience, upon whose surface are cast up, intermittently, patterns of incident which, though in themselves interesting, are likewise characteristic of, or symbolical of, the stream as a whole. Peer is a symbol for man the seeker; his experiences are typical of humanity. Yet he is given a touch of individuality. Bojer wishes, however, not to make his hero too individual. He desires us never to forget the allegorical implication. The technique aims, then, to keep the balance true between the individual and the typical, the concrete and the abstract. To slip from one to the other smoothly, both to generalize and to particularize without confusion, is the author's problem, one which he solves deftly:

He wanted to take firm root and be able to feel like others, that he had a spot in the world where he was at home.
Then came the sunny day when he stood by Merle's bed. . . .

A second instance:

And so the days go on.
Each morning Merle would steal a glance at her husband's face to see if he had slept. . . .
"What has taken you over to the farm so much lately?" she asked one day.

A third:

Then reaching home red and dripping, . . . etc. [following a generalized description of their winter days].
"Merle," said Peer, picking the ice from his beard. . . .

In all three instances the transition from the general to the particular is swiftly and unostentatiously effected. The pattern takes sudden shape like crystals in solution.

The converse of this process is observable in the analysis of the characters' thoughts. Incident becomes more biting and memorable when it has to do with the individual; thought becomes more significant when it transcends the individual and becomes universal:

At times, too, he would turn from the anvil and the darkness within and come out into the doorway. . . .
A man with a sledge-hammer in his hands instinctively looks up at the heavens. . . .
Peer looked at the clouds. . . . Rebellion against some one up there? But heaven is empty. . . .
But then all the injustice, the manifold iniquity.
Who is to sit in judgment on it at the great day?

In this, the analysis of Peer's thoughts merges very quickly with general philosophic speculation. The point of view is subtly enlarged and it is the author's thought, not Peer's, which we follow. It is the author's thought, too, which we find in the next passage, less skilfully arrived at and disguised:

Did he need money? No. Or was the work at a standstill? No. . . .
Happiness? Rest? Ah no! . . . You may stumble, you may fall—what does it matter? . . . The flame of the world has need of fuel—bow thy head, Man, and leap into the fire.

It is in thus eliciting his specific scene from the generalized background and in sinking the thoughts of his individual characters into a wider impersonal speculation, that Bojer achieves the effect of allegory which, at the same time, does not wholly sacrifice story interest. To the taste of some he will have sacrificed it too greatly. Better, it may be thought, to make characters labels for abstractions than half to individualize them, to arouse our interest in them as persons and then not adequately to gratify that interest. We remember them as sketches—life-like, provocative, but left incomplete while their creator speculates upon their significance in the scheme of things.

The Great Hunger, thus considered in its management of tempo and the resultant thinness of its human story, contrasts interestingly with *Maria*

Chapdelaine, which, too, is a story expressive of an idea, one less explicit, less philosophic to be sure, but definite enough. But whereas Bojer seems not so much to derive his philosophy from the contemplation of his human story but to devise a story as a medium for his philosophy, Hémon seems to think only of his characters. The thoughts to which that story gives rise are largely implicit. We formulate them for ourselves at the author's suggestion. He does not phrase them for us. Yet his seeming artlessness may very well be only the high refinement of technique. He may have perceived the greater effectiveness in art of indirection, and with an idea or attitude to express have cast about for characters, setting, and incident wherewith most effectively to clothe it. The book at any rate is there. The desired effect is achieved, and whether wholly conscious or largely instinctive matters not in the consideration of the technique employed.

The time covered in *Maria Chapdelaine* is only, as I recall, a year or two. We make the round of the seasons and witness the backwoods life in all its limited variety. Yet the time might have been much longer or shorter without materially altering the effect. The solidity of the impression which the book imparts is due, first, to the fixity of the scene: the log house in the clearing and the dark forest beyond the few meagre fields constitute the picture constantly before us, changing only superficially with the hour of the day and the passage of spring to summer and summer to winter. The group of characters is limited. We know them all, not profoundly with omniscient insight, but three-dimensionally as we know old acquaintances. They are not complex. They are simple, but real. The story, moreover, though slight is perfectly definite. The incidents are articulated. From the specific occurrence spring emotion and growth of character; from character incident inevitably develops. These people and the manner of their life are symbolic, to be sure, but the symbolism is, for the reader, sunk in his interest in the particular story. There is concern for their happiness; there is suspense, not breath-taking, but genuine.

In employing the word tempo to characterize the technical means whereby these effects are secured I seem, no doubt, to be trespassing upon the field of other terms—proportion, emphasis, structure. The word "structure" as employed in the consideration of a story is misleading, is no more than a figure of speech. The analogy of a novel to a piece of architecture is essentially false, for a story, like music, moves. It is conceived in time. Its essence is rhythm. The thing is not perceived as a whole in one view. It moves sequentially, from moment to moment. The relation of each part of it to that which immediately precedes and follows is more important, even, than the relation of the part to the whole. If it drags at any point our interest droops. If it hurries us along too rapidly it loses its contact with reality; its rhythm ceases then to be that of life and the story becomes something else—a vision of eternity crowded into an instant, or a nightmare in which time ceases wholly and we die of inertia. It is the function of the novelist so to adjust his story's speed that it suits the purpose for which he designs it, and as this purpose is, and must be, for the most part realistic, the best speed is that which accentuates slightly, or seems to, the speed of life. For in that slight accentuation lies the additional emphasis which differentiates art from actuality.

Scale is thus less important in securing effects than the adjustment of tempo to scale. A large impression of life may be conveyed in a story relatively short. *Maria Chapdelaine* is truly as epical, reflects as surely the slow tenacity of human life in its conflict with nature, as does Hamsun's *Growth of the Soil*. In its little year of simple living it suggests man in his relation to infinity, man circumscribed by birth and death. Or such is my feeling toward it. Yet in the reading it moves at a sufficient speed, the speed, in effect, of life. *Growth of the Soil*, having fewer incidents of a highly emotional value, and being, besides, much longer, seems, despite the time covered by the action, to move as one reads rather more slowly. The centre of interest being fairly constant the movement of the story is not, however, too greatly retarded. The development is sufficiently steady to hold the reader's interest and the effect of the long duration and the slow inevitable progress is, as I have characterized it, epical. This, in the reading, *Maria*

Chapdelaine is not, whereas in retrospect the two are in this respect comparable. Why?

As foreshortened in retrospect the two novels are comparable in that they set forth about the same quantity or mass of human experience. If one wholly disregards their purported duration— and in retrospect one does almost wholly so disregard it—the complication in each of incidents which constitute a pattern, and the weight in each of emotional experience are of about equal value. *Maria Chapdelaine* thus may bulk large in memory; it may be justly characterized as epical, whereas in the reading it seemed a slighter work, carrying much less metal than *Growth of the Soil*. There is implicit, no doubt, in such an estimate an argument in behalf of the novel with pattern or design as being more economical, as doing more in a given space, than the novel of a looser structure. It is a thesis which, not too dogmatically, I should defend. For it is emotion which gives meaning to experience. In retrospect it is the life crowded with emotion, in especial, *significant* emotion, which seems long; the life however long in years, yet filled only with trivial incidents and of experience barren in emotional significance, seems short. The novelist has, I take it, to weigh both considerations, in seeking his effect and the means to it: both the tempo of his narrative as it runs and the residual emotional impression, the effect, that is, which the book will have in memory.

Naturalistic fiction produces upon me a curiously ambiguous effect, much the effect, indeed, of *Clarissa Harlowe,* and for reasons very similar. Perhaps *Clarissa* is the maternal grandparent of all Naturalism.[1] However this may be, the constant shift in the point of view necessitated by the letter form, combined with the threshing over of the same incidents, creates a nightmarish effect of running on forever and with a progress so slow as scarcely to be discernible. Nevertheless when one has finished with *Clarissa* he has the sense of having brought a new planet into his ken. In naturalistic novels, it is not always so, this sense of having widened the universe. Even from the best of this genre, in which class I should place *Jean Cristophe,* I find that I carry away little except the memory of diverting hours—something truly. Too often I arise with the sense that life is inexpressibly tedious and protracted while one lives it from incident to incident, and yet is, in retrospect, exceedingly brief. It may, of course, very well be that this is precisely the effect at which the Naturalist aims. Life may seem so to him. How then is the effect produced?

In *Jean Cristophe* we have the entire life of a man, as it were a biography, in four volumes. Certain periods, episodes, and characters are vivid and memorable. I recall that the incidents of his childhood seemed to me especially good. Of later periods I recall few episodes and characters, nor even do I recall the effects of these periods upon

[1]For a discussion of Naturalism, see Chapter IV.

Jean Cristophe. They influenced the development of his genius in some way, but just how, if indeed I perceived as I read, I have now forgotten. The final impression is that Jean Cristophe arrived somehow at serenity and "passed over" cheerfully, but that his lifetime was no longer than that of a summer fly, however, mystically, more significant.

The memorableness of the childhood experiences is due, I think, not to their greater vividness but to the fact that Jean, as a boy, had more intimate relationships and dependencies than in his later more solitary life. His experiences illuminate not only him but those about him. They constitute a social life; and as they progress to ends more or less anticipated, to Jean's development as a musician, they have a rudimentary plot value. In the later books the grouping of characters is more casual. Few of them persist long, drifting into the story only to drift out again. Episodes only are memorable, whether because of some singular emotional content or because of unusual vividness in the telling. But the transitions from one incident to another and from one character to another create, in the reading, the sense of protracted time. Attention is fatigued by the flood of ever-fresh impressions. Though far from tedious, the book seems long in the telling. Jean lives a full lifetime; yet, looking back we think of that lifetime as short. His boyhood, in which the characters took on significant relationships one to another, is longer, in retrospect, than all of his middle years, the effect previously noted of the boyhood experiences in *The Great Hunger*.

The technical point I would raise is this: Could not the same effect be achieved in shorter space by even greater discontinuity in the narrative? The more logical and sequential the pattern of incidents, the greater is the ease with which the mind traverses it and in retrospect recalls it. A sequence wholly illogical, reproducing the stream of consciousness with no attempt to rearrange or order impressions, and endeavoring, in so far as words permit, to reproduce all, would in brief space create a powerful impression of "life"—as "life" is when not coerced and ordered by intelligence. A few pages depicting consciousness with a high degree of actuality would convey the sense of a very long period of time, though the impressions might be those of a moment. And this precisely is the illusion created by the work of Dorothy Richardson. In a page of hers reflecting the reverie of a few moments I have the sense of living æons. Time is suspended, as in a trance, after which, brief though it be, an eternity seems to have passed:

The thought of the five turnings to the station, all into long little roads looking alike and making you forget which was which and lose your way, was still full of pain . . . the relief of moving to Granville place still a relief, though it felt a mistake from the first. Mrs. Carrie's old teacher liking only certain sorts of people knew it was a mistake, with her peevish silky old face and her antique brooch. But it had been the beginning of London. . . . Bond Street that Sunday morning in the thick fog; these sudden pictures gleaming in a window, filmy . . . von Hier. Adelina Compayne, hanging out silk stockings on the top balustrade. "I *love* cawfy" that was the only real thing that had been said downstairs. There was no need to have been frightened of these two women in black silk evening dresses. None of these clever things were real. They said young Asquith is a really able man to hide their thoughts. The American Academy pupils talked together to keep everybody off, except when they made their clever jokes . . . "if any one takes that top bit there'll be murder, Miss Spink." When they went out of the room they looked silly. The young man was real somewhere else.

There are things to be said of this which are beyond my immediate purpose.[1] Suffice it that this is an instance, not extreme, of modern technique, the "actualism" which has been the outgrowth of naturalism. It widens the range of tempo, and suggests new effects such as Zola did not conceive. Pushed to the extreme, to the verge of unintelligibility, the method should make possible, in a few thousand words, the sense of time duration, of experience sounded to the utmost, which the more conservative naturalistic method requires its hundreds of pages to effect. In complete dissociation of ideas the sense of time would wholly disappear. Eternity would hover in the instant. Mind, I think, would cease to be. Pages of Gertrude Stein produce precisely this effect. Mind and will are paralyzed. One endures an eternity of torture awaiting the

[1]See Chapter IV.

final merciful release which does not come. Narrative writing when carried to this extreme ceases to be a temporal art altogether. The moment and eternity become synonymous.

So many points have been briefly touched upon in this discussion of tempo that a summary of them is desirable. Psychological time, for the novelist the one important time, has only an exiguous relationship to the calendar. The statement that months and years have passed has, of course, a slight emotional value, but its chief appeal is purely intellectual. It is informative rather than emotionally stirring. The novelist's concern is with the emotions of his reader and it is with an eye to them that he plans his incidents. He may, in his picture of experience, aim to reproduce as nearly as he can the pace of actual life, or to accelerate or to retard this pace. His method in any particular instance will be determined by the character of his story. And he has, moreover, to consider the immediate effect upon the reader of the tempo which he employs, and also the effect of the work when viewed as a whole in retrospect. For, the life depicted, whose pace seems slow as one reads, may in recollection seem transient, fugitive, as swift as a dream; or the life so intense that in the reading it passed in a moment may seem in retrospect rich and infinitely long. This is true, is it not, of experience? The crowded hour of glorious life may outweigh, in memory, the tedium of years; yet it passes more swiftly than any hour less intense.

Acceleration of story tempo may be secured in several ways. A close causal sequence of incidents gives an effect of rapidity. The steady adherence to one centre of interest likewise hastens the story speed. Last, and perhaps chief, the nature of the selected incidents, their emotional weight or interest, determines very largely the tempo. If the experiences are emotionally rich the action will be more rapid than if the incidents are emotionally barren. A dull and sluggish novel is one in which the moments of intense experience are few. Suspense, if not unduly protracted, has the effect of expediting the action. The mind runs forward to the anticipated event. Time, then, is all but annihilated; the action moves with the speed of light. Yet if suspense is unduly prolonged, the effect is just the reverse. The action seems, then, to pass out of time altogether and to become eternally fixed. Emotionally the effect is, in such a case, precisely that in which there is no suspense at all, for in the one instance the reader surrenders all hope of getting on, and in the other has never cherished it: in both he seems bound to the eternal *now*.

Tempo is retarded by the inclusion of much trivial detail, by all excurses and asides, whether author's comment or depiction of background; by frequent shifts in the centre of interest; and by a sequence of incidents whose causative relationship is not close and sharp. The formal mention of elapsed time has a minor contributory value in thus slowing the action. In general, speed is accelerated by a greater, an intensified coherence, by making life more logical, more causative in its sequence of events than is actually true of experience. Retardation is secured by exaggerating the incoherence of experience. The incoherence may be so extreme, as in some of the instances cited, that time, as a structural element in the story, may almost cease. Desirable as such a technical effect might, on occasion, be, as in depicting a mind momentarily stunned by a profound emotion, it would seem an impossible technique if employed throughout a long narrative. Fiction would then renounce its inevitable, its temporal, character.

Principles Governing the Selection of Detail, and the Relation of Detail to Realistic Effects

The "actualism" characteristic of the contemporary novel is the theme of a subsequent chapter; but there remain technical points of more general interest precedent thereto. For in stories of whatsoever type the reality of the fictive art is not, I conceive, factual but "real" in the Platonic sense. Not the literal data of sense experience but the essence of these is the prime concern of the novelist. The imagination distils the actual and embodies it concretely as truth in creations of its devising; creations which are, to be sure, built upon the reports of the senses, but selected from among them and rearranged to mark an emphasis expressive of an interpretation or point of view. The actual provides the raw material with which the imagination works. Also it is a snare which, in his absorption with its details, too often entraps the artist to forgetfulness of his true function.

Stevenson more than once laments the tyranny of the eye in fiction; elsewhere he denounces particularity of detail: "Roland advanced toward the house. It had green blinds and a scraper on the top step.—To hell with Roland and the scraper." Yet what more plausible in any imagined scene than to describe a host of details incident thereto and thus give it solidity and an air of factual reality? For a writer who delays in coming to grips with his subject, who has, perhaps, no very clear notion of the scene's relevancy to the whole of the story—who, in short, is feeling his way—nothing is more easy than to cling to the concreteness of details. Too often, it is evident, the author, like Little Red Riding Hood, is seduced by bright wayside flowers to forgetfulness of the waiting wolf.

Dependence upon the eye is most notably a characteristic of the contemporary novel. The present drift toward actualism has been fostered by it. It leads to impressionism and naturalism and other experimental methods which, notwithstanding their achievement and promise, have nevertheless complicated the novelist's problem, as artist, tremendously. In this respect I feel that the influence of the Russians has not been wholly good. One is always struck in a Russian novel by the wealth and vividness of its visual detail. These Slavs seem all endowed with extraordinary powers of visual memory and imagination. Yet the details in their vividness and copiousness are too frequently misleading. The novelist describes a scene, a chance character, a drawing room and its occupants with graphic particularity. The reader perceives place and persons vividly; he makes a mental note of them, believing them to have some relevancy to the future development of the story, only to discover often that they have none at all and are never afterward referred to.

Visual fulness and vividness in the depiction of scene and character are permissible artistically only as the emphasis is relevant to a larger purpose and fits into the story's scheme. In Turgénev, it was pointed out, the descriptions are often long; but they are always pertinent and woven integrally into the narrative; they are not mere incidental beauties. Subordinate characters, however vividly depicted, occupy precisely the places which the author desires and do not crowd the characters of chief importance. Not all authors are so skilful as Turgénev in this. The snare of particularity is one hard to escape. The following brief instances must suffice to illustrate contrasting methods. The first is from Willa Cather's *The Lost Lady*. Mrs. Ogden, so fully described on a chance social occasion, has no important part in the story and does not, as I recall, reappear. The second is from James's *The Wings of the Dove*. Here, too, the persons described have only a passing importance in the scene and do not enter into subsequent events. James, therefore, though he touches them off vividly, does so in a few words and without naming them, avoiding thereby a false emphasis.

Mrs. Ogden was almost unpardonably homely. She had a pear shaped face, and across her high forehead lay a row of flat, dry curls. Her bluish brown skin was almost the color of her violet dinner dress. A diamond necklace glittered about her wrinkled throat. Unlike Constance, she seemed thoroughly amiable, but as she talked she tilted her head and "used" her eyes, availing herself of those arch glances which he had supposed only pretty women indulged in. Probably she had long been surrounded by people to whom she was an important personage, and had acquired the manner of a spoiled darling.

The contrasting instance:

A real bishop, such as Milly had never seen, with a complicated costume, a voice like an old-fashioned wind instrument, and a face all the portrait of a prelate; while the gentleman on our lady's left, a gentleman thick-necked, large and literal, who looked straight before him and as if he were not to be diverted by vain words from that pursuit. . .

The due subordination of visual detail suggests, also, those novels which have as their origin a picture, a color contrast such as might inspire a painter, and the recollection of which is almost solely visual. Joseph Hergesheimer, I hazard, works largely from visual suggestion. *Java Head* is the picture of a Manchu lady exotically clad in golden silks and set against the gray background of a New England town and the grayer sea. *The Bright Shawl* is the portrait of a señorita among green palm trees looking over the blue waters beyond the rocky heights of Morro Castle. The novelist seeks to make this picture animate, to endow it with all the suggestions of romance. But the story fades, though the colorful image of the heroine remains in the memory. I wonder if, for the novelist, this is enough? The painter must reconcile himself to the limitations of his medium. The novelist has a wider scope. Movement is the essence of his art. Action, emotion, and the development of character are his legitimate game. By his achievement of these his success is measured and his work remembered.

The problem of the relevant detail, which is a vital one, lying at the very centre of the eternal riddle of what to put in and what to leave out, is peculiarly complicated in the art of fiction in that the aim of the novelist is seldom single and precise. Novels are both works of art and social commentaries. A good story may be one or the other of these; only rarely is it both. As a social commentary the principle which determines the selection of its incidents and scenes is not that of strict artistic pertinency, of the contribution of each detail to order, design, beauty. In that large and loose category of fiction, the purpose novel, the elaborate portrayal of social and natural backgrounds may be of prime importance; the fable may be no more than a convenient device for their display. The story is a sugar coating for a tract.

The generic term "novel" is thus made to cover a variety of narrative forms dissimilar in purpose, and it would add immensely to the clarity of technical discussion could these be divided into at least two groups, the "social commentary" and the "art novel." Unfortunately the genres are seldom distinct but overlap. Few novels are wholly artistic in aim; few are no more than social history cast in the form of fiction. However slight the fictive dress, to the extent which it is employed the novel is, of necessity, an art product to be judged by the criteria of art. Yet it is to this dual purpose which confusedly directs the novelist in his choice of incidents and scenes that incongruities, infelicities, and the inclusion of irrelevant details are largely due.

Examples of the purpose novel, the social commentary, are common enough. Kingsley's *Yeast* and *Alton Locke* are as good instances as any. In the first the author points out the pitiable condition of the country laborer; in the second he portrays the evils of the sweatshop. The story in both novels is a poorly conceived framework on which the descriptions, in themselves highly vivid and memorable, are hung. To the student of history or economics the books are valuable for the pictures which they give of social conditions seventy-five years ago. These pictures are more vivid than are the works of economists and social historians dealing with the same body of facts, for the fable and the characters, however thin and unreal, do, to some extent, evoke our imaginative sympathy. Our emotions are thereby more easily enlisted. Such pseudo-novels have, therefore, their use, however slight their degree of artistry; for to their humanitarian purpose, relevancy of detail, beauty of design, and truth in characterization have all been sacrificed.

In other purpose novels, such as those of Mrs. Gaskell, *Mary Barton* and *North and South*, the social background is sometimes better incorporated and made a more intrinsic part of the story. In these novels the fable is adequately designed, and characters sufficiently real are motivated by the forces of their environment to acts which are plausible. Yet the blending of two equal and dissimilar purposes is not complete, for in recollection it is the pictures of mill life, of industrial slums, and of the contests of capital and labor which remain. The story fades.

Any competent novel, realistic in its method, is necessarily to some degree a social commentary even though it have no purpose other than to tell a good story effectively. Its pictures of the social scene are largely by implication rather than consciously designed, and the subordination of parts is thereby much more artistic than in a novel written with a divided purpose. *Tom Jones* gives an excellent sense of eighteenth century life though it does not set itself to delineate that life. Its purpose is to record the misadventures of the hero. The nature of the social background is implied in a thousand involuntary touches. Sophia Western, we read, was accustomed to play her father to sleep "every day after dinner when he was drunk." In that detail, breath-taking in its casualness, lies more force than in the elaborate preachments of Sir Charles Grandison upon the evils of duelling. There is in *Tom Jones* less explicit a picture of customs and social institutions than in *Amelia*. In the latter the author is both Fielding the artist and Fielding the magistrate, depicting in his secondary capacity the evils of prisons. *Amelia* is an excellent novel, but as a story purely, as a work of art, it is not so good as *Tom Jones;* nor is its picture of eighteenth century life, though more detailed and consciously explicit, so compelling.

Jane Austen's singleness of aim, her seeming unawareness of all social conflicts and disparities as well as of the great world beyond her parish has frequently been remarked. There is in her restricted scene loss as well as gain. The artistic perfection of her work does not wholly offset its limited range. That she was wise not to attempt tasks beyond her is no doubt true. Her work nevertheless suffers when compared with that of those greater novelists in whose pictures of life are revealed the depth and breadth of society in all its variety and range, and whose emotional intensity and daring is likewise so much greater than hers. Perfect as is her craftsmanship it deals with a petty order of existence and with the surfaces rather than the profundities of passion.

The selection of detail is a two-fold problem and I have been led in my discussion from one aspect to the other. The tyranny of the eye which Stevenson deplores, and the seductions of particularity, constitute an artistic danger which has no necessary relationship to social purpose in the novel. Yet there is in fact such a relationship evident in the development of the novel during the last hundred years. The romantic novel which has exploited background and the social novel with a purpose have so stressed, for reasons other than artistic, details irrelevant to the story, that a confused tradition has been established. It has become almost a convention in the novel that anything which might plausibly accompany the story incidents—descriptive details of all sorts, of background, social customs, dress, and appearance, and, also, of historical events—may legitimately be included in the narrative and emphasized for its single intrinsic interest. No exacting relevancy has been asked. "Local color," "word pictures" are terms invented to define these by-products of fiction. They are often thought to be beauties. We hear it said of a novel that, though the story is uninteresting, it contains "beautiful descriptions."

Analogously the device, commonly employed, of setting fictitious characters upon too actual a stage is characteristic of an art increasingly literal in its method. In the theatre there has been a minor revolt against too realistic stage settings. Formal decorative backgrounds, wholly divorced from the actual, have been found stimulating and beautiful, contributing in their effect to the emotional tone of the play. Such methods receive little commercial recognition or popular appreciation. The current novel likewise abounds in the deadening actual and in its desire to be real succeeds only in becoming literal. A simple instance is the common use of place names and names of living persons to bolster the reality of the fiction. Names of streets, cities, rivers, mountains, and even public monuments have, it is conceded, a certain validity. They possess a more or less permanent identity. The name of Wanamaker or Marshall Field has no such justification. A department store is not only a baldly actual but, in the particular instance, an ephemeral thing. The novelist is concerned, so to speak, with the essence of department stores, not with a particular store known to us and arousing a chain of irrelevant associations. These irrelevant factual suggestions do not harmonize with the imagined, the "ideal" world of the artist's invention.

It is this employment of the actual which is so great a defect in Dreiser's work, as I elsewhere point out.[1] What it does in substance is to knock imagination on the head, to lead it up a blind alley

[1] See Chapter IV.

whence it cannot escape. The following excerpts, not from Dreiser, but from a writer employing the same photographic methods, will serve to illustrate:

He observed that the great castle of the Potter Palmer home was still dark and closed; something seemed to be going on at the Reynolds', and at Victor Lawson's house; and evidently there was a dinner at the Cranes'.

These are actual Chicago families and the use of their names in a novel not only clips the wings of fancy but seems somehow even indecent, like an attempt at familiarity.

The car, having passed through Lincoln Park, was rushing on beside miles of apartments, shops and motion-picture theatres and soon approached a gay, brightly lighted district of resplendent, garish buildings where, a few years ago, had stretched the wide lawns and winding roads and patches of bush and "woods" about family homes of which Eugene Field had sung in his poems. Not far away to one side had lived Eugene Field and over there had been the "Waller Lot" where children had done those redoubtable things told in the ballad which Gregg used to beg to be read to him over and over when he was a little boy. Now in their neighborhood and northward had crowded in an amazing conglomeration of "new people," eager to live in new, compact ways; and thousands of pretentious apartments—three, six, or sixty to a building—were sprung up to shelter them; movies and dance halls and "gardens" to amuse them. Respectable people, most of them, if extremely dressed in the modern fashion and if, by older standards of the vicinity, over fond of their new, conspicuous surroundings or loud or gauche in manner. For most of these people were on their way up from obscure localities; some from the blistered, grimy tenements of such dreary, west side streets as Elston and Halsted and West Division, where in the Italian or Polish or Scandinavian settlements their immigrant parents had begun to prosper; some from similar sections of Milwaukee or Toledo and such cities; but the most of them were from towns and little cities of Illinois, Indiana, Michigan and Wisconsin.

The passage is irrelevant to the narrative, for the hero is preoccupied at the moment with a grave mission and can have no eye for scene and its social implications. And in itself, regardless of its relevancy, so factual a description, heaped with names bearing with them each one some cluster of associations, is questionable art. It is journalism. The indefinable line which distinguishes art from actuality has been crossed and two worlds which, though similar, are not identical, have been confused.

An instance similar, if subtler, is to be found in Mrs. Wharton's dependence upon names in *False Dawn*. The story is that of the young man, commissioned by his father to buy pictures abroad, who falls under the influence of Ruskin, Brown, and Rossetti and purchases the wrong kind—pictures, that is, by men whose names are at the time unknown. The father, in true bourgeois fashion, has pinned his faith to names of recognized standing and disinherits his wayward son. Yet does not Mrs. Wharton in her satire, no less than the father in the story, weight her narrative with actual names, only different ones, and does not the fictional illusion suffer by the intrusion? A picture by Rossetti is one thing; it takes on an identity and permanence peculiar to itself and may legitimately be made the theme of fiction; but Rossetti the man and critic is of a different order of reality. James in *The Aspern Papers* thinly disguises Clare Clairemont and Byron as the chief characters of his story, but the disguise suffices to make the story art.

Mr. Wells, in his more journalistic fiction, sins frequently in this respect. The mention of living novelists—I think in *Joan and Peter*—has a flat effect. At times he crowds his page with contemporary allusion. The result is not at all one of heightened realism. The passages seem to be, and are, journalistic merely. This is the raw material of fiction not yet assimilated and transmuted by the imagination into art. The method is the more unpardonable in Wells in that he very well knows better and in his best work attains a truly imaginative plane. *Tono-Bungay* is one of the best pictures in fiction of certain aspects of the modern world; but it is not literal. Wells here gets to the essence of his idea and fashions a fable suitable to its expression. The patent medicine, tono-bungay, is a symbol, as the life of its inventor is a symbol. Nor are there evident in the story actual persons, characters inevitably less lifelike and compelling than those imaginatively conceived.

That particularity of detail, especially visual detail, is in itself vivid and interesting, whether strictly relevant or no, much modern fiction and the mail-order catalogue attest. A good catalogue, especially if illustrated, is indeed more entertaining than many novels. The lists and pictures of farm implements, guns, fishing tackle, tools, accordions, and automobile accessories have much of the charm of Arnold Bennett's stories of the Five Towns. They invoke innumerable sense memories; they stimulate the imagination. Bennett, it must be admitted, in his best work adds something to his details. From the host of sense impressions emerges, now and then, a flash in which life, lying back of all this stuff of sense experience, is more vividly apprehended. In this spiritual implication the method of particularity finds its partial justification. So, too, though to a less degree, in the work of Dorothy Richardson. Nevertheless the artistic justification is not, to my mind, complete. The great writer achieves not only these moments of vividness, but also a beauty of design of which they are a subordinate, though an essential part.

CHAPTER IV

ACTUALISM

Realism is too loose and controversial a term to permit precise definition. The "realistic" novelist may, however, be distinguished by his purpose, various as his product is. He seeks, I take it, to see life without prejudice, and if there is such a thing as truth to experience, to report it with as much fidelity as his limitations permit. He endeavors to live without anodynes; he does not blink because life is unpleasant. Such at least is his endeavor. His success is another matter; nor will any two novelists equally sincere and painstaking report life in identical terms. Yet however various and discrepant the works of the great novelists, it is obvious, I think, that fiction in the last seventy-five years has, in its efforts to be realistic, merely reflected the philosophic and scientific temper of the age. Not only have novels such as those of George Eliot, Hardy, and Samuel Butler, been influenced by the findings and the philosophic implications of science, but in one genre, the naturalistic, novels have been indebted to science for their actual form, their technic.

It should be noted parenthetically that an art which feels itself bound to report its observations with the utmost fidelity to "reality," as it perceives reality, is immensely more difficult than an art—call it "romantic" if you like—which professes no such allegiance. The novelist whose imagined world need only be consistent with itself, whose concern is primarily with the beauty and ingenuity of his patterns, has a single problem; whereas the task of the realistic novelist is twofold: he must be faithful to his findings in his study of life, however contradictory, harsh, and inharmonious these may be; and he has also the task of fashioning these into a thing of beauty. If Mr. Cabell in the world of his creation, divorced in time, place, and morality from the world about us, seems to realize a beauty not to be found in the work of Theodore Dreiser, be it remembered that Dreiser, doggedly faithful to his philosophy, his point-of-view, has far the more difficult task. The art of a realist or naturalist, such as Dreiser, is cabined and confined by the intellectual honesty of his endeavor. His successes are hard won.

Naturalism as Defined by Zola

It is in a twofold aspect that naturalism must be considered: as a contribution to knowledge—as science—and as an artistic method. That it is scientific in intent is apparent in Zola's definition of it in *The Experimental Novel.* "The experimentalist," Zola has remarked, "is the examining magistrate of nature; we novelists are the examining magistrates of men and their passions."

Zola's philosophy and the philosophy, I take it, of all true naturalists is determinism. Human conduct is the inevitable product of hereditary forces modified by environment. The experimentalist in fiction seeks, then, by his selection of characters whose hereditary "values" are known and by placing these characters amid forces of environment whose strength likewise is calculated, to observe the inevitable results. The results are presumably fruitful in their revelations of human passion, motive, and conduct. They constitute truth.

The theory suffers at the outset, however, in that it is based wholly upon a false analogy. Once this fallacy is revealed, as it easily can be, the whole pretensions of naturalism to value as science can be dismissed, and further discussion of it be confined to its æsthetic method. The fallacy is this: in laboratory science the same experiment conducted under similarly ideal conditions by various observers will come inevitably to the same results. These results are measurable by instruments, by tests which are impersonal and not subject to vagaries of temperament. An old scientist and a young one, a man or a woman, a hedonist or a Puritan will get the same results from the same combination of chemicals in a test tube. With the novelist such unanimity of result is impossible, for there is no material or abstract scale of values by which results may be measured, nor any agreement, save in the most general sense, as to the way in which the experiment shall be conducted. Zola conceives a priest of a certain temperament and beliefs led by the practices of his church to the renunciation of his vows and the formulation of a social philosophy. The result is merely Zola's belief as to the conduct of his character. Another novelist taking a similar character might arrive at different conclusions. There is always an incalculable factor in the mind of the novelist and, no doubt, also in the minds of his characters, if they are genuinely alive, which makes human conduct unpredictable and all prophecy merely speculative. The findings of the novelist cannot yet have, if ever, the validity of science.

It is for their æsthetic method, not for their contribution to science, that novelists of the naturalistic school are important. Their influence upon modern fiction has been considerable. They have revolted against what, in their eyes, are the artificialities of plot. For the novelist to plan his story, to know precisely at what end he would arrive and to lead his characters through a series of invented situations to that end, has seemed to the naturalist to falsify life, to transform it from a free growing organism into something dead, making it a contrived thing. A novel so built is not a plant or tree but a structure, a building, or a geometric design. Character is made subservient to situation, rather than situation subservient to character.

Great novelists, it may be remarked, have always been aware of this element of artificiality in their art and have not hesitated to alter their stories in the process of their creation rather than force characters into too rigid a mould. Scott, it was earlier noted, constantly altered his stories as he wrote, though not, I fancy, at the dictation of his characters. Trollope, essentially a character novelist and weak in invention, is a better instance of a writer anticipating the essentials of the naturalistic method long before the progress of science had led to so explicit a theory and method as Zola's. His method is evident in the Barsetshire stories, which had their inspiration in the old clergyman seen in the cathedral close of Salisbury. In the effort to realize this character, to surround him with plausible circumstance, and to develop situations which would reveal the nature of life in cathedral towns, Trollope was led on to the whole of his admirable series of novels which tell the story of Barchester and its inhabitants. In these, plot is wholly subordinate and grows naturally from the possibilities of the characters. They, in truth, create their own story.

Trollope is always faithful to his guiding principle that character should determine incident rather than be cramped by it. A very admirable instance is the case of Lily Dale, the heroine of *The Small House at Allington*. In this story the heroine is jilted by the worthless lover and vainly sought by the good young man. At the end the situation is unresolved and we look for its continuance in some sequel, which promise is kept in *The*

Last Chronicle of Barset. In this the hero renews his suit, with signs of wavering in the heroine. The way is cleared for the *scène à faire* in which she shall yield and the reader's romantic hopes be gratified. The author too, it is apparent, is hopeful; he wishes his heroine to reward her faithful lover. Yet when Trollope comes to the scene, try as he may he cannot make her succumb. She hesitates, but her nature is such, and the wound of her first love so lasting, that she must reject her admirer. The author defers to her deepest nature, of which, until the crucial moment, he was not himself sure, and regretfully denies us a romantic but false conclusion.

Such a method as Trollope's, no less than his admirable conscientiousness, is a joy to his readers, who share with the author a sense of exploration. The characters may be looked to for words and deeds off their own bat, not such, only, as are prescribed for them by the author. Spontaneity, waywardness, the air of life itself spring from characterization so unforced by the circumstance of plot. Plot nevertheless there may be, on the large lines of a Gothic cathedral, whose symmetry is undisturbed by the efflorescence of gargoyle and stained glass. A fine scene in nature may likewise bear a considerable burden of irrelevant detail without artistic loss, with gain even of exuberance. Design, structure, pattern within which character seems nevertheless free to act of itself, however paradoxical a combination, is the achievement of the best novel-

ists as it is the greatness of Shakespeare. Turgénev we observed, in *Fathers and Children,* despite the great care with which his fable is constructed, contrives to let his characters shape their
own story. If by naturalism were meant only naturalness, truth to life, its discovery would long
antedate Zola.

Zola is to me most readable when his theoretical
naturalism is tempered by his native artistry. The
differences in his manner are exhibited in such
contrasted novels as *Lourdes* and *Paris.* In the
former irrelevant details are heaped up without
mercy. The long train journey to the shrine is an
artistic nightmare. Every cow in the passing landscape, every porter and watchman at the stations
en route is seemingly enumerated. Why? There is
no reason save that cows and porters might plausibly be there and that Zola with the eye of a jour-
nalist so visualized them. That these details achieve
more than an unendurable monotony is not apparent.

In *Paris* plan and a selective principle are evident at the outset. The novel is built on a large
scale, involving several groups of characters. Yet
these are so naturally interrelated, and the lines
of development are so clearly indicated that the
story moves surely, though slowly, to the conclusion inherent in its origins. There is here sufficient
plot executed in terms of unforced characterization. Many of the details are, no doubt, not wholly
essential; background seems at times too fully de-

scribed. The impression of the whole is, nevertheless, essentially unified: society in all its various
classes is depicted as functioning like some immense organism. The picture, though elaborate, is
clear, reminding one of Balzac's works and not
unworthy of him. That so notable an effect is
achieved is due very largely to the tempering of
naturalistic theory with the more traditionary
practices of realism.

Conceivably a man's history might be related
with such fulness of detail that to follow it would
ask a lifetime of reading. To write such, is presumably the secret ambition of some of our contemporary novelists. James Joyce devotes a gigan-
tic work to the incidents of a day; Dorothy Richardson pursues her relentless course as though
Miriam were the heroine of the Elsie books. The
practical difficulties in the way of such an ambition though great are not insuperable. The artistic
difficulties are more formidable. On what principle,
it may be asked, are the incidents in the life of the
story's hero to be selected? Some selection there
must be; not *everything* can be told. Two criteria
for selection there are: the incident may be told
because it is vivid, interesting in itself; or because
it is, in some way, significant, falling, that is, into
a pattern whereby the author imposes some sort
of an interpretation upon experience.

Only occasionally in a novel is the experience of
a character told with such vividness that it can be
said to vie with the vividness of life itself. It is a

rare and cherished moment when the reader loses himself wholly in the sensations of another and forgets his own existence. On such moments the writer cannot wholly depend. He must be economical in their use. Words are a dull medium, not apt to delineate the sharp thrusts of sensation. The most vivid writing is dim as compared with life, no less than the colors of the painter are dim as compared to the hues of nature. It is in the significance of his details, their relation, that is, to others in a design, that novelist and painter find their strength. If he has no design, perceives no significance, the odds are that the novelist will write a book of which the reader will ask, Why should I read of a life apparently as meaningless as my own and considerably less intense?

The Method of Dreiser as Illustrative of Naturalism

The work of Theodore Dreiser, most notable of American naturalistic novelists, is inevitably called to mind by these reflections, especially as it exhibits, in my judgment, both the merits and the defects of the method. Back of Dreiser's craftsmanship lies his artistic heritage—he professes admiration for Hardy and Zola—and the philosophy which leads him to adopt naturalism as the medium for his art. This philosophy may be compactly put in a quotation from his own writings: "I do not know what truth is, what beauty is, what love is, what hope is. I do not believe any one absolutely and I do not doubt any one absolutely." Huxley and Spencer early emancipated his mind from conventional beliefs. He has no faith in any supernatural power or design, but is nevertheless sure that "life was intended to sting and hurt" —the philosophical paradox which was noted in Hardy. Dreiser is of the mid—or late—Victorian school of scientific pessimism. Were his theology to be exactly defined it would be agnosticism rather than atheism.

Life, to Dreiser, is inexplicable in its origins and without purpose; it is a drift, a confusion of experience without intelligible emphasis and productive of pain. Its only bright or tolerable moments are those in which the hunger for power, for sexual gratification, and for artistic expression (this latter no more than the accumulation of art objects) are satisfied. Around these episodic highlights lie the gray commonplaces of experience in which no one thing is more important than another.

A technique adequate to and expressive of this philosophy while possessed, at the same time, of beauty, is obviously not easy to acquire. The author is, first of all, denied any logical stopping-point for his fiction unless it be the death of an important character. It is precisely at such a point that both *Sister Carrie* and *Jennie Gerhardt* come to rest. The heroines have concluded one cycle of experience, that is all. In *The Financier* and *The*

Titan the story stops when it does merely because the author chooses to have it so. It might, in either, end sooner or be continued indefinitely. Life is a patternless endless thing, a gray stream of paper pouring from the press and cut at arbitrary intervals into lengths for convenience in handling.

The problem of selection, if a story is without a particular goal, is difficult. Selection of some sort there must be, but what shall determine it? It is noteworthy that in his first two and, to my taste, most effective novels, Dreiser achieves a greater unity than in his later ones. In both the centre of interest is firmly established in the heroine and in the one or two characters most intimate with her. In *Sister Carrie*, Hurstwood and Carrie divide the interest, with a wholly minor emphasis upon Drouet. In *Jennie Gerhardt*, the heroine is chief, with her lovers subordinated. A few characters only, in each book, occupy the stage and are closely observed. And in each the life depicted rises from its casual commonplace origins to a series of emotional experiences more or less intense and then drops again. The graph described can scarcely be called an arc, for an arc implies a symmetry which these stories have not. They possess, however, a certain unity. The author has unravelled one thread from the gray fabric of life and implied that all other threads resemble it.

It is in the selection of incidents to reveal his characters that Dreiser's method fails, I think, most notably. Incidents of structural or moral

significance are barred by the author's negative
philosophy. They should then, to interest us, be so
colorful and varied, be told with such emotional
power, that we shall enjoy them for their own
sakes. The picaresque novel is no more than this.
Candide, as wholly disillusioned a book as any of
Dreiser's, is of this order, but gay, and witty, and
caustic. In Dreiser the picaresque has been reno-
vated by science and all its gaiety blighted. To
read one of Dreiser's novels, especially of the first
two, is to be powerfully impressed. A second is less
striking, and with each successive novel the impression is feebler.

The negation of belief which is Dreiser's philosophy asks for its interesting embodiment endless wit and invention such as Voltaire possessed
but which Dreiser has not. The succession of Cowperwood's mistresses is, in recital, very dull. If,
from each, Cowperwood learned something, if we
perceived his character altering with every affair,
then these erotic adventures would have meaning.
Yet they have no more significance than the liquor
which he consumes or the pictures which he buys.
They attract his fancy and satisfy a hunger; that
is all. Hurstwood in *Sister Carrie* lingers in memory when all the financial marauders and their
mistresses have vanished. He is endowed with a
kind of pathos; his personality gradually fades
and dulls to its final extinction. In Hurstwood
Dreiser puts that grave query to life which Flaubert embodies in the dissolution of Madame Bo-

vary. It is a moral query, essentially. Yet to ask it repeatedly, with infinite variety and interest, would task the most gifted and ingenious novelist.

Dreiser is a gay dog in a very dreary fashion. And why should any one read a book which is duller and less exciting than the most commonplace existence? Dull lives in fiction must be so movingly portrayed that the contemplation of them is exciting. The feat has been achieved. Arnold Bennett in his best work, in the *Old Wives' Tale* and in *Clayhanger*, has done it. Bennett of course believes that every life, however trivial its circumstance, is exciting. The sense that I am I is a recurrent wonder and all experience magical. Lacking this zest, this sense of wonder, Dreiser is thrown back upon an æsthetic pattern, which his philosophy denies, and upon the resources of a technical dexterity.

These as exhibited in the power to reveal emotion poignantly Dreiser seldom displays. He attacks a situation by frontal assault. That indirection which is the chief resource of art he does not possess. Nor does he display skill in selection— in his later novels less even than in the early ones. What motive leads him to describe, as in *The Financier*, all the legal mechanism incident to Cowperwood's trial, even to the fortuitous descriptions of the criminals whose trial precedes his? These characters have nothing to do with the hero. Their appearance is a factual coincidence, nothing more. Again when Cowperwood's household goods are sold we have a detailed account of the various art objects whose acquisition has been previously told. The very names of the purchasers are given. There is, for another instance, a wholly superfluous description of the building in which the banking firm of Jay Cooke was housed. Instances of this sort could be endlessly multiplied from any of Dreiser's novels. An old newspaper gives the picture of a past generation with equal vividness and no less significance. The reader, bewildered and irritated by this mountain of irrelevant facts, may easily overlook or forget Dreiser's great and redeeming virtue, his intellectual honesty.

Dreiser's defects of method are not necessarily inherent in the technique of naturalism. Selection is, to be sure, more difficult in so loose a design than in one employing the old-fashioned plot. The merit of the naturalistic method is that it avoids the rigidities of plot and, at its best, creates a more convincing picture of the flow of experience and the accidents of destiny than, let us say, a novel so neatly plotted as Galsworthy's *Country House*. It is to the naturalistic method that are due such notable works as *Jean Cristophe* and *Pelle the Conqueror,* the latter, surely, one of the great imaginative works of our time.

"Jean Cristophe"

Jean Cristophe follows its hero from infancy to the grave; it is in the biographical form to which naturalism readily lends itself. The centre of interest is always the hero, Jean. Life is seen throughout from his eyes. We identify ourselves with him and live, vicariously, his life, while, at the same time, we see him as the author would have us. Of plot, in the usual sense, there is little. In his youth he is influenced by characters who soon drop out of the story never to reappear. Thus throughout the various stages of his career he has friends and acquaintances who contribute to his development and then vanish from the story, or, occasionally, are reintroduced only for a moment. The effect created is that of experience itself. Continuity lies only in the persistence of the one central figure. The technical problem is to select experiences which are significant, which modify the personality of the hero and feed the growth of his genius.

The experiences of the hero do, in a large way, so contribute to his growth, though in terms of morality it may not be easy to declare precisely how. There are erotic episodes reminiscent of Cowperwood's affairs, but which reveal in the women causes for surrender subtler than physical desire, and which widen our knowledge of human nature. In the hero himself these experiences express, moreover, various spiritual hungers, the search for some satisfaction never attained. Life in *Jean Cristophe,* if enigmatic and not easily summarized in a neat ethical formula, is at any rate a liberalizing experience. It is depicted as a good in itself and its ending is not felt as a meaningless cessation. Jean pursues his pilgrimage across the stream to some new realm of experience and growth. Rolland's philosophy, however mystical, gives him an attitude toward life which determines his selection of incident.

The Method of Nexö in "Pelle the Conqueror"

Pelle the Conqueror has rather more pattern then *Jean Cristophe*. The inter-relations of characters are more completely depicted, the group is more coherent. There is, in short, some plot; though not enough to give an impression of rigidity, of life cramped and forced into moulds, yet sufficient to create expectation and suspense. Surely suspense is legitimate in the most rigorous realism, for there is suspense in life itself. Experience, even though it falls into no single pattern, is separable into a series of broken inconclusive patterns which the novelist may, for emphasis, accentuate and complete. This Nexö has done, with the result that the story is more memorable than *Jean Cristophe* and the fable with its chief episodes is more vividly recalled—one test of good craftsmanship.

Nexö's greatest power lies in the perfect frankness and naturalness with which he records the most homely, sordid, and even bestial facts of human experience. No novelist, unless it be Hamsun, is so wholly unforced and undramatic in the depiction of facts in themselves disagreeable but which in his large scene are no more than details. These

Scandinavian realists accept life more wholly, more
sanely, one feels, than do we, with our taboos and
our obliquities. James Joyce in *Ulysses* is no less
frank, but his swaggering emphasis, his deliberate
bravado, is the unwholesome display of one to
whom life is revolting and who vacillates between
the extremes of sensuality and asceticism. Nexö
portrays life unflinchingly but with a casualness, a
freedom from false emphasis, which is wholly disarming. He is no more coarse nor prurient than a
text-book on physiology. No citation divorced from
its context can do justice to this quality in Nexö,
his wholly unemphatic acceptance of all experience, however coarse and brutal. The brief excerpt
from *Ditte,* which follows, is not exceptional; yet
the revolting character of the tenement house to
which this description is incident could not be half
so well conveyed in a more exclamatory and sympathetic manner. To the children, whose experience
this is, the manner of life is not revolting but interesting:

When they were sitting by the window it was possible to have it open; otherwise they had to keep it shut
—because of the rats. They were walking along the
roof-gutter, appearing suddenly out of a drain pipe as
if it were the top of a staircase—right in front of one's
nose—walking the whole round, bustling and sniffing
the air, looking ever so funny. When the rain drove the
children out of the yard they took possession of the
roofs of the outhouses and gambolled about down there.
But in the night-time it was still worse. When the moon
shone into the yard one could see them literally lying in

wait in the entrances to the cellars; and no sooner had the baker put his sheets of bread out to cool on the roofs of the outhouses than the rats were at it, before he'd even had time to turn away. Old Rasmussen had seen it when she sat up with the women of the building who were expecting babies. One could actually see the rats getting their noses burned on the hot rolls. Then they'd whirl round, squealing and rubbing their noses with their paws.

The sufficient if not elaborate design of *Pelle* and of *Ditte* and the unforced character of the realism, technical excellences both, spring from a philosophy which provides a selective principle. Nexö accepts all of life because life to him has meaning, because all experience, even the most bestial, contributes to the growth of soul. The particularity of detail, the unflagging factual quality of his work, is not an end in itself but a means to the development in his hero and his heroine of those spiritual qualities which enable them to find themselves and achieve a fit place in society. Their experiences have both an individual and a social bearing. Surely peasant life has never been so graphically portrayed as in the first volumes of *Pelle* and of *Ditte,* nor has the thesis been elsewhere so powerfully proclaimed that from the coarsest physical surroundings character may spring, and the finest spiritual qualities have their roots in muck. The mystical enlargement of soul which is Jean Cristophe's achievement seems vague and thin beside an idealism so robust as this.

Although it is the fictional biography of its hero,

Pelle, unlike *The Way of All Flesh,* does more than depict an individualistic morality, or, like *Jean Cristophe,* record the development of genius. Its theme is a larger one, the discovery of the self in its social relations. Pelle's experiences have a twofold purpose, individual and social. It is only at the last, when he is happy in his work as a labor leader, that the conflict of ideals is resolved. In this fusion of individual and social morality, the naturalistic technique falls into line with the traditional purpose of the novel. The emphasis is upon Pelle, but background is more constant, more important, than in a novel like *Jean Cristophe.* Minor characters, too, loom larger; their development, though minimized, is not overlooked, and they persist longer in the action. Thus, for instance, Pelle's wife, his adjustment to her and hers to him, is sufficiently depicted, for it is a step in his adjustment to society. Plot in the old rigidly predeterminded sense there is not, but the mesh of social relationships is complex. We have here more than the story of a single life.

Neither Rolland nor Nexö is in his philosophy of life, strictly speaking, a naturalist. The heroes of each have an individual endowment which is more than the product of inheritance played upon by environment. Neither author accepts a mechanistic philosophy; to both, human life is more than an experiment in animal behavior. Yet each employs a technique derived from the naturalistic method of Zola. A more rigidly naturalistic technique than theirs is productive, I think, of less interesting fictional results. For the purpose of art it is necessary to predicate of humanity an incalculable factor. If life is no more than a chemical formula, why write realistic fiction at all? Novels for entertainment, merely as anodynes to the pain of existence, there will always be. But the serious novelist would be better occupied with experimental psychology than with fiction. Fiction on the mechanistic formula, as a hand-maiden to science, cannot, I think, endure.

Naturalism as practised by Nexö, though it returns, in a sense, to the traditional purpose of the novel to portray the life of an individual in relation to society, does so with a difference. The old picaresque novel followed the fortunes of a single character. It portrayed the seamy side of the social fabric, but uncritically. The biographical novel of a later development, such as *David Copperfield,* depicted the individual in his pursuit of wife and fortune and left him at last ensconced in his comfortable niche. In neither form was the hero put through any course of questionings as to his social adjustment. That was wholly a material thing, a matter of rank, fortune, and family relationships. Structurally speaking this adjustment was wholly a matter of plot, the resultant of a series of complicated incidents working out to a predetermined end. The naturalistic fiction of our day, as exhibited in the work of Nexö, takes neither the individual nor society so much for granted. It questions both and is satisfied with no passive relation of the one to the other. It breathes the air of inquiry. Product of the scepticism of experimental science it seeks in its fictive instances to find new answers, a new morality, individual and social, to replace what science has destroyed. It builds new hypotheses by means of a new method which, while indebted to science, is not science but art.

The Growth of Naturalism and Its Derivation from Scientific Philosophy

The worlds of science and of art, although concerned equally with the facts of experience, are essentially diverse, for in the apprehension of these facts lies an insuperable difference in purpose and method. The facts of science must be standardized and constant. They are, emotionally speaking, dead facts, divorced from their relation to the individual percipient. They are devoid of morality and beauty, even of interest in the sense that one fact is innately more interesting than another. Interest implies an emotional judgment with which science is not concerned. Yet it is with this emotional response to experience that literature is, or at any rate until our day has been, wholly concerned.

The effects of science upon literature, even to the development of a new technique, as in the instance of naturalism, are sufficiently manifest. Literature is quick to adopt a new vocabulary and to exploit new fields. More profoundly, science has altered our attitude toward life, has contributed to the new philosophy which has sprung from the warfare of science and religion of two generations ago. The upshot of that conflict was the denial of religious authority. "Revealed" religion received then its deathblow, and though the world at large only now dimly perceives the fact, science has been aware of it for fifty years. The effects of the new philosophy upon the novel and its technique are manifest prior to the conscious theory and experimental method of Zola.

In George Eliot, most widely educated of the mid-Victorian novelists and quickest to respond to the scientific, theological, and philosophical advances of her day, the result of the overthrow of authority was not, interestingly, to unseat the moral judgment but to strengthen it. With the loss of external sanctions she reasserted more firmly her religious convictions. The universe became for her a place of moral struggle, of a spiritual evolution analogous to the evolution of life forms. "The army of unalterable law" was for her a host no less of ethical than of scientific import. However inscrutable might be the origins of things, for her the fact remained that this was a moral universe, one in which moral effort or lack of effort bore its inevitable fruit. Her books all bear witness to her faith. In them selfishness spells spiritual disaster; unselfishness, growth and happiness. Her books have therefore plan, structure, moving from their premises to calculable and predetermined ends. They have the logic of a mathematical demonstration. Yet tacitly she assumes that in this universe of moral law the individual has freedom to choose his course. He may, like Godfrey Cass, choose the selfish path and find unhappiness. Or, like Silas Marner, he may care more for another than for himself and so be happy. In either case the result is predetermined in the choice, but the choice is free.

Though George Eliot avowed a disbelief in God, her practical philosophy implies his existence under some other name. The plan of her books, more than any overt acceptance or denial, expresses her; just as in Shakespeare the belief in a moral order is implicit in his manipulation of human destinies, in the disintegration of personality through sin and its growth through the exercise of virtue. Essentially this also is manifest in Meredith. Meredith is less the explicit moralist than George Eliot; his philosophy is not so simple. Virtue does not necessarily find, with him, any earthly reward, nor does he imply any subsequent. Richard Feverel and Nevil Beauchamp come to unhappy ends, broken in the contest with human selfishness and blindness. Yet his admiration is for them rather than for the worldly-wise. Virtue to him is a good in itself, like the beauty of earth.

There is thus manifest in Meredith, in the form of his novels, a more real, if less conscious, acceptance of the new scientific spirit and attitude, however ethically uncompromising he may be, and however touched his novels are with a mysticism and a joy in life which George Eliot has not. Though fate is not with him that demonic force which it is with Hardy, the drift of circumstance is tragic. In the conflict with life the idealist suffers. The little accidents are, on the whole, against him, though they are of human contriving rather than the result of blind mischance. Thus the death of Lucy Feverel and the misfortunes and death of Nevil Beauchamp. The catastrophe in each instance lies in the tragic drift of circumstance rather than in an adequately motivating cause. Hence the debatable artistry of these conclusions, elsewhere discussed.[1] Their explanation lies in Meredith's philosophy, his reading of life.

I have spoken of the "drift of circumstance" in Meredith's novels, and, in two tragic denouements, of the lack of specific cause structurally adequate to them. Neatness of design, the calculated balancing of parts, the end wholly explicit in the premises is not, as in George Eliot, characteristic of him. His novels resemble broad rivers flowing serenely, with no sense of haste but with sure power, to inevitable consummations. Structural incident is, in a sense, of no importance—that is to say, the *particular* incident. It is as unimportant as the boulder or hill slope which deflects the stream. The stream has a hundred possible paths to its goal and inevitably finds its way thither. So in Mere-

[1]See Chapter III.

dith it is character which determines destiny. Lest the figure of speech cloud the point, observe, specifically, the series of incidents which in *Beauchamp's Career* leads to the horse-whipping of Dr. Shrapnel and its consequences. There is in this no forced or plotted crisis. Though its ostensible cause is Captain Baskelett's pique and intoxication, its deeper motivation lies in the inevitable enmity of Baskelett and his kind for Dr. Shrapnel and Beauchamp. The specific incident is no more than driftwood borne by deep currents.

I have reverted to this technical point, this determination of incident by character, because Meredith's novels mark a development from the neatly plotted novel to one of freer design. They, like the novels of Trollope, anticipate the naturalistic method, and while subscribing to no theory of art or science are the unconscious product of a new philosophy. Meredith, though he does not part wholly with the past, faces the future. In his art as in his politics, he is a conservative radical. In his novels while there is yet plot, design, it is not a mould into which the story is poured, not a shell enclosing it.

It is the defect of Hardy's novels, as I have elsewhere pointed out,[1] that for the old cramped philosophy he substitutes another no less confining. The action of his stories is as rigidly determined by his conception of mischance as it could be by any other narrow creed whatsoever. Character does not determine destiny but destiny claps char-

[1] See Chapter III.

acter into a strait-jacket. The contrast of the old age, redefining its Calvinism in new terms but essentially unchanged, and a new age of broader outlook is exhibited in Hardy and Meredith, both in their avowed philosophies and, more revealingly, in the structure of their works.

Butler, in *The Way of All Flesh,* cuts loose almost wholly from the past. The theme of the book is precisely that, a denial of the old coercions—philosophical, social, and moral—and a cheerful experimental attempt to find something in their stead. It is the book's moral freedom which is most notable. Ernest, ridding himself of old taboos, discovers in the course of various vicissitudes a new morality: that whatever makes him happy is good. His conduct is as experimental as science itself. The author's formula is simple. It is not apparent that he knows himself what is to happen to Ernest, but taking us by the hand he leads us to observe the tragedy and absurdity of his hero's divagations.

Butler anticipates the work of the conscious naturalists, Zola and his imitators. Of late naturalism has followed the two divergent lines predictable in its origins. In Nexö it has returned, with an important modification in technique, to the traditional problem of the novelist: the study of the individual in his social relations; individual and social morality are reconciled, as in the instance of Pelle. In its other development it has sought to portray with a fidelity never before achieved the exact nature of the individual consciousness. It is in the work of Dorothy Richardson and of James Joyce that this most recent technique is best exhibited.

Naturalistic Technique in Dorothy Richardson and James Joyce

Miss Richardson's novels I find hard reading. Of the several which I have tried I think I have read none from cover to cover. Yet their method is extremely interesting and episodically they are often vivid. So incoherent are they, however, despite the constancy with which the centre of interest is held, that they wholly lack suspense. There is no emotional inducement to continue with them. Pattern, if they possess such, is not evident. And I submit that, without evidences of pattern, the sequential character traditional to fiction wholly ceases to be. If one can take up the story at any place and proceed indifferently either backwards or forwards, a novel, whatever its merits, can only by courtesy be called narrative. It is but a slight exaggeration wholly to deny this narrative interest to the work of Miss Richardson.

It is her evident purpose and triumph to reflect the stream of consciousness, the actual complex of sense perception, memory, and formulated thought, with greater fidelity to fact than ever before achieved. In the management of the point of view there could be no completer effacement of the author. The centre of interest, also, is abso-

lutely fixed. We enter into Miriam's consciousness and live her life; the identification is absolute;
the illusion of vicarious experience is unbroken.
There is, of course, selection. It being physically
impossible to give us all of Miriam's consciousness,
day in and day out, the author must content herself with typical excerpts, chosen more or less at
random. That, at least, is the effect which they
create. The moments chosen may coincide with incidents in Miriam's life which are deemed important; but wherein this importance lies does not
appear, unless they are remarkable for a certain
freshness and sharpness of impression which sur-
passes that of other incidents. It seems to be the
writer's thesis that amid circumstances the most
usual there are more vivid moments, moments in
which we realize the poignant wonder of experience, come closest to some inner reality. These
moments are an end in themselves and thus worthy
of record.

Yet one wonders why such a description as the
following is introduced. That Miriam should have
observed "The Australian" with such intentness
is possible. But why give all the details unless the
girl is to have, as she does not, some further significance in Miriam's life?

Miriam noticed the hoarse hacking laugh of the Australian. Her eyes flew up the table and fixed her as she
sat laughing, her chair drawn back, her knees crossed
—tea was drawing to an end. The detail of her terrify-
ingly stylish ruddy brown frieze dress with its Norfolk

jacket bodice and its shiny leather belt was hardly distinguishable from the dark background made by the folding doors. But the dreadful outline of her shoulders was visible, the squarish oval of her face shone out —the wide forehead from which the wiry black hair was combed to a high puff, the red eyes, black now, the long straight nose, the wide laughing mouth with the enormous teeth.

The next passage which I select, from *Interim,* compares interestingly with the passage from *The Tunnel* quoted in another place.[1] The general method is the same in the effort to depict the flux of consciousness, that mixture of sense impressions, associated memories, and formulated thought which at any moment constitutes a state of mind. *Interim,* however, is a later book, and my impression is that Miss Richardson is becoming more orthodox in her manner. It seems a more coherent book, more easily intelligible, than *The Tunnel.* There are, it is true, more difficult passages in *Interim* than the one cited, but I judge it to be fairly representative. The mental state, the mixture of observation and reflection, is rendered faithfully, and the reader takes pleasure in guessing the associations which bridge the apparent gaps. It is, however, a pleasure which wears rather thin on repetition, and when, after innumerable passages of a like sort, the heroine, Miriam, seems to get nowhere in particular, I put the book aside. Immensely difficult as it is so to record the flux

[1] See Chapter III.

of consciousness, vivid as is the description, the result is less interesting than direct experience. On the score of intensity fiction cannot compete with life. Only as it gives significance to life through the beauty and implications of its patterns can it seize and hold us long. The excerpt follows:

She set out from the house of friends to meet the darkened daylight . . . perha,ᵣs the sudden tapping of thunder-drops upon her thin blouse. The street was a livid gray, brilliant with hidden sunlight.

The present can be judged by the part of the past it brings up. If the present brings up the happiness of the past, the present is happy.

Purgatory. The waters of Lethe and Eunoe's "forgetfulness and sweet memory"; and then Heaven. The Catholics are right about expiation. If you are happy in the present something is being expiated. If life contains moments of paradise you must be in purgatory looking across the vale of Asphodel. You can't be in hell. . . . Yet hell would not be hell without a knowledge of heaven. If once you've been in heaven you can never escape. Yet Dante believed in everlasting punishment.

Bathing in the waters of Lethe and Eunoe unworthily is drinking one's own damnation. But happiness crops up before one can prevent it. Perhaps happiness is one long sin, piling up a bill. . . . It is my secret companion. Waiting at the end of every dark passage. I did not make myself. I can't help it.

Brilliant . . . *brilliant;* and some one was seeing it. There was no thunderstorm, no clouds or pink edges on the brilliant copper gray. She wandered on down the road hemmed by flaming green. The invisible sun was everywhere. There was no air, nothing to hold her body separate from the scene. The gray brilliance of the sky was upon the pavement and in the green of the park, making mauve shadows between the trees and a mist of mauve amongst the further green. The high house-fronts stood out against the gray, eastern-white, frilled below with new-made green, sprouting motionlessly as you looked . . . white plaster houses against the blue of the Mediterranean, gray mimosa trees, green-feathered lilac of wisteria. Between the houses and the park the road glared wooden gray, dark, baked gray, edged with the shadowless stone gray of the pavement. Summer. Eternity *showing*. . . .

The Euston Road was a narrow hot channel of noise and unbreathable odors, the dusty exhausting cruelty of the London summer, leading on to the feathery green floored woods of Endsleigh Gardens edged by gray house fronts and ending in the cool stone of St. Pancras Church.

In the twilit dining-room one's body was like a hot sun throbbing in cool dark air, ringed by cool walls holding darkness in far corners; coolness poured out through the wide open windows toward the rain-cool gray façades of the opposite houses, cool and cool until the throbbing ceased.

Miss Richardson's work is naturalistic, but also —so complicated is our modern terminology—impressionistic. Her point of view never varies. Always we see through Miriam's eyes and if reality is thereby distorted, it is a distortion inevitable to the method. Truth for the author lies in telling us precisely what Miriam thought and felt and saw; it is life seen through and colored by a particular temperament. In so far as words are competent to that end we actually live the life of an imaginary being. James Joyce in *Ulysses* has, evidently, the same end in view, though in this novel we enter successively into the lives of a number of characters with a resultant richer effect and a greater avoidance of the monotony which seems inevitable to Miss Richardson's method.

Ulysses I have seen described as a masterpiece, a work of curious and complicated design, its various parts—corresponding to the members of the human body—symbolizing some profound and ribald criticism of existence. I suspect it instead of being a hoax put upon the critics and a serious public; for much of it is surely unintelligible unless one has a key which the author does not provide, and like many a work of genius it is impossible to read it through. Yet parts of it are of great technical interest. Joyce too, like Dorothy Richardson, is concerned with the immediacy of experience; his effort is to depict the flux of consciousness wholly and exactly. In the first citation Mr. Bloom's thoughts, though casual, are perfectly intelligible. It is easy to follow the thread of association. As compared with the excerpt from *Interim* this is ordered and lucid and imposes little strain upon the reader:

Gaswork. Whooping cough they say it cures. Good job Milly never got it. Poor children! Doubles them up black and blue in convulsions. Shame really. Got off lightly with illness compared. Only measles. Flaxseed tea. Scarlatina, influenza epidemics. Canvassing for death. Don't miss this chance. Dog's home over there. Poor old Athos! Be good to Athos, Leopold, is my last wish. Thy will be done. We obey them in the grave. A dying scrawl. He took it to heart, pined away. Quiet brute. Old men's dogs usually are.

A raindrop spat on his hat. He drew back and saw an instant of shower spray dots over the gray flags. Apart. Curious. Like through a colander. I thought it would. My boots were creaking I remember now.

Presumably the next passage, if it has any meaning at all, suggests the broken pictures and half memories evoked by the music of the band. But who will have patience to disentangle its suggestions? An author, if he wishes to be read, must put himself to more inconvenience to be lucid than is here perceptible:

Bronze by gold heard the hoofirons, steelringing Impenthnthn thnthnthn.
Chips, picking chips off rocky thumbnail, chips.
Horrid! And gold flushed more.
A husky fifenote blew.
Blew. Blue bloom is on the
Gold pinnacled hair.
A jumping rose on satiny breasts of satin, rose of Castile.
Trilling, trilling. Idolores.
Peep! Who's in the . . . peep of gold?
Tink cried to bronze in pity.
And a call, pure, long and throbbing. Long indying call.
Decoy. Soft word. But look! The bright stars fade.
O rose! Notes chirruping answer. Castile. The morn is breaking.
Jingle jingle jaunted jingling.
Coin rang. Clock clacked.

Avowal. *Sonnez.* I could. Rebound of garter. Not
leave thee. Smack. *La cloche!* Thigh smack. Avowal.
Warm. Sweetheart, goodbye!
Jingle. Bloo.
Boomed crashing chords. When love absorbs. War!
War! The tympanum.
A sail! A veil awave upon the waves.
Lost. Throstle fluted. All is lost now.
Horn. Hawhorn
When first he saw. Alas!

etc.

In the preceding instance a kind of psychological shorthand is employed and there is little effort
so to order the ideas that they are given any coherence. Their associations are too difficult to follow, more difficult than the previous excerpt from
Dorothy Richardson. In my concluding instance,
one of the few quotable passages from the thoughts
of Mrs. Bloom, there is little real incoherence. The
associations and suggestions as they arise are intelligible enough, but by the omission of all punc-
tuation and sentence structure Joyce secures an
unbroken continuity which mirrors with artistic
fidelity the flux of consciousness.

. . . I'll go to Lambes there beside Findlater's and get
them to send us some flowers to put about the place in
case he brings him home tomorrow today I mean no no
Friday's an unlucky day first I want to do the place up
someway the dust grows in it I think while Im asleep
then we can have music and cigarettes I can accompany
him first I must clean the keys of the piano with milk

whattl I wear shall I wear a white rose or those fairy
cakes in Lipton's I love the smell of a rich big shop at
7½ d a lb or the other ones with the cherries in them
and the pinky sugar 11d a couple of lbs of course a nice
plant for the middle of the table Id get that cheaper in
wait wheres this I saw them not long ago I love flowers
Id love to have the whole place swimming in roses God
of heaven theres nothing like nature the wild mountains
then the sea and the waves rushing then the beautiful
country with fields of oats and wheat and all kinds of
things and all the fine cattle going about that would do
your heart good to see rivers and lakes and flowers all
sorts of shapes and smells and colors springing up even
out of the ditches primroses and violets nature it is as
for them saying theres no God I wouldnt give a snap
of my two fingers for all their learning why dont they
go and create something I often asked him atheists or
whatever they call themselves go and wash the cobbles
off themselves first then they go howling for the priest
and they dying and why why because theyre afraid of
hell on account of their bad conscience ah yes I know
them well who was the first person in the universe before there was anybody that made it all who ah that they
dont know neither do I so there you are. . . .

That the impressionistic method can be made
tremendously effective when sparingly employed
and when its vivid moments are both emotionally
and structurally relevant is, I think, demonstrated.
When pushed too far, when unrelieved, its effect
is that of a piano played fortissimo or of a singer
who shouts at the top of his voice. Henry James
can create the effect of an explosion by three quietly
spoken words withheld until the proper moment.
A shriek, if it is but one of a succession of shrieks,

is merely deafening. That is much the effect of a book written wholly in the impressionistic method. In the next instance to be quoted, from Joyce's *Portrait of the Artist as a Young Man*, the effect is powerful because the experience marks an emotional climax for which we have been prepared. We have been identified with the character, whose mind has become disordered by remorse and religious terror. The distortion of reality, madness virtually, is thus credible:

He came down the aisle of the chapel, his legs shaking and the scalp of his head trembling as though it had been touched by ghostly fingers. He passed up the stairway and into the corridor along the walls of which the overcoats and water-proofs hung like gibbeted malefactors, headless and dripping and shapeless. And at every step he feared that he had already died, that his soul had been wrenched forth of the sheath of his body, that he was plunging headlong through space.

He could not grip the floor with his feet and sat heavily at his desk, opening one of his books at random and poring over it. Every word for him! It was true. God was almighty. God would call him now as he sat at his desk, before he had time to be conscious of the summons. God had called him. Yes? What? Yes? His flesh shrank together as it felt the approach of the ravenous tongues of flames, dried up as it felt about it the swirl of stifling air. He had died. Yes. He was judged. A wave of fire swept through his body: the first. Again a wave. His brain began to glow. Another. His brain was simmering and bubbling within the crackling tenement of his skull. Flames burst forth from his skull like a corolla, shrieking like voices:

"—Hell! Hell! Hell! Hell! Hell!

Impressionism unrelieved as in *Pilgrimage* and too little relieved as in *Ulysses* is unbearably monotonous. Emphasis, too, is lost. Its effective employment is further complicated by the question of the point of view. In Dorothy Richardson's work there is no difficulty in this respect. The point of view is omniscient wholly of the one character; and in *Ulysses,* consecutively omniscient of several characters, without at any time permitting the intrusion of the author in the conduct of his story. If the author, however, tells the story in his own person, a difficulty at once arises. The distortions of reality incident to viewing an experience through the eyes of a character are wholly different in their effect from similar distortions viewed through the eyes of the author. The confused perception is justified only by the mood which alters reality. Truth lies in depicting for the reader what is in the mind of the character. The author, on the contrary, presumably sees reality as it is, undistorted, uncolored by a particular mood. His description of scene should then, if it is to be believed, be a normal one, without exaggerations and discolorations.

Two contrasting excerpts from Evelyn Scott's *Narcissus* bring out very well this relevant and irrelevant use of the impressionistic method:

The light rushed out and bathed the indistinct walls. The carpet was bleached with it. There was a circle of radiance low about the desk where the lamp stood. Julia had not answered. Her shoulders, turned to him, resisted him. Her head was bent forward, away. She was moving some papers under a book. Her bare hand and arm appeared startlingly alive, saffron-colored in the glow, trembling out of the dim blackness of her sleeve. There were blanched reflections in the lighted folds of her silk skirt.

That all of the details here are strictly essential is, no doubt, debatable. It is Julia's mood, suggested in her posture and her averted face, which is the important thing. The light reflected in the folds of her skirt has no character or emotional value. It does, however, contribute to the sharply defined picture, and this picture is seen wholly through the eyes of the man.

In the second excerpt, the scene has no relevancy to the mood of the character. Indeed, from the context it is evident that he does not see it, for his thoughts are turned inward; and it is with his mood, rather than with the externally observant eye of the author, that the reader is presumably identified. The impressionistic description by the author seems, then, irrelevant and untrue:

He passed along the neat sidewalks, his head bowed. His air of abstraction was ostentatious. He wanted to enjoy uninterruptedly the relaxation of self-loathing. There were deep, violet-red shadows on the newly-washed asphalt street. The tree-tops were still and glistening against the line of faintly gilded roofs. The grass blades on the ordered lawns were green glass along which the quiet light trickled. Well-dressed children played under the eyes of nurse-maids. A limousine was drawn up in the shrubbery that surrounded a Georgian portico. Lawrence decided that he was relieved by the failure which separated him from the pretensions of success.

In the last sentence the thought of the character is linked up with the scene, but the transition in mood whereby his self-loathing has been dissipated and his attention caught by the external scene is not intelligible. The author's description and the character's absorption in his mood have, until this point, been wholly disparate and unlinked.

Pictorial Origins of Impressionism and Expressionism—Their Contrasted Methods

The pictorial origin of literary impressionism has been made clearly evident by the citations. In painting, the term "impressionism" implies the effort to depict the exact visual impression of a moment without rectifying this by a studied comparison with the facts; without, that is, reading into the impression what is known to be there though unperceived. Thus, simply, the modern landscape painter does not paint innumerable leaves to his tree nor waves to his ocean. He paints, instead, the masses of light and shade which constitute the visual impression and which, in the observer, memory, with the aid of intellect, resolves into their particular identities. Virtually all modern landscape painting is, in this respect, in its greater fidelity to sense perceptions, impressionistic as compared with the work of Ruysdael or Hobbema. In its more extreme practice it records the findings of an instant, with too evident distortion of the actual as perceived in a longer and steadier view. Between this extreme and the distortion of visual truth which lies in reading into perceptions too much of the knowledge born of previous experience, lies the larger body of modern landscape painting.

Expressionism in painting pursues a radically different method. The artist has, let us say, observed a contrast of light and shadow falling upon a wall. In this he finds a suggestion, the abstract theme for a picture. Or again in the skyline of a city street he observes a composition of lines and masses which he finds pictorially suggestive. He thinks over these suggestions, endeavoring to disentangle from them their essential elements, to simplify them. The ideas or themes thus freed from irrelevances he then seeks to *express,* to find for them, that is, the dress which will set them forth clearly and powerfully, freed from all distractions. In this recreative process it is likely that the two ideas which sprang up at different times and as the result of diverse stimuli may coalesce. Light and shadow, lines and masses may all find their adequate symbols in a picture of trees on a snowy hillside, reflections in a pool, or haystacks and barns in a field. The symbols are, in a sense, unimportant; that is to say the essential ideas may be expressed by innumerable devices at the choice of the artist. He selects the one which happens to suit him, or, as is often the case, he repeats his idea many times in a variety of forms, seeking thus to exhaust its possibilities or to chance upon the one perfect medium for its expression.

The creative processes in these two forms of painting, impressionism and expressionism, are mentally, it is obvious, utterly diverse. In expressionism, between the initial suggestion and its incarnation in some arrangement of lines and colors, lies an analytical and selective process. Thought, deliberation, choice are prerequisite to its employment of symbols which are not an end in themselves but important only for what they convey of the artist's thought. Expressionism does not aim at immediacy of effect. It seeks a permanent *something* embedded in hosts of visual experiences and beneath all manner of physical forms. It is, in a sense, abstract. Whistler's desire to paint a picture wholly in lines and masses which should have no correspondence to the world of objects, which should be wholly divorced from actuality, is the wish for a kind of short-hand or algebraic formula intelligible only to other artists but to them affording a profound and incommunicable joy.

Expressionism in literature becomes easier to understand in the light of its analogy to the art of painting. More or less expressionism has always been the method of the great novelists, of those who, reflecting upon life, have come to certain conclusions about it, and have seen in it themes to be dressed forth in appropriate character and incident. They have found beneath the flow of experience something universal and permanent and this they have endeavored to express. Analysis, simplification, the deliberate choice of symbols have constituted their method. Allegory is the most naive, most obvious product of it. The novels of Turgénev likewise are expressionism, for in them the abstract idea or theme is set forth in its appropriate fable, a fable so interesting in itself, so animate, that its abstract origin and inner meaning do not obtrude but are wholly implicit.

Galsworthy and Bojer are, of contemporary novelists, most obviously expressionists. In both the somewhat abstract nature of the theme and the process of its incarnation in character and incident are apparent—perhaps too apparent for the taste of many, too little removed from allegory. *The Country House* and *The Great Hunger* are not very different in genre from *Pilgrim's Progress*. As such they offer nothing essentially new in method. Nor does Marcel Proust, whose work in *Swann's Way* is expressionistic in another fashion, in its detached episodes rather in the idea or structure of the story as a whole, offer anything new. His work carries to a new pitch of perfection a method of expressionistic description as old, surely, as *Tristram Shandy* and *The Sentimental Journey*.

Pilgrimage, I have remarked, makes the depiction of the stream of consciousness an end in itself.

If it has a larger or more abstract purpose, such is not evident. *Swann's Way*, likewise, is interesting chiefly for its episodes. These, it is true, are strung upon a slight thread of plot, but this possessing only the faintest story interest. One may open the book anywhere with enjoyment. Read its incidents in inverse order and the pleasure is no less than when they are read in the order of time. The book is a series of impressions, of golden moments, of separate jewels each cut and polished with the utmost art. Yet these impressions are built up in a fashion wholly different from that which Miss Richardson employs.

The whole essence of Proust's method is its retrospective character. It views experience through the mellowing influence of time. The immediacy of the impressionistic manner is abhorrent to it. Above all it is selective. Memory is the first agent to selection, for in remembered experience that which is emotionally irrelevant, which is extraneous to the essence, drops away. Only the mood remains, often with few associated details. In the literary expression of the mood, then, it is necessary to recapture details congruous to it, capable of conveying it. And if memory cannot supply these, as usually it cannot, the imagination must be invoked. New details must be invented and these harmonious with, and expressive of, the mood. The experience thus recreated may, and usually must, as *fact* differ sharply from its original. Its essential truth, its reality, lies in the fidelity

with which the impression, the mood, as persist-
ing in memory, is set forth. It is Proust's distinc-
tion that he creates an impression with exquisite
fidelity and fulness, building it up with infinite
detail:

They were rooms of that country order which (just
as in certain climes whole tracts of air or ocean are
illuminated or scented by myriads of protozoa which
we cannot see) fascinate our sense of smell with the
countless odors springing from their own special virtues,
wisdom, habits, a whole secret system of life, invisible,
superabundant and profoundly moral which their atmosphere holds in solution; smells natural enough indeed,
and colored by circumstances as are those of the neigh-
boring countryside, but already humanized, domesti-
cated, confined, an exquisite, skilful, limpid jelly, blending all the fruits of the season which have left the
orchard for the store-room, smells changing with the
year, but plenishing domestic smells, which compensate
for the sharpness of hoar frost with the sweet savor
of warm bread, smells lazy and punctual as a village
clock, roving and settled, heedless and provident, linen
smells, morning smells, pious smells; rejoicing in a
peace which brings only an increase of anxiety, and in
a prosiness which serves as a deep source of poetry to
the stranger who passes through their midst without
having lived amongst them. The air of those rooms was
saturated with the fine bouquet of a silence so nourish-
ing, so succulent that I could not enter them without
a sort of greedy enjoyment, particularly on those first
mornings, chilly still, of the Easter holidays, when I
could taste it more fully, because I had just arrived
then at Combray: before I went in to wish my Aunt
good day I would be kept waiting a little time in the
outer room, where the sun, a wintry sun still, had crept

in to warm itself before the fire, lighted already between its two brick sides and plastering all the room and everything in it with a smell of soot, making the room like one of those great open hearths which one finds in the country, or one of the canopied mantelpieces in old castles under which one sits hoping that in the world outside it is raining or snowing, hoping almost for a catastrophic deluge to add the romance of shelter and security to the comfort of a snug retreat; I would turn to and fro between the prayer-desk and the stamped velvet armchairs, each one always draped in its crocheted antimacassar, while the fire, baking like a pie the appetizing smells with which the air of the room was thickly clotted, which the dewy and sunny freshness of the morning had already 'raised' and started to 'set,' puffed them and glazed them and fluted them and swelled them into an invisible though not impalpable country cake, an immense puff pastry, in which, barely waiting to savor the crustier, more delicate, more respectable, but also drier smells of the cupboard, the chest-of-drawers, and the patterned wallpaper I always returned with an unconfessed gluttony to bury myself in the nondescript, resinous, dull, indigestible and fruity smell of the flowered quilt.

The excerpt is necessarily rather long, for the whole effect lies in the copiousness of the detail, in the minuteness with which the impression is built up. There is in the method itself nothing essentially new. In *Tristram Shandy* and in *The Sentimental Journey*, you will find scenes contrived with similar art, designed likewise to convey a single emotional impression; scenes moreover which are an end in themselves and whose relation to the story action, to plot, is of the slightest. In Sterne the episodes are shorter, are more sentimental, and have more character value than in Proust—are not so, in a sense, impersonal. But the essence of the method is the same. The artist is seeking to convey a mood, a shade of sentiment, and casts about for details which, harmoniously blent, will express it. In Mrs. Radcliffe, likewise, are to be found scenes descriptive of background which are harmoniously contrived for emotional effect, but which may even be false to fact. Yet their essential thinness and falsity are in part compensated for by the emotional unity which they attain. They are pretty, pleasing, like a painting of Watteau's.

The following, from *The Mysteries of Udolpho*, is characteristic of Mrs. Radcliffe's facile brush. The specific touches which she ventures are few and gleaned, no doubt, from books of travel. The description resembles one of those romantic paintings of the old school in which a variety of unlikely objects is agreeably assembled on one canvas:

The travellers, as they descended, gradually exchanged the region of winter for the genial warmth and beauty of spring. The sky began to assume that serene and beautiful tint peculiar to the climate of Italy; patches of young verdure, fragrant shrubs and flowers looked gaily among the rocks, often fringing their rugged brows, or hanging in tufts from their broken sides; and the buds of the oak and mountain ash were expanding into foliage. Descending lower, the orange and the myrtle every now and then appeared in some sunny nook, with their yellow [sic] blossoms peeping from among

the dark green of their leaves, and mingling with the
scarlet flowers of the pomegranate and the paler ones of
the arbutus, that ran mantling to the crags above; while,
lower still, spread the pastures of Piedmont, where
early flocks were cropping the luxuriant herbage of
spring.

Though the appeal to the eye is not graphic in this
description, and though the scene as a whole may
be essentially false to any specific view, emotionally it is unified, better suited to its romantic context than a scene more sharply etched and authen-
tic. If it does not greatly add to the story, neither
does it detract. The mind of the reader slips over
it conscious only of a mildly pleasant sensation.
As an exercise of the synthetic imagination it is
not without its merit.

The tremendous burden of such a method as
Dorothy Richardson's is, as I have pointed out
elsewhere,[1] that of a tempo which is almost un-
bearable. The incoherence imposes a strain upon
the mind which few readers will endure. In Proust
there is no incoherence, but one has the sense of
enchantment, as though spell-bound in some garden of Midas. The story does not move at all,
virtually; there is almost no sense of chronology
and growth. It is as though the past were some
vast storehouse of Indian stuffs to be rummaged
at will. The novel is a collection of priceless bits
which form no whole. Oddly, the structural effect, or lack of it, is precisely the effect which

[1]See Chapter III

Dorothy Richardson achieves by dissimilar methods. Impressionism and expressionism here touch hands and may, to the casual glance, be confused.

Mrs. Woolf's method in *Jacob's Room* is no doubt explained in a passage near the end of the book in which she discusses characterization in these words:

It is no use trying to sum people up. One must follow hints, not exactly what is said, nor yet entirely what is done. Some, it is true, take ineffaceable impressions of character at once. Others dally, loiter, and get blown this way and that. . . .

There is also the highly respectable opinion that character-mongering is much overdone nowadays. After all, what does it matter—that Fanny Elmer was all sentiment and sensation, and Mrs. Durrant hard as iron? that Clara, owing (so the character-mongers said) largely to her mother's influence, never yet had the chance to do anything off her own bat, and only to very observant eyes displayed deeps of feeling which were positively alarming. . . .

Some are driven back to see what the other side means—the men in Clubs and Cabinets—when they say that character drawing is a frivolous fireside art, a matter of pins and needles, exquisite outlines enclosing vacancy, flourishes, and mere scrawls. . . .

It is thus that we live, they say, driven by an unseizable force. They say that the novelists never catch it; that it goes hurtling through their nets and leaves them torn to ribbons. This, they say, is what we live by—this unseizable force.

The author seeks to suggest the force, not to enclose, define, and limit it. Her characters are plastic, are even at the end of her story still in process of change. We have had glimpses of them and in a sense know them as we know people whom we have met—casually, that is. But they remain essentially enigmatic, victims of the unseizable law, mysterious as life is mysterious. Jacob, the central character, is portrayed almost wholly by the impressions which he makes on others. Yet these impressions are neither very numerous nor varied. To women he is invariably "distinguished," "awkward," and, apparently, lovable. One of his friends speaks of him as the greatest man he had ever known—just why we do not perceive. Of Jacob's literary tastes we learn a good deal, but these, after all, tell us little that is important; taken in conjunction with other characteristics they may mean something. Jacob is but one of the "procession of shadows" which, the author says, is life. This being so, "why are we yet surprised in the window corner by a sudden vision that the young man in the chair is of all things in the world the most real, the most solid, the best known to us—why indeed? For the moment after we know nothing about him. Such is the manner of our seeing. Such the conditions of our love."

Jacob does not, I think, however enigmatic, make so great an impression of solidity as this. He is suggestive. We supply him with qualities of our own devising; and this no doubt is an excellent thing, this collaboration. Yet the question inevitably arises, Why did not the author, if such was her method, employ it more rigorously? Jacob is not wholly portrayed in the comments and impressions of others, nor in word and deed. Sometimes we look into his thoughts and mood; he soliloquizes for us. He tells us, indeed, surprisingly little that matters:

"It is those damned women," said Jacob (to himself), without any trace of bitterness, but rather with sadness and disappointment that what might have been should never be. . . . She reminded him of Sandra Wentworth Williams. . . . He was extraordinarily moved. . . .

Such passages, rather rare, contribute nothing essential, and are the more remarkable in a book which employs a distinctive method and appears to be wholly self-conscious and deliberate.

An anomaly of the method lies in the author's omniscience of minor and even casual characters while the chief character is portrayed almost entirely from the objective point of view. Thus:

But there was a time when none of this had any existence (thought the young man leaning against the railings). Fix your eyes upon the lady's skirt; the gray one will do—above the pink silk stockings.

We have forthwith the anonymous young man's improbable recreation of the past, the picture of the seaside resort at various stages of its history. This seems a wholly superfluous device. And again, characterized and named, is the elderly lady who rides up to Cambridge in the same railway carriage with Jacob. Yet she is introduced only to tell us how Jacob looked:

> Taking note of socks (loose), of tie (shabby), she once more reached his face. She dwelt upon his mouth. The lips were shut . . . etc.

This would seem an elaborate contrivance for a simple matter. The elderly lady never reappears in the story.

It may be said in justification of this method, which seems at first sight to attain only a false emphasis, that a novel so peopled with minor characters and mere hangers-on achieves just that shadowy degree of reality which the author professedly seeks. The method is, then, deliberate, but whether successful or no is quite another matter. Certainly *Jacob's Room* is a fatiguing book. Attention is distracted and strained amid so many characters so slightly sketched and with no more than a descriptive purpose. The transitions from one to another, like the sudden transitions in time and place, exact an incessant reorientation which is wearying. Not always are the shifts marked even by a break in the page or a dotted line. Thus in the fifth chapter the initial scene is in Jacob's room with Jacob looking out of the window. The second paragraph is reminiscent of eighteenth century life amid these scenes. The third describes the motor buses on Oxford Street, names some of the occupants, among them "little Johnnie Sturgeon" who descends and is "soon out of sight— forever." When Jacob, whom we have left in his room, descends, likewise, at St. Paul's, the reader experiences a shock.

The method imposes great, even illegitimate, demands upon the reader. It must be a nimble imagination which would follow the author:

> The light drenched Jacob from head to toe. You could see the pattern on his trousers; the old thorns on his stick; his shoe laces; bare hands; and face.
>
> It was as if a stone were ground to dust; as if white sparks flew from a livid whetstone, which was his spine; as if the switchback railway, having swooped to the depths, fell, fell, fell. This was in his face.

It is much to be conveyed by any face. And the imaginative reader has, I believe, suffered Jacob's internal revolution; is in fact identified with Jacob before the author's concluding declaration of the point of view recalls him to the rôle of spectator.

Swiftness of transition or omission of transition, however a strain on the imagination, has its compensations in brevity; much brick and mortar stuff, the substance of many novels, is wholly done away with. But too elastic a use of the point of view is another matter. We are frequently unsure in *Jacob's Room* whether we view the character from within or without, whether as invisible spectator we identify ourselves with the author or with the character. Particularly is this true in the descriptions of scene. Mrs. Flanders seats herself in the Roman fortress with its "magnificent view—moors behind, sea in front, and the whole of Scarborough from one end to the other laid out flat like a puzzle." Here surely we see either through her eyes or take our stand beside her. Yet in succeeding paragraphs we forget her and are taken into the city: into the aquarium, upon the pier, to the esplanade where we listen to the band; we see the mysterious young man whose speculations were previously quoted. Only after a long circuit do we return to Mrs. Flanders. It is not through her eyes that these things have been seen, but the author's.

Impressionism, of which *Jacob's Room* is an excellent instance, too often has borrowed from painting without clearly perceiving that in a sister art the methods to the same end must necessarily differ. Lessing's distinctions among the arts have not yet, so far as I know, been successfully challenged. Painting, which is static, can only suggest movement. Narrative, which moves in time with the utterance of words or the tracing of symbols, is at its weakest in the description of scene. The good novelist, therefore, blends his description with action. Scene is depicted as it enters into the mood of his characters, altering that mood and in turn discolored by it. Therein lies the truth of impressionism: to the novelist the value of a scene lies in the response of his characters to it. It has no other truth, no other justification for being. If as narrator he describes a scene which is not blent with the emotions of his characters, he is devising a decorative adjunct to his story. If he describes it impressionistically, discolored, that is, by a mood of his own, not that of a character, he is endeavoring to practise two arts at once and at the cost of truth. For to the author, it is assumed, the scene must exist as it is, uncolored by mood, undistorted by passion. The distortions permissible to a character are not permissible to him.

Too much of the description in *Jacob's Room* is extraneous. It is vivid description but the reader forever questions its relevancy. True, these scenes were, the characters moved amid them. Yet save as the characters are influenced by these scenes, are conscious of them, what place have they? The scenes are background, it may be said, against which the characters are revealed. But what if they are not? Jacob, the child, sleeps in his room:

Outside the rain poured down more directly and powerfully as the wind fell in the early hours of the morning. The aster was beaten to the earth. The child's bucket was half-full of rain water; and the opal-shelled crab slowly circled round the bottom, trying with its weakly legs to climb the steep side; trying again and falling back, and trying again and again.

This is wholly pictorial, not narrative in quality, unless the crab has some recondite significance. It is vivid enough, but a more exacting artistry would question its right to be.

Jacob's Room, like most experiments in impressionism, suffers the divided purpose and the antithetical method of painter and novelist. Its flashes of description, its vivid epithets, are striking as one reads, but soon forgotten. The scenes are not blent with the emotions of the characters, are not seen through their eyes. Scenes exist only for themselves; they are not, usually, narrative in quality. A passage of Proust's expressionism, depicting experience rebuilt from memory, its essence extracted, and the scene delineated with the emotional color proper to its percipient, is striking in its method and memorable for its truth. Expressionism is but a modern name for a method as old as story-telling. Narrative is expressionistic in essence. Impressionism in narrative, I believe to be a technical method whose possibilities extend only to details, to contributory effects.

If to the criticism of *Jacob's Room* it be objected that the discontinuity, the incoherence, the vividness of detail, and the inconclusiveness are designed—that such is the picture of life the author wished to create, the only answer there can be is that so broken an effect is not enough for the novelist, that he must have some sort of a pattern, some sort of an artistic philosophy. If he has not, if his aim is purely pictorial, the novel is not the proper art form for him. That life may be meaningless, purposeless, and incoherent has been the thesis of novels which have employed methods more authentically narrative. *Madame Bovary* is such a book. Yet whereas its pessimism is as deeply rooted as that of *Jacob's Room*, its lucid coherent method puts its question to life masterfully, and its individual scenes, because related one to another, are memorable. The very background— the farm, the provincial town, the places of Madame Bovary's assignations—is distinct. Its quietness achieves what violence cannot. Perfectly it exploits the possibilities of the narrative method and never steps beyond. It does not exact too much of its reader. It asks of the imagination, sympathy, not gymnastic exercises. It has, in short, beauty. Beauty, it would seem, is calm, not violent. Its effect is of a whole which makes its constituents memorable; not of vivid constituents which will not blend to unity.[1]

In Mrs. Woolf's *The Voyage Out* one of the characters says:

You ought to write music . . . music goes straight for things. It says all there is to say at once. In writing, it seems to me, there's so much scratching on the box.

It is in the effort to avoid the "scratching" that the author denies the reader his accustomed clues to transitions and achieves thereby a rapidity which in itself is surely commendable. The difficulties of her method do not spring from this but from the causes I have mentioned and from an-

[1]In a later book, *Mrs. Dalloway,* Mrs. Woolf achieves, I think, the beauty and unity which I do not find in *Jacob's Room.*

other, the long impersonal author's comments, a curious reversion in kind, however different in manner, to the leisurely practices of the Victorian school. That the method owes anything to music is not apparent to me, though the resemblance to pictorial art is evident. Narrative and music, kindred arts in that both move in time, should seemingly lend each other devices in method more congruous than those which painting can lend to narrative. It is odd that in an age so experimental as our own some innovator has not composed a novel in the symphonic manner. I can recall none, though May Sinclair, indefatigable experimenter, must surely have written one.

Miss Sinclair's variety of "manners" lends her novels great technical interest. In one book or another she has experimented with naturalism, impressionism, expressionism, and psycho-analysis. She does not in any of them, however, wholly discard the conventional plot. Always there is a story to tell and the manner of the telling is never permitted to corrupt the essential structure. Miss Sinclair in thus clinging to the old while testing new technical devices reveals a sound instinct for craftsmanship, for it may very well prove that all these innovations in method will ultimately result in no new genres in fiction but will offer merely new tools for old tasks. Certainly in this scene from *Mary Olivier* Miss Sinclair, working in the manner of Dorothy Richardson, has surpassed her model in compactness and coherence:

She thought: "I'd have known. If I'd been here it wouldn't have happened. I wouldn't have let him. I'd no business to go away and leave him. I might have known."

"Lord, if Thou hadst been here our brother had not died."

The yellow coffin swayed before her eyes, heaped with white flowers. Yellow and white. Roddy's dog. His yellow dog with a white breast and white paws. And a rope around his neck. Roddy thought he had hanged him.

At seven she got up and dressed and dusted the drawing room. She dusted everything very carefully, especially the piano. She would never want to play it again.

The next citation, also from *Mary Olivier,* is impressionistic in manner but expressionistic in substance. Its staccato details resemble the sharp impressions of a single occasion; yet it is not in reality a single experience that is told but a number of experiences compressed into one and their essential character stressed as in the manner of Marcel Proust. Significance is thus achieved, together with implication of the heroine's character whose summarized impressions these are:

The soiled light; odors from the warm roots of girls' hair; and Sunday. Sunday; stale odors of churches. You wrote out the sermon you had not listened to and had not heard. Somebody told you the text, and you amused yourself by seeing how near you could get to what you would have heard if you had listened. After tea, hymns; then church again. Your heart labored with the strain of kneeling, arms lifted up to the high pew ledge. You breathed pew dust. Your brain swayed like a bladder, brittle, swollen with hot gas-fumes. After supper, prayers again. Sunday was over.

I can take space for but one more illustration which, despite the movement which the writer contrives to put into it, seems to me essentially "mannered," the kind of thing impressionism becomes unless the point of view is most religiously held. In this passage the reader is not conscious of perceiving the scene through the eyes of the heroine but through those of the author. It is decorative rather than built into the narrative and made indistinguishable from the action. It is, besides, too long, has the air of a tour de force, and it does what the impressionists so often and so ineffectually attempt, it stresses color. The canny writer gets his color effects by indirection, swift allusion, and effective figures of speech. It is fatuous to attempt too open rivalry with the art of painting:

Stone walls. A vivid country, caught in the net of the stone walls.

Stone walls following the planes of the land, running straight along the valleys, switchbacking up and down the slopes. Humped-up, gray spines of the green mounds.

Stone walls piled loosely, with the brute skill of earth men, building centuries ago. They bulged, they toppled, yet they stood firm, holding the wild country in their mesh, knitting the gray villages to the gray farms, and the farms to the gray byres. Where you thought the net had ended it flung out a gray rope over the purple back of Renton, the green shoulder of Greffington.

.   .   .   .

Broad sheep drives cut through the moor. Inlets of green grass forked into purple heather. Green streamed through purple, lapped against purple, lay on purple in pools and splashes.

Burnt patches. Tongues of heather, twisted and pointed, picked clean by fire, flickering gray over black earth. Toward evening the black and gray ran together like ink and water, stilled into purple, the black purple of grapes.

Psycho-Analysis in Recent Fiction

Mary Olivier besides reflecting the influences of naturalism and impressionism is indebted also to the new psycho-analysis. The mother's jealousy of her daughters, desiring their talents for her better loved sons; the father's jealousy of his sons because they absorb his wife's affection—these are themes which, if not wholly modern, are undoubtedly derived from Freudian suggestion. The pressure of these jealousies upon the heroine and her struggle to realize herself, to find an inner self-sufficiency despite them, is the theme of the book.

In *The Three Sisters* a Freudian complex is studied more exhaustively and exhibited only too consciously and neatly, after the fashion of an experiment. The father in this story, a sensual man denied expression of his sex life by reason of his separation from his wife and, as a clergyman, not daring to find illicit experience, endeavors to thwart the marriage of his three daughters. These exhibit various phases of sex repression. Ally, the youngest, shamelessly pursues the one eligible young man and failing to secure him marries a farmer. With marriage she becomes a perfectly normal woman. The second sister, Gwenda, clearly perceives the nature of her instincts and, perceiving, is able to master them; but only to her own undoing, for the sacrifice she makes enables the eldest sister to capture her lover and dooms her to a starved existence. The eldest sister merely follows her instincts, while refusing to admit their true nature; she pursues her man relentlessly and cruelly but disguises her motives always even to herself.

One passage from *The Three Sisters* will suffice to demonstrate the author's complete scientific awareness of her problem and her too open presentation of it. Fact here is not subdued to art, nor the direct method of science translated to the indirect method of fiction:

Mary thought, "Wednesday is his day. On Wednesday I will go into the village and see all my sick people. Then I shall see him. And he will see me. He will see that I am kind and sweet and womanly." She thought, "That is the sort of woman that a man wants." But she did not know what she was thinking.

Gwenda thought, "I will go out on the moor again. I don't care if I *am* late for Prayers. He will see me when he drives back and he will wonder who is that wild, strong girl who walks by herself on the moor at night and isn't afraid. He has seen me three times, and every time he has looked at me as if he wondered. In five minutes I shall go." She thought (for she knew what she was thinking), "I shall do nothing of the sort. I don't care whether he sees me or not. I don't care if I never see him again. I don't care."

Alice thought, "I will make myself ill. So ill that they'll have to send for him. I shall see him that way."

The novel smacks too much of the case-book; the illustrations are worked out too completely to a demonstration, to be wholly satisfactory. And comparison with *Wuthering Heights* is inevitably challenged, in setting and in characterization. There are few books which would not suffer by such a comparison and *The Three Sisters* is none of the exceptions. It is too self-conscious. The background of reading and the scientific method employed are too obvious. Emily Brontë was happily ignorant of psycho-analysis as a term and as a theory though aware of the essential mind-stuff with which psycho-analysis has to do. Instinctively she groped beneath superficial motives to subconscious motives more profound. Her characters obey these motives in their conduct, but she does not explain, is not aware even that there is anything to explain. Her characters in word and deed unconsciously explain themselves.

The essence of psycho-analysis is no modern discovery. Hawthorne in *The Scarlet Letter* and *The Marble Faun* was concerned with the psychology of the subconscious and it is his greatness as an artist that he suggests the deep motives of conduct without too fully elucidating them. They remain as they are, for all the theories of modern science, mysterious. *Wuthering Heights* also is a triumph in the same field. Nor were the older psychological novelists, even when dealing for the most part with human motives of a more obvious and intelligible order, unaware that human beings act often in accordance with motives which they do not understand or acknowledge. Bulstrode in *Middlemarch* is a fine study of unacknowledged motive dominating the actions of a man whose professed motives are utterly different. And of another character George Eliot remarks:

> And without his distinctly recognizing the impulse, there certainly was present in him the sense that Celia would be there, and that he should pay her more attention than he had done before.

George Eliot was too good a student of human nature to be unaware of the part played in conduct by unconscious motive. She anticipates the modern psycho-analytical novelists in repeated instances. It was her good fortune, however, to have no theory to maintain. The occasional passages of her analysis of the subconscious are simple enough. The appeal to the reader in the first citation to reflect upon his own experiences, could be spared:

> One thing Stephen seemed now and then to care for and that was to sing; it was a way of speaking to Maggie. Perhaps he was not distinctly conscious that he was impelled to it by a secret longing—running counter to all his self-confessed resolves—to deepen the hold he had on her. Watch your own speech and notice how it

is guided by your less conscious purposes, and you will
understand the contradiction in Stephen.

The second instance is more deft:

If the truth should be that some undermining disease
was at work within him, there might be large opportunity for some people to be happier when he was gone;
and if one of those people should be Will Ladislaw, Mr.
Casaubon objected so strongly that it seemed as if the
annoyance would make part of his disembodied existence.

This is a very bare, and therefore incomplete way of
putting the case. The human soul moves in many chan-
nels, and Mr. Casaubon, we know, had a sense of recti-
tude and an honorable pride in satisfying the requirements of honor, which compelled him to find other
reasons for his conduct than those of jealousy and vin-
dictiveness. The way in which Mr. Casaubon put the
case was this," etc.

Other passages from the older novelists antici-
patory of psycho-analysis and its methods could be
cited, but I shall content myself with one concluding instance from George Moore's *Evelyn Innes*.
In this scene, conscious and unconscious motive
and desire, the intelligence of the nerves and the
instincts of the blood, are intelligibly blent and
conveyed:

She was trembling, and had no strength of will to
refuse to ask him in. She would have had the strength
if she had not been obliged to give him her hand. She
had tried to bid him good-bye without giving her hand,
and had not succeeded, and while he held her hand her

lips said the words without her knowing it. She spoke unconsciously, and did not know what she had said till she had said it.

And while they waited for tea, Evelyn lay back in a wicker chair thinking. He had said that life without love was a desert, and many times the conversation trembled on the edge of a personal avowal, and now he was playing love music out of "Tristan" on the harpsichord. The gnawing creeping sensuality of the phrase brought little shudders into her flesh; all life seemed dissolved into a dim tremor and rustling of blood; vague color floated into her eyes, and there were moments when she could hardly restrain herself from jumping to her feet and begging of him to stop. . . . She heard him speak of the handkerchief motive, of thirty violins playing three notes in ever precipitated rhythm, until we feel that the world reels behind the woman, that only one thing exists for her—Tristan. A giddiness gathered in Evelyn's brain, and she fell back in her chair, slightly to the left side, and letting her hand slip toward him, said with a beseeching look:

"I cannot go on talking, I am too tired."

The work of Freud in stressing the importance of subconscious motive and repressed desire has led many contemporary novelists to attempt the exploitation of new fields. Hawthorne, to be sure, had traversed them, but his findings were suggestive only, not explicit. The scientist brings to the light that at which the artist had only hinted. The consequence has been the discovery of a new country to be exploited for its local color, exploitation attended with all the haste and ravage and superficiality which marks the expansion of colonial empires. For it cannot be demonstrated that the Freudian theories have as yet, in their influence upon fiction, produced much that is either informing or beautiful. If the theories have in themselves much widened our field of knowledge—an issue which is debatable—the novelist has certainly done little but repeat them in the guise of fictional illustrations and with a distortion which robs them of scientific truth.

This distortion is manifest in the attribution to sex impulse of so vast a part of human conduct. Biologically it may be true that all feeling can be traced to primitive hungers—to the desire for food and sex expression. These hungers, thinly disguised, may, in particular instances, survive. Yet for the novelist the fact remains that the vaster part of the emotional life has to do with motives which, whatever their purely animal origins millions of years ago, have been transformed to something else. Complexes and repressions, the significance of dreams—all the matters of interest to the psychiatrist in his diagnosis of a pathological condition—are dangerous tools in the hands of the novelist. If he is not cautious in their use he becomes, like the medical specialist, too wholly concerned with "cases," with the exceptional instance. This precisely is the effect which the novel of the psycho-analytical school creates. "Surely," exclaims the startled reader, "these people are mad!"

To depict a kind of madness is, I take it, the purpose of D. H. Lawrence in *Women in Love*. For to free conduct from its various inhibitions, to portray primitive impulses, is, if the subject be presumably a normal social being, to depict him as mad. Madness is nothing more, surely, than unchecked obedience to impulse, the surrender of the conscious will to the unconscious. This theme is explicitly avowed in *Women in Love:*

"Perhaps there was an unconscious will behind it," said Ursula. "This playing at killing has some primitive *desire* for killing in it, don't you think?"

And again, in a passage which expresses much of the unrest of our age and the extravagances of its fiction:

". . . Never carried away, out of themselves, always conscious, always self-conscious, always aware of themselves. Isn't *anything* better than this? Better be animals, mere animals with no mind at all, than this, this *nothingness.* . . . Isn't the mind . . . our death? Doesn't it destroy all our spontaneity, all our instincts? Are not the young people growing up to-day, really dead before they have a chance to live?"

Animalism plays a considerable part in *Women in Love,* both in the purely physical desires and surrenders of the characters, and in the depiction of rabbits, cats, and Highland cattle. The conduct of these creatures has vague analogies to human impulse; it stirs to inexplicable cruelties. Gudrun, excited by the herd of cattle, strikes Gerald in the face—just why isn't apparent, and yet you feel she very well might. It's a half mad world, one in which the characters look over the edge of the abyss and speculate upon what it would be like to hurl themselves in. Their surrenders aren't complete but tentative, and accompanied by a vast deal of speculation which springs from that self-consciousness they endeavor to escape.

Women in Love cannot by any standard, even that of the new fiction, be considered a successful work. It is loaded with philosophic speculation which endeavors to express the unutterable. It is charged with "black electricity" which, after a few passages like the following, becomes absurd:

> The Pussum sat near to Gerald, and she seemed to become soft, subtly to infuse herself into his bones, as if she were passing into him in a black, electric flow. Her being suffused into his veins like a magnetic darkness, and concentrated at the base of the spine like a fearful source of power.

Lawrence is endeavoring to express the inexpressible. It is the defect of *Women in Love* that he makes a frontal attack upon his objective instead of resorting to those indirections wherewith art achieves its end. All his philosophizing is so much tediousness. And as for his story, it drifts, following the impulse of the moment, and getting nowhere in particular. It has the effect of an improvisation, of the talk of a man endeavoring to find out what he thinks.

The very ineffectiveness of the book is enlightening to one who seeks to find out what novelists of the psycho-analytic school are "at." If it be compared with other work of Lawrence in which, it seems to me, he succeeds admirably in doing what he sets out to do, a whole object lesson in technique is revealed. Lawrence's successes lie, chiefly, in his short stories or tales. In *England, My England,* or in *The Captain's Doll,* for instance, his method is effective. He *suggests.* What is it he suggests? Something not easily put into words: deep impulses, primal sympathies with the world of animals, sex attractions which are half sex repulsions. As you read, your imagination is stimulated. You are aware of the mystery of life. To reawaken in new ways the sense of wonder is the prime purpose of poetry and one of the ends of fiction. In such a story as *The Fox* it seems to me that Lawrence does this.

I believe it to be a significant fact that Lawrence succeeds much better in his short tales than in his novels, excepting always *Sons and Lovers.* In the relative failure of his novels he is at one with the rest of the modern experimenters with new methods. Dorothy Richardson's novels are interesting in pages or chapters, rather than as a whole. Proust's work, exquisite in its parts, is no more than its parts. It has no organic wholeness. It would be quite as effective were it printed as a bundle of sketches. The modern novels employing any of the new methods seldom, for me, hold their interest to the end. The fact may argue a defect in me, but I prefer to think the defect in the work. For I can still read and reread novels of the old school, however long. Naturalism, impressionism, expressionism, psycho-analysis lack something.

The Need of a New Philosophy Anticipated by New Technical Methods

It is a life all surfaces, pictorial and behavioristic, that much of the new fiction portrays. There are frequent vividness and occasional beauty. Subtle and poignant sensations are sought and snared in new words and images. Pessimistic philosophies enwrap themselves picturesquely in clouds of immitigable gloom. Flippant allusions to a deity little more real than Olympian Zeus are so common as no longer to titillate. Morality, it is universally conceded, is wholly a convention and outgrown. There are no longer accepted standards either of conduct or art. The aim, therefore, is to startle by some fresh audacity or some new trick of method. Conservative persons cherishing memories of a quieter time are naturally shocked by these ebullitions as by the unorthodox conduct of the young. Yet it is a more hopeful phenomenon than adherence to old models and respectful deference to the past. It displays the essential thing, vitality. A point of view, a philosophy, is sure to come, for men have never lived for long without one. And with the new philosophy will come, too, new manifestations of beauty achieved in part by new technical devices.

Much of the new fiction is episodically interesting; some of it may have a scientific value—though I doubt it. Yet its chief merit is the contribution which it is making to the technical resources of the novelist. If these new technical methods have as yet seldom been put to any notable use the fault lies in the spirit of the age. The old philosophies are no longer adequate. The tight little world of religious affirmations and simple morals has gone glimmering, and no new philosophy has arisen to replace what is lost. Or if such a philosophy, or various philosophies, exist, they have not inspired the writers of fiction, and the mass of novel readers is not yet ready for them.

It is a superficial criticism that the modern school of fiction lacks "plot" unless the significance of plot is weighed. Plot in the narrow mechanical sense of prepared surprise and of incidents carefully articulated is of secondary importance, though stories skilfully employing it will, no doubt, always have their place. Plot in the larger sense of characters and incidents artfully marshalled to an end, which is the expression through a design or pattern of some philosophy, æsthetic or moral, in which the author believes, is, I conceive, essential to any powerful and enduring work. Lacking this it can be no more than a string of incidents or a document possessed of social and scientific rather than æsthetic significance.

There are notable exceptions to the general lack, in contemporary fiction, of purpose and meaning and, consequently, of design. Hamsun, Bojer, and Nexö, though employing the technique of naturalism, express, all of them—Bojer and Nexö more explicitly than Hamsun—a philosophy. Precisely what this philosophy is it may not be easy to say, but it has obvious resemblances to the theory of creative evolution as Bergson has defined it. For the older theological conceptions imposed upon man from without it substitutes a purpose conceived by man himself. Man becomes the creator of his God, moulder of his own destiny. Laboriously he must examine his personal morality and adjust it to the society in which he lives. He must create an ideal for himself and for society and rely only upon his own strength to achieve it. In all three of these novelists man is more than an individual victimized by his own unintelligible impulses. He is a conscious will, groping, but finding his way ever more clearly to an end. In depicting this struggle and this end the obligation lies upon the novelist to select and arrange his incidents. Structure, design, is inevitable.

The philosophy of the creative evolutionist is not necessarily the only one possible to the novelist of to-day. It is, however, one which has borne fruit; in the light of it notable works have been written. It conceives of man as a social being; and no philosophy, I should hazard, can be of æsthetic value to the novelist which is less than that. The interest and justification of the novel lie in its picturing for us endless instances of individuals adjusting themselves, amid all manner of circumstances, to life; or coming to disaster in the failure so to adjust themselves—which inversely attains the same philosophic end. In this very large sense fiction and all art has, I take it, a "moral" purpose. Without this purpose, without some philosophy, art, however interesting in its details of method, can achieve no larger unifying design and cannot, consequently, endure.

Ephemeral much of contemporary fiction, even the most serious fiction, necessarily must be, lacking, as it does, any philosophy to guide it. Yet with rare exceptions novels must ever be relatively short-lived. They are not the less important because of that. They pass into the consciousness of their readers and there attain their immortality, clarifying impulse, determining conduct, enlisting the sympathetic emotions. They constitute a vast civilizing agency. They are a means whereby men can observe with detachment their individual and social problems and thus be aided in their solution. It is not easy to conceive any other agency equally competent to this end.

I have grouped in this chapter under the caption "Actualism" a number of tendencies in modern fiction rather diverse in kind and not all strictly technical in their nature. Psycho-analysis, for instance, is not properly a technical method, unless its use of animal symbolism be considered as such. It implies rather a widening of the novelist's field to include, more deliberately than heretofore, the subconscious and to give to the subconscious a more important place in determining human conduct. Expressionism likewise is not essentially a new method though perhaps more consciously pursued than heretofore. Nevertheless the term "actualism" will serve as well as another to label something common to all the experimentalism of the day.

Recent developments of fictional technique have aimed most notably to depict as closely as possible the actual flux of consciousness, the genuine stuff of experience. Greater intimacy and vividness are their achievement, and these are desirable qualities. In their utilization to more clearly perceived ends lie the possibilities of the novel's future growth as an art form and as a civilizing agency. Yet whatever the enlargements of the novelist's field and increase of his technical resources in the coming age, the old requirements of art remain: there must be selection among means to the achievement of some preconceived end; that end is an explanation of life or some aspect of life in the light of a personal philosophy; and last there must be indirection of approach, for unless it conveys its meaning by symbols, rather than by explicit moralizing, art ceases to be art at all, but is science, philosophy, or sociology, and the æsthetic pleasure which it is its legitimate purpose to create no longer appertains to it.

INDEX